The Edinburgh Companion to Contemporary Scottish Poetry

Edinburgh Companions to Scottish Literature

Series Editors: Ian Brown and Thomas Owen Clancy

Titles in the series include:

The Edinburgh Companion to Robert Burns
Edited by Gerard Carruthers
978 0 7486 3648 8 (hardback)
978 0 7486 3649 5 (paperback)

The Edinburgh Companion to Twentieth-Century Scottish Literature
Edited by Ian Brown and Alan Riach
978 0 7486 3693 8 (hardback)
978 0 7486 3694 5 (paperback)

The Edinburgh Companion to Contemporary Scottish Poetry
Edited by Matt McGuire and Colin Nicholson
978 0 7486 3625 9 (hardback)
978 0 7486 3626 6 (paperback)

Forthcoming titles include:

The Edinburgh Companion to Muriel Spark
Edited by Michael Gardiner and Willy Maley
978 0 7486 3768 3 (hardback)
978 0 7486 3769 0 (paperback)

The Edinburgh Companion to Robert Louis Stevenson
Edited by Penny Fielding
978 0 7486 3554 2 (hardback)
978 0 7486 3555 9 (paperback)

The Edinburgh Companion to Irvine Welsh
Edited by Berthold Schoene
978 0 7486 3917 5 (hardback)
978 0 7486 3918 2 (paperback)

The Edinburgh Companion to Scottish Romanticism
Edited by Murray Pittock
978 0 7486 3845 1 (hardback)
978 0 7486 3846 8 (paperback)

The Edinburgh Companion to Contemporary Scottish Poetry

Edited by Matt McGuire and Colin Nicholson

Edinburgh University Press

© in this edition Edinburgh University Press, 2009
© in the individual contributions is retained by the authors

Edinburgh University Press Ltd
22 George Square, Edinburgh

www.euppublishing.com

Typeset in 10.5 on 12.5pt Goudy
by Servis Filmsetting Limited, Stockport, Cheshire, and
printed and bound in Great Britain by
CPI Antony Rowe, Chippenham and Eastbourne

A CIP record for this book is available from the British Library

ISBN 978 0 7486 3625 9 (hardback)
ISBN 978 0 7486 3626 6 (paperback)

The right of the contributors
to be identified as authors of this work
has been asserted in accordance with
the Copyright, Designs and Patents Act 1988.

Contents

Series Editors' Preface

In 1919, T. S. Eliot (or perhaps a sub-editor) posed the provocative query, 'Was there a Scottish Literature?' and critical angst on this subject has ensued over the ninety years since. The view of the editors of this series – and a prime motivation for its production – is that however valid the question within one concept of literary tradition, it does not make sufficient room for the nature of literatures produced by multilingual and multivalent cultures. The question was always more complex than Eliot seemed to allow. Further, by their nature, certain Scottish literary works have also been subsumed into the corpora of other literary traditions – for instance, medieval Irish, Latin, or modern English. Such intercultural richness and hybridity, we argue, is not a weakness in a literature's history, but a token of international openness and cosmopolitan potential.

Study and research, not to mention creative writing, since 1919 and perhaps especially of the last twenty years, make Eliot's still historically interesting query redundant as a serious contemporary enquiry. To be fair, the political and educational structures are still in place that at times separated Scottish literature in Gaelic from that in English or Scots – and led sometimes to amnesia regarding that in other languages like Latin. But that Scottish literature was, and is, is clearly recognised. It glories in the resources of historic canons in at least four languages that each stand as internationally important, worthy of careful study and richly enjoyable, and it is now absorbing work in, or influenced by, languages from Scotland's newer vibrant language cultures.

Much new scholarship supports the authoritative, accessible, succinct and up-to-date studies comprising the various volumes of the *Edinburgh Companion to Scottish Literature*. These recognise that worldwide interest in Scottish literature, both in universities and among the reading public, calls for fresh insight into key authors, periods and topics within the corpus. Each of these three categories of *Companion* is represented in the 2009 publications. This first tranche of our new series marks the vigour and rigour of the study of Scottish literature and its enjoyment. It sets aside old questions, and gets on with the acts of studying and enjoying.

Ian Brown
Thomas Owen Clancy

Introduction – Feeling Independent

Matt McGuire and Colin Nicholson

It is widely acknowledged that the late twentieth century was a dynamic, productive and innovative period in Scottish literary history. A flourishing of creative and scholarly endeavour, along with a rejuvenated Scottish publishing industry, radically transformed the cultural landscape north of the border. In *The Scottish Novel since the Seventies* (1993) and *Scottish Theatre since the Seventies* (1996), both edited by Randall Stevenson and Gavin Wallace, critics began to chart these energies and undercurrents, while simultaneously legitimising these decades as a distinct moment in the evolution of Scotland's literary output. On the stage the 1970s had witnessed the emergence of a deliberately self-conscious drama, where playwrights like Stewart Conn, Hector MacMillan, John McGrath, Ian Brown and Donald Campbell sought to interrogate the Scottish past and in doing so shed new light on the country's present predicament. If the 1980s saw the resuscitation of certain perennial themes – questions of language, nation, community – there is also a sense in which such preoccupations were subject to rigorous transgression and transcendence. Similarly, if the 1920s invoked a mythical Scotland, contemporary writing would debunk such notions by re-orientating itself within global fields of reference. In Kathleen Jamie's landmark poem 'The Queen of Sheba' it is an outsider, the eroticised female Other, who rides in from the East to pour scorn on small-town Scotland and its couthy prejudices. While Alasdair Gray's *Lanark* (1981) set a time bomb inside Scottish culture, it also belonged to wider developments within the novel, influenced by postmodernism and the French *nouveau roman* of the 1950s, whose practitioners include writers like Salman Rushdie (1947–), Gabriel Garcia Marquez (1927–) and, earlier, Jorge Luis Borges (1899–1986). In a local context Gray's novel was symptomatic of broader movement within Scottish fiction, characterised by self-confidence and textual innovation in novelists as diverse as James Kelman (1946–), Iain Banks (1954–), Janice Galloway (1955–) and A. L. Kennedy (1965–). The 1990s would see commercial success build on this critical acclaim with best-selling writers like Irvine Welsh (1958–), Ian Rankin (1960–), Val McDermid (1964–), Louise Welsh (1965–), and

1

Alexander McCall Smith (1948–) bringing Scottish writing, for the first time in many instances, to the attention of a global audience.

So how does poetry find space amidst all this critical attention and expansive creativity? The effective revival of Scottish aspirations to self-government in the late twentieth century offers a compelling point of comparison with the agenda advanced by MacDiarmid and others in the 1920s. Given that the currents of contemporary Scottish poetry have inevitably been responsive to changes in the socio-economic and political environment over recent decades; the failed referendum in 1979, the rise of Thatcherism and the restoration of a Scottish parliament in 1999 cannot help but suggest useful reference points. Alan Riach picks up on these correspondences in his contribution to the current *Companion*. When Donny O'Rourke's anthology *Dream State* was re-issued in 2002 its editor could claim that the poets, more confidently than the politicians, were dreaming a new state.[1] However, as other chapters here demonstrate, recent poetry is as often characterised by a desire to distance itself from any explicit politics of nationalism, and to explore and chart a host of alternative agendas. Cairns Craig's chapter on Kenneth White develops Marco Fazzini's comparative treatment to demonstrate a largely forgotten European dimension in Scotland's historic intellectual relationships. In these contexts it is worth considering – as several of our contributors do – Alexander Moffat's painting *Poets' Pub* (1980) which provides another defining moment in this evolving story. Moffat's picture recreates the bohemian poetry scene that gathered around the Rose Street pubs of Edinburgh during the 1960s. While excluding White, the painting features ten poets, the grand old men of Scottish letters (who never in fact came together in the group Moffat represents), gathered around the central figure of MacDiarmid. The lack of women in the picture reflects the gender-skewed nature of the poetry, a scheme of preference that would be radically reconfigured by the emergence of women writers during the 1980s including Liz Lochhead, Kathleen Jamie and Jackie Kay. Fiona Wilson addresses and explores the impact of these female voices in her chapter on 'Scottish Women's Poetry since the 1970s'. While MacDiarmid's centrality in the Moffat painting enshrines his place at the gravitational centre of Scottish literary life, other contexts are busily establishing themselves. Born in the nineteenth century (1898) and having lived through both World Wars, MacDiarmid's death in 1978 in many ways signalled the end of an era. In these terms, it is worth recalling that O'Rourke's *Dream State* gathered together a generation of poets born after 1955, and emerging in the 1980s outwith the immediate and looming presence of MacDiarmid.

Poetry in Scotland has generally been more democratically accessible than the high modernism of MacDiarmid and the exclusivity of literary cliques would suggest. This is a country where lively and widespread folk and ballad traditions operated long before the advent of mass literacy. Moreover, the work of Robert Burns is woven into the cultural DNA of Scotland in a way that is almost unrivalled in other countries around the world. One might think of Whitman in America, or Neruda in Chile; but neither of these figures quite matches Burns in terms of either popular appeal or cultural dissemination. And as recent events surrounding the 250th anniversary of the poet's birth demonstrate, Burns is no mere tourist sideshow, but an intellectual and emotional resource whose work is a palimpsest upon which subsequent generations of Scots continue to write and rewrite the story of their lives. Beyond that, contemporary Scottish poetry has been notably broad in its appeal, capturing the attention of diverse audiences in a way which the 1920s generation failed to do. As sign and symbol of this success, Scottish writers continue to figure prominently on the prize circuit for contemporary poetry: Kathleen Jamie won the Somerset Maugham Award (1995), the Geoffrey Faber Memorial Prize (1996 and 2000), and the Forward Poetry Prize (2004); Carol Ann Duffy received an OBE (1995), a CBE (2001), and won the T. S. Eliot Prize (2005); Jackie Kay received the Somerset Maugham Award (1994) and an MBE (2006); Don Paterson has won the T. S. Eliot Prize twice (1997 and 2003). John Burnside, shortlisted for the Forward and T. S. Eliot prizes, won the Whitbread Poetry Award in 2000. Robin Robertson won the 1997 Forward Poetry Prize, the Aldeburgh Poetry Festival Prize and the Saltire Society First Book Award. In 2004 the Poetry Book Society named him one of the 'Next Generation' poets, and the American Academy of Arts and Letters gave him the E. M. Forster Award. In 2005 he was shortlisted for the T. S. Eliot Prize and won the 2006 Forward Poetry Prize (Best Poetry Collection of the Year). In 2008, Mick Imlah won the Forward Prize. From an earlier generation, Douglas Dunn won the Somerset Maugham Award (1969), the Geoffrey Faber Memorial Prize (1976), and in 1985 the Whitbread Book of the Year Award. Meanwhile, Edwin Morgan has picked up more prizes and awards than you can shake a stick at; and Kenneth White has won the 1983 Prix Médicis Étranger, the French Academy's Grand Prix du Rayonnement in 1985, the Prix Alfred de Vigny in 1987. In 1993 he was promoted from Chevalier to Officier dans l'Ordre des Arts et des Lettres.

Recent decades have also seen the number of anthologies of Scottish poetry on the rise including *The Poetry of Scotland* (1995), *Scottish Love Poems* (2002), *Modern Scottish Women Poets* (2003), *The Edinburgh Book of Twentieth-Century Scottish Poetry* (2005) and *100 Favourite Scottish Poems* (2006). While local publishers such as the Edinburgh-based Canongate, and Luath Press have been responsible for some of these projects, 2006 also saw the re-issue of *The Penguin Book of Scottish Verse* as part of the Penguin Classics series. Alongside this, Faber re-issued its 1992 anthology edited by Douglas Dunn, *The Faber Book of Twentieth Century Scottish Poetry* (2006).

Despite an impressive exhibition of writing in the creative arena, there remains a conspicuous disparity between the sheer volume of poetry produced in Scotland and critical commentary dedicated to it. Christopher Whyte's *Modern Scottish Poetry* (2004) is almost alone in attempting to chart the terrain of post-war Scottish poetry in all three of the nation's main languages. Even so, his survey format makes for uneven treatment and offers little scope for extended discussion of individual writers: with a time-scale that ends in the 1990s, moreover, Whyte makes no mention of Jackie Kay, John Burnside, Robin Robertson or Don Paterson. As part of the development of a necessary critical task, this *Companion* combines thematic chapters with others where the primary focus is on the work of a single poet. It addresses the major themes of contemporary Scottish poetry: the influence of tradition (both national and international); the language question and writing in Gaelic, Scots and English including their variant forms; the rise of women's writing; the relationship between poetry and politics; and the importance of place to the Scottish imagination. It also discusses writing by poets who live and work within wider senses of community; what Kirsten Matthews refers to as 'a democracy of voices'. The volume ends with chapters devoted to close readings of work by key poets: Edwin Morgan, Kenneth White, John Burnside, Aonghas MacNeacail, Kathleen Jamie, Robin Robertson and Don Paterson. These chapters evince a broad range of interests, while also offering detailed analysis of the many ways writers broach their subject matter.

The temptation to subtitle this Introduction 'Already Gone Cosmopolitan' was strong. Such a move would acknowledge the strength and accept the validity of Berthold Schoene's argument that Scottish writing has for long been signally in advance of strategies of reading developed to integrate a culture of creativity that is by any measure remarkable for a small European state.[2] On the evidence of the poetry discussed in the following chapters, when Schoene further suggests that contemporary writers by and large avoid any restriction on what being a Scot means to them, he describes a widely assumed liberty and a natural inheritance. After Margaret Thatcher rode to power in 1979 against a Scottish agenda for reclamation and reconstruction, Scotland's electorate responded by wiping her party out of parliamentary representation north of the border. As a suitably ironised phrase from Kathleen Jamie's *Jizzen* (published in the same year as the partial restoration of Scottish self-government in 1999) has it, 'History in a new scheme' is not surprisingly the order of the day for poets sensitive to changing landscapes of possibility.[3] While Scottish writing has never been short on radical self-criticism of political, social and personal kinds, including a sometimes scathing and as often hilarious tendency to satirical assault, a sense of reaching out to find what satisfies and fulfils, and the urge to work it into living relationship are distinctive features of innovative writing across the twentieth century and into the present.

It has already come to seem more than just a trick of hindsight and changed political circumstance that Donny O'Rourke's *Dream State* poets, included because they were breaking out of any obligation to pre-existing categories for identity and relationship, now read like significant contributors to poetry's longer story of imaginative independence. How could it be otherwise when O'Rourke claims Edwin Morgan, already in his seventies when *Dream State* first appeared, as the anthology's 'presiding spirit'? [4] More than any other Scottish poet in the last half-century Morgan has committed himself to experimental exploration in the fields of imaginative invention. This most rooted and locally sensitive writer assumes the world's republic of letters as his natural habitat, while scouting pathways to the moons of Jupiter and beyond. He eats taxonomies for breakfast, chronologies for lunch, genealogies for supper; crashing frontiers wherever he finds them inhibiting potential, and mining traditions for what is useful, exploding them where they constrict initiative. If the politics of his aesthetic traces its pedigree back to Aristotle, for whom the *politeia* constituted the structure of relationships in a given community, Morgan's libertarian poetics projects innovation as the condition of writing where change is a function of continuity and transformation a continuing promise. Because his panegyric is invitational, others might follow or not as they choose; take up his lead or fashion their own. With heterogeneity incorporated as norm, heteroglossia as reconstructive tactic and alterity as both subject and object of desire, the ways in which personalised orientation have become the signature, stuff and substance of the generation that came after Morgan suggests that his invitation – and his exemplary demonstrations of what might issue from it – is proving irresistible. Scottish writers continue to explore and invent contexts for creative self-management; habitually dissolving or ignoring prescribed (or prescriptive) definitions and assumptions. In this way they challenge and transcend the valorising habits of customary thinking, so that self-identifying relationship can be reconfigured.

Given additional exigency by changed and changing circumstance, Edward Soja's imperatives in *Postmodern Geographies* (1989) have long been a Scottish priority:

> We must be insistently aware of how space can be made to hide consequences from us, how relations of power and discipline are inscribed into the apparently innocent spatiality of social life, how human geographies become filled with politics and ideology.[5]

Two years after Soja's book appeared, Fredric Jameson was calling for:

> a new kind of spatial imagination capable of confronting the past in a new way and reading its less tangible secrets off the template of its spatial structures

– body, cosmos, city, as all those marked the more intangible organisation of cultural and libidinal economies and linguistic forms.[6]

This kind of spatial imagination is familiar territory to several of the poets featured in the present *Companion*. Its forms are regularly exercised by writers for whom 'real people in a real place' generate thoughtful feeling focused on evolving perceptions of lived experience.[7] As the cutting edge of language, poetry is alert to the constitution of interior and social space; such forms of attention make all imaginative writing political, and the poem's particularities particularly so, since its spaces also include and express the asymmetrical relations of power identified by Soja. In these circumstances it becomes a condition of the poem's personalised engagement that each writer 'from his or her own perspective [challenges] hegemonic constructions of place, of politics and of identity'.[8] All of which makes for rich pickings in the quality and range of work produced, partly because of a distinctive linguistic and cultural variety. Scottish difference inevitably pluralises access to perception and cognition, as surely as a crafted authenticity of speech – and fidelity to the sound worlds it inhabits – multiplies 'the metaphor of locality' while clarifying specific voice. In the imaginative processing of diverse material, 'social location [becomes] less an individual than a multi-dimensional experience, a collective engagement of mutually implicated identities'.[9]

The mutual society of the poem activates a dialogic impulse that is for many a necessary adjunct to writing in a democratic society; and 'true democracy', moreover, 'lies in the equality and equal power of all parties to that dialogue'.[10] Until such conditions properly obtain, Jacques Rancière (1940–) suggests: '[E]quality has no vocabulary or grammar of its own, only a poetics.'[11] A Scottish pedigree for this mode of thinking is not far to seek. We have recently been reminded that largely through the work of John Macmurray (1891–1976), 'the dialogic conception of the self' continues to be 'a fundamental aspect of Scottish thought';[12] to the extent that a poetics of equality informs the congenial society Macmurray frames, and for which 'the democratic slogan, "Liberty, equality, fraternity"', is adequate to his activist sense of community as 'the self-realisation of persons in relation'.[13] Macmurray's project clarifies the last of the three mysteries that Edwin Muir believed preoccupied our minds: 'where we came from, where we are going, and since we are not alone . . . how we should live together'.[14] Except that they are initially contemplative, the discriminations of poetry involve similar engagements for selfhood and alterity. Language is inherently other-centred – 'I speak and you hear me, therefore we are' in Julia Kristeva's memorable formulation.[15] But the poem must still reach out to find an audience, shaping the responses by which it is to be measured, through an interactive and personalised dialectic that is the grounding pleasure of its text. In a self-governing community,

Macmurray suggests, persons 'are constituted by their mutual relation to one another'. He also accepts that much needs to be done to establish this mutuality as a basis for social action: 'We have to discover how this ultimate fact can be adequately thought, that is to say, symbolised in reflection'. [16]

Poetry is both thoughtful reflection and symbolic disclosure, as Gaston Bachelard acknowledged in *La Poétique de l'Espace* (1958), published a few years after Macmurray delivered his Gifford Lectures at Glasgow University. *The Poetics of Space* became more widely influential in translation, and is of continuing relevance in so far as it addresses Macmurray's call for further discovery. For Bachelard 'the joy of reading appears to be the reflection of the joy of writing, as though the reader were the writer's ghost', in a context and relationship where 'poetic expression, although it has no vital necessity, has a bracing effect on our lives':

> The poetic image is an emergence from language, it is always a little above the language of signification. By living the poems we read, we have then the salutary experience of emerging . . . A great verse can have a great influence on the soul of a language. It awakens images that had been effaced, at the same time as it confirms the unforeseeable nature of speech. And if we render speech unforeseeable, is this not an apprenticeship to freedom? What delight the poetic imagination has in making game of censors! Time was when the poetic arts codified the licenses to be permitted. Contemporary poetry, however, has introduced freedom in the very body of the language. As a result, poetry appears as a phenomenon of freedom.[17]

This seems to be where we are now.

CHAPTER ONE

The Poetics of Devolution

Alan Riach

The occasions of poetry – the momentary intuition that raises you in the hours before dawn, the commission to contribute to a public event, the compulsion to gather your forces in the context of a cultural argument about language and political authority – are inevitably numerous. In the period from 1994 (which saw the publication of the first edition of *Dream State: The New Scottish Poets*) and 2008 (the year of Edwin Morgan's 88th birthday), they are both liberated into a greater diversity than earlier eras and at the same time endangered by the ethos of distraction that seems characteristic of the early twenty-first century.

A few dates might help contextualise the contemporary scene historically. In 1979 a referendum in Scotland delivered a majority in favour of devolution but the vote was disqualified by Westminster; soon after, Margaret Thatcher's Conservative government was voted into power on the tide of a British election. This double negation of a national declaration certainly helped energise writers, intellectuals, artists and critics through the 1980s and 1990s in producing work which took as its emphatic gravitational centre the various locations and identities that comprise the nation of Scotland.

Cultural history and literary criticism by such as Roderick Watson, Cairns Craig, Marshall Walker, Douglas Gifford, Dorothy McMillan and new writing by Alasdair Gray (1934–), Edwin Morgan (1920–), Liz Lochhead (1947–) and many others reconfigured and reasserted the dynamics of Scotland's cultural character.[1] In 1997, another referendum delivered an increased majority in favour of devolved political authority and tax-raising powers. In 1999 the resumed Scottish Parliament was established and for the occasion, two contemporary writers delivered complementary poems celebrating and commenting on the potential the event represented.[2] Iain Crichton Smith (1928–98), alluding to the closing comment made upon the ending of the previous Scottish Parliament in 1707, 'There's an end of an auld sang!' wrote 'The Beginning of a New Song': 'Let our three-voiced country / Sing in a new world . . . ' Hoping that the new Scotland might be 'true to itself and to its origins', this secular prayer ended:

Inventive, original, philosophical,
[Let] Its institutions mirror its beauty;
Then without shame we can esteem ourselves.

The eighteenth-century idea that a parliament could be a kind of polyphonic song, and the twentieth- or twenty-first century hope that a nation's institutions might mirror its beauty are both potent images, staggeringly unfamiliar to the escalations of what Walter Benjamin called 'the age of mechanical reproduction'.[13]

At around the same time, Anne Frater (1967–) wrote (in Gaelic) a feminist poem taking the questions of language, political power and national identity into a metaphorical realm to deliver an equally memorable message about what the best way forward might be: Divorce.

He bought you like a slave
thinking
that because he paid with gold
you would be submissive.

Time and again
he raped you . . .

This is 'Saying "No" in thunder'. Frater's poem has none of Crichton Smith's tentative optimism; its Scotland is still beautiful, but its need to 'remember' is urgent, because only by not forgetting might we be self-consciously motivated to the point of taking action:

Beautiful Alba
remember
the noble woman that you were
and end this marriage
before the three hundred years have passed.[4]

A few years later, Edwin Morgan was commissioned to write a poem which came to be published under the title, 'For the Opening of the Scottish Parliament, 9 October 2004'. Morgan being too ill to attend, it was read at the opening ceremony of the new building by Liz Lochhead, standing beside Sean Connery and not far away from Scotland's First Minister. On 16 February 2004, at a celebration in the nursing home where he was living, aged eighty-three, Morgan had been appointed the first-ever National Poet of Scotland, effectively Scotland's first Poet Laureate, with support from all political parties. At that point he passed on his official title as the Poet Laureate of Glasgow, with the approval of Glasgow City Council, to Liz Lochhead. The point about this is that both Morgan and Lochhead self-consciously let their voices ring out in this reconfigured political arena. It was perhaps as courageous of them as it had been for the Scottish Government to invite them to do so. It was certainly pleasing to see quotations from poems adorning the walls of the resumed Parliament at Holyrood. This was more than tokenism, as Morgan's poem shows.[5]

In 2007, the Scottish National Party was voted into power in a minority government. This was the (to many, unexpected) breakthrough moment of their history, following their formation as the National Party of Scotland in 1928. In every country, poets have always been involved in the political moment to some degree but the questions poetry asks of politics are never easily answered. How does poetry connect with history? Some poets directly comment on events and characters, moments and conflicts, specific to the political day; there are others who resolutely turn away from such commentary. Even good things can grow stale or lose tension. At the end of a poetry festival in St Andrews in 2007, Alastair Reid (1926–) burnt a copy of his famous poem, 'Scotland', which describes someone exclaiming in praise of a beautiful day, fresh after rain, to be answered by a miserable old woman insisting: 'We'll pay for it, we'll pay for it, we'll pay for it!'[6] Reid had had enough of this woman's vile self-righteousness and the familiarity of the poem had dimmed the freshness of the day it describes so well, so he set it on fire in front of a hundred other Scottish poets. Not arch but exemplary. Time to freshen up.

Two immediate traditions cut across each other in the hinterland of this age. Both are old history now. Yet both are fresh to every new generation, to make of them what they will, depending on how they encounter them, and on how able they are. Each supplies vital components of the currency of contemporary Scottish poetry, its political responsiveness and social presence.

One is based in the ballad tradition but encompasses vernacular poetry in the Scots language, from Barbour (c. 1320–95) and Henryson (c. 1460–1500) on. Its rooted nationality is inescapable and, especially since the 1960s, has been easy to caricature. Marion Angus (1866–1946), Violet Jacob (1863–1946), MacDiarmid, William Soutar (1898–1943) point forward to recent and contemporary poets such as William Neill (1922–) and Rab Wilson (1960–). These poets are adept in traditional verse-forms and conservative stanzaic structures.

The other comes from English-language American poetry, pre-eminently from the 1950s, from the Beat, Black Mountain and San Francisco Renaissance groups (if groups they can be called), gathered in Donald Allen's influential 1960 anthology *The New American Poetry*.[7] These two traditions overlap and are not absolutely mutually exclusive. Tom Scott (1918–95) would seem to belong to the former as Alan Jackson (1938–) to the latter, yet Duncan Glen (1933–2008) draws on both very specifically: in language, from the former, in verse-structure from the latter. For Glen, a native Scots tradition and the 'postmodern' American one, come together. Shrewd, quizzical and reflective, he wrote a conversational long line in the language we call Scots. He acknowledged an affinity with Whitman, not as stentorian prophet, but rather as loafer, an observant eye, a quiet man given to a multitude of perspectives. Linguistically he was in a direct line with Burns and Henryson, but formally he was more closely in tune with William Carlos Williams (1883–1963), Lawrence Ferlinghetti (1919–) or the loose-shouldered versification of Ed Dorn (1929–99). His poems drift and dally attractively, often low-voltage but sometimes achieving an intensity of restrained charge, as in the elegy for his father, or the good-humoured recognition of personal limitation that informs 'The Hert o Scotland'.[8] In this poem, he ruefully says that while he would wish to write grandly of Scotland, he knows no Gaelic and there are innumerable parts of the country to which he has never been. A gentle satire on nationalist exceptionalism, the poem nevertheless registers an affirming desire to see national identity on a human scale. Glen bridges the MacDiarmid era to the contemporary scene. Robust yet tentative, his poems explore contexts of self-limitation, domesticity, relativity and caution. Douglas Dunn (1942–) shares this caution, but his poetry since his return to Scotland has addressed a related sense of compromised or qualified national commitment, in language and political self-determination. Formally, the conservatism of his poetics has served him well with personal subjects fraught with emotion, such as the elegies for his wife. The Introduction to his anthology of *Twentieth-Century Scottish Poetry* makes a passionate claim that neglected traditions should be reclaimed by a wide hinterland of poetry readers. His poems, particularly those addressing Scottish identity, engage and unfold an argument, sometimes with apparently carnaptious attitude yet assiduously in pursuit of a secure political position, like a bristly hedgehog trundling across a dangerous road with unpredicted determination. Robert Crawford (1959–), like Dunn, a professor at St Andrews University, seems committed to celebrating the diversity of identities the nation might empower, with more than one poem entitled 'Scotland' and a number of very different characters and characteristics depicted in his shifting kaleidosocope. Some poems indicate his interest in the topography and intellectual history of his favoured place (and he has edited a valuable anthology of St Andrews writing). The mix of opportune boldness and caution is sometimes felicitous, sometimes awkward. In 'Scotch Broth' a 'big, teuchtery face' rises through 'carrots and barley' towards the poet's descending spoon, while in 'A Scottish Assembly' we are reminded of the hubris of the 'handicapped printer' who began to put together 'The ultimate encyclopedia'.[9]

One of the most notable advances in recent years has been the production of poems by women delivering an understanding of experience that no man could convey. Slim books of poems by the novelists A. L. Kennedy (1965–) and Janice Galloway (1956–) are indications of the imaginative strengths at work.[10] To take another American co-ordinate point, the poem 'Diving into the Wreck' by Adrienne Rich (1929–) remains a classic account of the work of modern poets who, because they are women, have had to dive and swim down, to rediscover the wreckage of patriarchal assumptions, take what treasures might be found, abandon the objectification of the obsolescent figurehead at the prow, and discover ways of writing appropriate to their own purposes and experiences.[11] The accomplishment of various poets is already major: Liz Lochhead and Veronica Forrest-Thomson (1947–75), Jackie Kay (1961–), Kathleen Jamie (1962–), Carol Ann Duffy (1955–) are only the most conspicuous names.

The idea of the poetic imagination confronting political reality directly is integral to the work of feminist poets. Obvious examples are Jamie's 'Mr and Mrs Scotland Are Dead' and 'The Queen of Sheba', unhesitatingly proclaiming the demise of 'Wee Wifie' mentality; or Carol Ann Duffy's pillar-box-eyed disdain for all the male posturing in the limelight which obscures the wives of the world's more famous men, in 'The World's Wife' (entertaining squibs happily rubbing shoulders with poems of real indignation). As if to underline the reflexive charge that nationalism is masculinist, both Duffy in 'Originally' and Jackie Kay in 'In my Country' insist in different ways upon the relativity of identity, the security of universals that counterpoints any sense of exclusive nationality. Both consent to their identification with Scotland but both insist on the porous nature of that designation. In Kay's poem, 'an honest river / shakes hands with the sea' is a universal context for a particular encounter between the poet and a 'slow watchful' and suspiciously hostile woman who asks her, 'Where do you come from?' We might infer from the question, and since Kay is currently well-known as a public figure, through readings and public appearances, that the colour of her skin is being referred to, though there's nothing in the poem to confirm this. Her answer is beautifully pitched: '"Here," I said. "Here. These parts."' That is, perhaps, somewhere near the honest river and the sea, and the neighbourliness of shaking hands.[12] The poem's 'Here' might be Scotland but its universal references remind us that absolute exclusiveness in national identity is inadequate to human experience. To exaggerate this point, however, would be to risk the pieties of political correctness. At which point it is helpful to recollect Edwin Morgan's Demon poems of 1999:

My job is to rattle the bars. It's a battle.
The gates are high, large, long, hard, black.
Whatever the metal is, it is asking to be struck.
There are guards of course, but I am very fast

And within limits I can change my shape.
The dog watches me, but I am not trying
To get out, nor am I trying to get in.
He growls if I lift my iron shaft.
I smile at that, and with a sudden whack
I drag it lingeringly and resoundingly
Along the gate; then he's berserk: fine![13]

The Demon is the cure when tranquillity turns to complacency. The Demon is a vitalising spirit, real and living in us. He reminds us that a literary education helps us read the world more richly and critically, rather than passively submitting to the poetics of utopian universalism; neither resting on the data of historical foundations nor acquiescing easily in the platitudinous orthodoxies of the status quo. If all poets are of the Demon's party, so are all good readings.

To over-simplify, one might characterise a nationalist 'poetics' setting itself in opposition to British imperialism. This situation, it can be argued, still pertains. If you're not for independence, you're inevitably unionist and fall into the trap of British, rather than Scottish, nationalism. And British nationalism is simply English nationalism. The demographics prove it: fifty million English as opposed to five million Scots. In a UK population of fifty-five million, why should five million have any special rights?

The results for poetry are visible enough. Certain poets, happy to be included in accounts of modern British or English poetry, and also included in histories of modern Scottish poetry, have a fair amount of critical coverage, while certain poets, setting their co-ordinate points in self-consciously national Scottish contexts, are excluded. What has been working against both the nationalist and imperialist agendas, inevitably, has been the ascendancy of what might be denigrated as 'rootless' cosmopolitanism. The critical opening for this was the novel *Cain's Book* (1961) by Alexander Trocchi (1925–84) which introduced the word 'cool' to Scotland. Its culmination, perhaps, is in the poetry of Muriel Spark (1918–2006), icily ironic, uncannily balanced on spikes. Though she said she always thought of herself as a poet, and novels like *The Ballad of Peckham Rye* (1960) acknowledge their affinities gladly, the cosmopolitan sensibility is not nationalist.

In this context, Edwin Morgan's work remains the central challenge. *The Second Life* (1968) presented not only the festive celebration poem 'Trio' but also the brutal sexual violence of 'Glasgow Green'. Morgan's challenge is therefore to be affirmative about what is worthwhile and understanding of the cost at which it arrives, to be national and specifically international, located in a favoured place but free to roam, drawing nourishment from roots in Scotland (most vividly explored in his favourite of his own books, *Sonnets from Scotland*, 1986), but when it comes to an intergalactic, voyaging imagination, unafraid to be uprooted and airborne. Perhaps this is why his example is so pervasive through the self-consciousness of the contemporary scene and the ephemera of its occasions. For example, Lesley Duncan runs a daily online poetry webpage and a daily poem in the newspaper *The Herald*. When that paper organised a poll of their reading favourite paintings, Morgan responded with a sequence of poems keyed to that paintings, which *The Herald* then printed. These poems were then published as a book with reproductions of the paintings, entitled *Beyond the Sun: Scotland's Favourite Paintings* (2007). The question arises, who are these poems to be read by? Who are they for? The answer has to be, not a target audience, and not, even given the emphasis of the title, an exclusively national one, but the widest possible constituency. Ephemeral as their occasion may have been, the poems include one of the best of Morgan's later years, a response to and named the same as the artist Joan Eardley's seascape 'Flood-Tide'. She is depicted avoiding salon-parties and sherry, 'Striding into the salty bluster of a cliff-top' and painting the storm, as a solitary clover is blown onto the canvas:

> and then it's fixed,
> Part of a field more human than the one
> That took the gale and is now
> As she is, beyond the sun.[14]

Poets are not always alone, friendly with only their friends. Sometimes we find them in groups of loose configuration, and very occasionally they will issue a manifesto for some set purpose. Unfortunately, there have been very few groups committed to the manifesto in Scotland in recent years, and very few publications that have set out only to make a specific impact, then stop, as the New Zealand magazines *AND* and *Rambling Jack* did in the 1980s and 1990s. Recent poetry groups such as Jim Carruth's splendid Mungo's Mirrorball or David Manderson's Tchai Ovna reading groups in Glasgow (and there are other local groups throughout Scotland) have, to varying degrees, developed their venues with reliable listeners and readers who perform their work to critical appreciation. This is not the same, however, as close written criticism.

Consider: the constellation of writers in proximity to Glasgow University (with varying degrees and kinds of affection for it), including Alasdair Gray, Tom Leonard and Liz Lochhead; those in or close to St Andrews, including Douglas Dunn, Kathleen Jamie, Robert Crawford, John Burnside and Don Paterson; in Edinburgh, Stewart Conn (1936–), Dilys Rose (1954–), Ron Butlin (1949–), Brian McCabe (1951–); W. N. Herbert (1961–) is based in Newcastle but his poetry is rooted in Dundee; in or from Shetland there are Alex Cluness (1969–), Christine de Luca (1947–) and Robert Alan Jamieson (1958–). There are poets particularly adept in the Scots language, William

Hershaw (1957–) and Tom Hubbard, for example; poets associated with Dumfries and Galloway, Angus MacMillan, William Neill (1922–), John Manson (1932–), Liz Niven (1952–) and Tom Pow (b.1950). There are poets whose geographical co-ordinate points are located in other areas of Scotland: George Gunn (1956–) in Caithness, Sheila Templeton in Ayrshire and vernacular poets like Sheena Blackhall (1947–) in Aberdeenshire. Individual voices from a slightly older generation include Kenneth White, Thomas A. Clark (1944–), Alan MacGillivray (19–) and J. B. Pick (1921–). The poetry of Gael Turnbull (1928–2004) and Ian Hamilton Finlay (1915–2006) still seems pretty contemporary partly because it shows a clear affinity with White and Clark, while Ian Hamilton Finlay's son Alec Finlay (1966–) followed his father's example not only in his own aesthetic precision and sharp but generous humour, but also in his publishing of others in a freshly-imagined series of anthologies including *Wish I Was Here*, collecting work by writers whose ethnic or cultural history complicates any simple, single sense of what being 'Scottish' might be; and another, *Without Day*, collecting essays, poems and sometimes surreal sketches commemorating, celebrating or questioning the resumption of the Scottish parliament.[15] The occasional poignancies and bitternesses, and the sometimes wild humour in these collections are directly responsive to the context of devolution and incipient independence, yet this does not disqualify their aesthetic priorities and pleasures.

One might describe the individual characteristics of all the poets listed so far: urbane, oblique, élitist, civic, droll, playful, reductive, festive, linguistically zestful, politically direct. These terms might be applied selectively. And there is room for dissent, voices that do not harmonise in this polyphony. One thinks of the gentle humour and close focus on nature in the poems of Gerry Cambridge (1959–) or Ken Cockburn (1960–), with his anthology about the Tweed in Alec Finlay's series or his poetic responses to the John Murray archive in the National Library of Scotland; one thinks of the strong, occasional but tough poems by Jenni Daiches (1941–) or Tessa Ransford (1938–), founder of the Scottish Poetry Library, whose time spent in India gives her work a distinctively sharp perspective on notions of the native and the foreign; or of Alison Fell (1944–), Mandy Haggith (who has her own take on the territory around Lochinver made memorable by Norman MacCaig), Gerry Loose (1953–), Frank Kuppner (1951–) (who has the singularly attractive knack of always seeming on the point of something great), Gerrie Fellows (1954–) (whose New Zealand background supplies another freshening, most vividly present not only in subject matter but in poetics), Kate Clanchy (1956–), Jen Hadfield (1978–), Cheryl Follon (1978–), Bashabi Fraser (1954–), Kevin McNeil (1972–), Kokumo Rocks (1965–), and others, many of whom are collected in the last twenty pages of the anthology *Scotlands*, edited by Douglas Gifford and Alan Riach.

There are intellectually demanding poets such as David Kinloch (1959–) and Iain Bamforth (1959–) and the beautifully poised poems by Richard Price (1966–), most haunting in their evocation of domestic circumstances, relationships between parents and children. Price coined the term 'Informationists' to refer to a loose group including Peter McCarey (1956–), whose work for the World Health Organisation in Geneva has given him a global provenance and experience of poverty and privilege, which, married to unfailing intellectual standing and a marvellous domestic tenderness (the elegies for his parents and his love poems are as memorable as his long, multi-track, complex narrative poems) give his poems a distinctiveness unmatched by any of his contemporaries. His three poems on the run-up to the devolution referendum of 1997 are stunning. The first (number 3) ends:

> And when I fly away from Scotland,
> packing it carefully down in cotton wool for another year,
> when I think of it, near as old as any tree,
> am I using a Roman stone for a step? Is this the last
> light from a done star reeling into my eye like a measuring tape?[16]

McCarey is producing the most progressive, aesthetically politicised poetry on the contemporary Scottish scene. He has never been taken up by a major publisher and his most recent, perhaps most impressive, work is an epic, multi-faceted virtual volume of oblique lyrics collected as *The Syllabary*.[17]

There are the London Scots, Robin Robertson (1955–) and Mick Imlah (1956–2009). Imlah's revisioning of familiar Scottish characters in *The Lost Leader* (2008) is deeply impressive and could only have been written from the perspective of distance and oblique but accurate capacities for measurement he has assiduously cultivated. There are the Cambridge Scot Drew Milne (1964–), and the international Scot, Angus Calder (1942–2008). More than merely Anglo-Scots, these poets draw particular strengths: Robertson from a caustic distance from specific locations in and around Aberdeen; Imlah from a metropolitan gravity unembarrassed by clichés of Scottishness that can spin new, compassionate ways of seeing stock figures and characters from Scottish history; Milne from a specific group of Cambridge poets; and Calder from his experience of the colonial and neo-colonial world, from Kenya to New Zealand, to Tollcross, Edinburgh.

There are important poets who have worked extensively and directly in the new Scottish Parliament and in schools throughout Scotland, evangelically promoting the awareness and practice of poetry amongst Members of the Scottish Parliament and schoolchildren (sometimes equally intractable readers). These include James Robertson (1958–), Matthew Fitt (1968–) and Liz Niven. There are exceptional poets, who have been exploring their own vision for decades, including most impressively Stewart Conn (1936–), whose lyric, farming world, reveals darknesses and balances that are delicately poised on the edge of the abyss. *Stolen Light* (2000) remains a deeply resourceful collection. Conn is both rural and urban, learned and simple, delightful and humble before the unanswerable. Similar qualities inform the work of both John Purser (1943–) in Skye and Roderick Watson (1943–) in Stirling, both of whom have produced memorable work, impossible to categorise, directly engaged by the intuitions, the dreams, of political identity; both sustained by hard material understanding of what William Carlos Williams called the 'thingness' of the world and the transmissions – musical, emotional, that cross between the 'things'.

Any one of these poets might be the subject of a full, extended critical account: an essay, at the very least. Which is to say that what Scotland needs is not more good poets, but more good readers.

I noted above that after the debacles of 1979, the 1980s and 1990s saw a major efflorescence of work in cultural history and criticism across all the artistic disciplines, and of creative writing across all the genres, reconfiguring and reasserting the independent character of Scotland's history and arts. The first edition of the anthology *Dream State: The New Scottish Poets*, edited by Daniel O'Rourke, appeared in the epicentre of this, in 1994. In the Introduction, the editor claimed that, confronted with desolation and despair, the nation's poets were at the forefront in imagining an alternative vision for the future. Eight years later, the second edition appeared, edited by Donny O'Rourke.[18] The future had begun. The second edition appeared in a newly devolved Scotland. The editor's name had become less formal, more itself. Even the meaning of the title seemed changed. The first seemed like a description of unrealised potential, a 'DREAM state', an imaginary nation. The second seemed like a command, order or invitation to imagine action: 'dream STATE!' In other words, it IS possible. A postcard was produced at the time of the 1997 referendum with a map of Scotland covered with the slogan: 'Counter-argument: Yes we can.'

What is evident in both editions is the engagement with play, an openness in form and attitude, an appetite for subjects otherwise excluded from the realms of the poetic, from Angela McSeveney's 'Changing a Duvet' to Gillian Fergusson's 'Pram Rage'. The poets in both books – most reappear, though not all and some in the second edition are new – draw on both native Scots traditions in terms of attitude, countenance and location but they are all well-informed by the American tradition noted above. To varying degrees they also draw on two Scottish poetic traditions, figured in Hugh MacDiarmid and Edwin Morgan. From MacDiarmid's middle and later poetry, through *In Memoriam James Joyce* (1955) with its computer-like resources of reference, seemingly endless shifts, twists and turns of allusion,

and continuous, massive weight of direction, to the enablement of Morgan's
Collected Poems (1990), with its exemplary diversity of games and strategies,
its developing vision and commitments. If Morgan and after him, Lochhead,
remain figures of enablement, that can be seen in perspective. Just as Seamus
Heaney's poetics of negotiation are so much more tractable than Yeats's
poetics of form, spine and rootedness, so Morgan's poetics of experimental-
ism and play are so much more friendly and easy than MacDiarmid's poetics
of the rebarbative, combative and contentious. This is not to underestimate
the intensities of risk in the lives of either Heaney or Morgan, and it is also
to welcome the access of an expanded provenance for poetry in play (which
need not lack seriousness). But it is to recognise a context for the contemporary we should not forget, and to remind ourselves that watertight compart-
ments are only good for sinking ships – that there is much still to learn from
both Morgan and MacDiarmid. Their example is of a practice of intellectual
and writerly openness to experience, in life and in poetry. And the open
complexity of all human experience is precisely the domain of poetry and all
the arts. Understanding this is – and remains – a form of resistance against
the vanity of all efforts to bind and contain imaginative life, against the
mechanical excess of systematic meaning to which the contemporary – even
in its endorsement of play – seems prone. It is to teach that intelligence and
sensitivity reside with an irreducible openness, never with the closed.

Andrew McNeillie has a pertinent poem entitled 'Cynefin *Glossed*'.
'Cynefin' means a sense of belonging, at-homeness. And McNeillie has his
own mixed loyalties – his father was Ian Niall, a very fine novelist from
Galloway in Scotland, author of *Wigtown Ploughman* (1939), *No Resting Place*
(1948) and *A Galloway Childhood* (1967), among many other neglected and
badly under-valued novels. Niall moved south and McNeillie grew up in
Wales but also lived in Ireland for a long time, so his own experience leads
him exactly to what this poem is asking us to consider. This is how it ends:

> tell me in a word how
> you'd express a sense of being that
> embraces belonging here and now,
> in the landscape of your birth and death,
> its light and air, and past, at once, and what
> cause you might have to give it breath?[19]

The poem jags the reader to 'tell me in a word how . . . ' and the word is
'Cynefin' – but the language of the 'gloss' – and the poem – is English.
McNeillie's profound question about language and belonging recollects the
Brechtian formulation that 'Identity' is a function of position and position is
a function of power. The questions raised here energise the contributions to

McNeillie's important journal *Archipelago*, published outwith and in opposition to metropolitan centralism, 'rootless cosmopolitanism' or the authority of the big – or merely reputable – publishing houses.[20]

In 1983, joint winners of the Saltire Book of the Year Award were Edwin Morgan's *Poems of Thirty Years* and Derick Thomson's *Creachadh na Clarsaich/ Plundering the Harp*, happily connecting in celebration the work of two men whose parallel careers at Glasgow University ran alongside their burgeoning poetic production. Teachers and artists both, they were exemplary in their discipline and commitment to the work of giving their best in the ways of both the academic and the creative imagination – not always so productively interwoven. In 2003, Liz Lochhead's *The Colour of Black and White* and Edwin Morgan's *Cathures* marked a wonderful moment of the continuity noted above, as Morgan, Glasgow's first Poet Laureate, was to pass that mantle to Lochhead while he went on to be appointed first National Poet of Scotland in February 2004. *Cathures* was a crowning work of surprises including exhilarating visions of Glasgow past and present, new verse forms, an aurochs, moving meditations on time and mortality – nowhere more expressive than in 'Pelagius', a key poem in the Morgan oeuvre, celebrating mankind's endless original innocence and capacity to learn and grow. Lochhead's book similarly embraced matters of language and identity, place and time, the title itself challenging absolute oppositions with the notion of chiaroscuro, shades and tones.

There is a kaleidoscope of new directions, from the highrollercoastery, panopticonoclastically exuberant, sometimes shuddering to a serious full-stop and trembling-pause poetry of W. N. Herbert to the various identities, sometimes dramatic monologues, even theatrical convocations of voices, in the poetry of Jackie Kay and Carol Ann Duffy. These poets all have the one essential skill of the playwright: the ability to create others. Morgan displays this; MacDiarmid does not.

There is the phonetic punch of Alison Flett's *Whit Lassyz Ur Inty* (clearly 'after' Tom Leonard but no simple mimicry); and there are the swing, rock and jazz idioms of Andrew Greig (1951–), learning from the American poet Ed Dorn the use of personae that might cheekily slip by the weighty constraints of magniloquence implied by an older generation. As Hugh MacDiarmid was to that great generation of post-World War Two poets of whom Morgan is the last survivor, so Morgan himself is to the contemporary, from around 1984 to at least 2008.

In that period, there are poets of real stature and achievement (such as Stewart Conn) who are not easily seen in a school or group, with qualities of measured attentiveness and qualified ironies, sometimes bittersweet, acquired tastes. Alongside the work of older poets, a range of first books of continuing interest – names to keep an eye open for – include work by Donny O'Rourke, Elizabeth Burns, Raymond Vettese (1950–), Ken Cockburn, Anne MacLeod

(1951–) and Roddy Lumsden (1966–). It's worth emphasising again that the voices of women and the poetic expression of the experiences of women are much stronger in the last twenty-five years than they would have been in a sampling of poetry from, say, 1957 to 1982. Any contemporary anthology of Scottish poetry cannot but be rich in poetry by women. The presiding spirit here perhaps is Liz Lochhead, sustaining the human touch that crosses over and corrects any tendencies to self-righteousness, primness, or merely self-important fighting factions, to remind us of the opening she made in the 1970s, again with the help and example of Morgan. In Morgan's plenum of personae, the autobiographical, lyric 'I' is immersed in a multitudinous company, and only prominently present in *The Second Life* (1966), *The New Divan* (1977) and *Love and a Life: 50 Poems* (2003)'. Lochhead's progress charts a trajectory from lyric, autobiographical poems, through dramatic personae to fully developed plays for theatre. It may be that their development of others' voices has heralded a plenitude of poetic voices in the contemporary scene, none of them dominant in the way of 1950s or early 1960s patriarchalism. This in itself may be described as a 'poetics of devolution' and yet it is not a poetics of devolution that is required but a poetics of independence. Mimicry can help bring about learning, but independence of voice in long conversation or dialogue is always required. Contemporary voices are vitalised by such long conversations, most profitably with the dead. Thus, a 'purely' contemporary poetry scene is as likely to be as vapid, self-regarding and as vitiated by time as a 'purely' national identity will be riddled by difference in an age of dislocation. On its own, pluralism is a celebration of distraction and advertises only the surface. As such, it is heartless. As the American poet Stephen Rodefer says in *Four Lectures*: 'I like your voice. Look where it comes from.'[21] That advice invites you to recognise Edwin Morgan's question and answer in the opening lines of his poem for the anthology published in 2005 to commemorate the 700th anniversary of the death of William Wallace, *The Wallace Muse*:

Is it not better to forget?
It is better not to forget.[22]

Whatever we might vote for, this should help to keep us uncomfortable, critical, capable of praise, and able to recognise the gaps in communication the technologies of our society cannot occupy without poetry and the other arts, that it neglects, trivialises or obscures at its evident peril.

CHAPTER TWO

Scottish Women's Poetry since the 1970s

Fiona Wilson

We have been categorised. The gemme's a bogey. (Janet Paisley, 'Poets or What?')[1]

When I was approached to write this chapter, my first impulse was to ask if it would appear with a companion piece on, say, 'Scottish Men's Poetry since the 1970s'. For if 'women poets' may be considered to embody a special category among writers, surely the same may be said of 'men poets' too. After all, male writers – like female writers – live in sexed bodies; their day-to-day experience is shaped by the subtle (and not so subtle) promptings of gender. To ignore this reality is to treat masculinity as transparent and normative, a condition from which the Scottish woman who puts pen to paper can only be seen as somehow perversely deviating, marked as different whether she wishes to be so defined, or not. To accept the term 'woman poet', Tessa Ransford has argued, 'is to accept a limitation, however well meant'; elsewhere, Christopher Whyte has stated that the use of the phrase in the Scottish context represents an 'ungrateful label', meaning not only that it ignores the long history of writing by Scottish women, but also that it lends itself all too easily to institutions looking to cordon off and contain writing by women poets.[2] In this light, as we shall see, most of the poets discussed in this essay have, at some point, expressed discomfort with the idea of being classified as 'woman poets' – a discomfort further exacerbated by their widely divergent opinions as to the meaning of Scottishness.

I began with a problem then, a problem of terms, which was also, of course, a problem of language. How helpful was it really to group together the likes of Liz Lochhead (1947–), Carol Ann Duffy (1955–), Jackie Kay (1961–), Janet Paisley (1948–), Angela McSeveney (1964–), Dilys Rose (1954–), and Kate Clanchy (1965–) under the unified banner 'Scottish Women Poets'? Might an essay like this reproduce the very problems identified by Ransford and Whyte? Might it shunt the writers named here off to a kind of literary annexe, where they would be condemned to talk exhaustively of 'female' topics, while the rest of the volume set off to that popular howff 'The Poets'

Pub' to discuss matters of more universal interest? Might it fall into the trap, identified by Denise Riley, of assuming that the subject of 'women' has a synchronically and diachronically consistent meaning – or as Douglas Gifford and Dorothy McMillan more engagingly put it in their excellent introduction to A History of Scottish Women's Writing (1997), of creating a 'smooth story of sisterhood and continuity [by] papering over the cracks'?[3]

The risk was significant, but, as I came to realise, far from an argument for not writing this chapter. For one thing, female topics (whatever they are) are surely just as universal as any other (the notion of universality being highly contested anyway). For another, The Edinburgh Companion to Contemporary Scottish Poetry clearly has no wish to fence off women poets by gender alone; deeply engaged commentary on a range of women writers is present throughout this volume. Moreover, in the end, without disputing the points made by Riley, Gifford and MacMillan, a perfectly valid argument can be made for the historically specific use of the term 'woman poet' within the parameters of the less than four decades 'since the 1970s'. For it is fact, pure and simple, that, in the course of this brief period, Scottish women writers have produced an unprecedented quantity of remarkable poetry; it is fact (just as pure, but not so simple) that this phenomenon has utterly altered Scottish literature.

To grasp fully the extent of the shift that has taken place in Scottish writing in the last forty years one need only consider the painting referred to above, Alexander Moffat's The Poets' Pub (1980), with its iconic depiction of the 1960s poetry scene as a lively, affable and all-male night of beer and craic in Milne's Bar, Edinburgh. The image is somewhat fictionalised in so far as the poets represented – George Mackay Brown, Robert Garioch, Norman MacCaig, Hugh MacDiarmid, Sorley MacLean, Edwin Morgan, Iain Crichton Smith and Sidney Goodsir Smith – never actually met as a group. Yet, the painting is accurate enough in its portrayal of a cultural moment in which Scottish women who wrote were largely marginalised, if they were visible at all. The sole non-symbolic female figure (a naked Muse is included) in the painting is a faceless bystander, an 'extra' as it were, firmly removed from the centre of the action.

How times have changed. It is not just that the joint has been thoroughly crashed (though the door now swings on its hinges and women poets, it seems, are three deep at the bar); it is more that a certain dialogue about Scotland – a dialogue about language and identity formerly exemplified in the work of MacDiarmid and MacLean et al. – now includes women too. But what does it mean to be included in the national conversation after centuries of virtual invisibility? According to Alice Entwhistle, the work of Scottish women poets is 'often complicated by a sense of estrangement from the aesthetic tradition embedding their nation's communal imagination and memory'.[4] While I would not wish to claim 'estrangement' as the concern of women poets alone (or, for that matter, a subject of interest to all Scottish women who write; it is certainly not), issues of identity – and, yes, alienation – are recurrent among the writers selected here. Also recurrent are: a concern with stereotypes and, more broadly, with representation in general; a fascination with margins, borders and acts of transgression; an insistence on the material presence of the body; and, finally, in terms of style, a strong interest in the use of the dramatic monologue. No doubt, many of these attributes can be traced to the historical circumstances of the late twentieth century, to the emergence of the international women's movement and, in Scotland particularly, to the reclaiming, and redefinition, of national identity in the wake of devolution. Still, while historically grounded, this article offers no over-arching developmental narrative. I do not pretend to describe either a tradition or a school (though the poets discussed here may share certain aspects of style and of content, they are quite various in their attitudes to, for example, feminism and Scottish nationalism); neither do I offer a comprehensive survey. Rather, I present a series of interventions into the writing of a group of women poets whose work has altered what we mean when we talk now about contemporary Scottish poetry.

If any single writer can be described as pioneering the public role of the Scottish woman poet, it is surely Liz Lochhead, who began writing in the 1970s, when literary culture in Scotland, as elsewhere, was very much male dominated. Initial influences included the Irish poet Louis MacNeice (1907– 63) and Roger McGough (1937–), as well as the circle of writers brought together at Glasgow University by Philip Hobsbaum: Jeff Torrington (1935- 2008), James Kelman (1946–), Alasdair Gray (1934–) and especially Tom Leonard (1944–). If the Hobsbawm group was key in nurturing Lochhead's talent, however, it also inevitably highlighted her difference. 'My country was a woman,' Lochhead once said in an interview with Colin Nicholson, invoking Virginia Woolf and precisely putting her finger on her sense of herself as allied with, and yet distinct from, her male peers.[5] Necessarily, then, a central concern in Lochhead's writing has been the deliberate, often painful, attempt to forge identity, an activity repeatedly represented as conflicted when it seeks to engage with issues of gender, as well as of nation.

Lochhead's consciousness of writing from a gendered point of view is evident from her first published book, *Memo for Spring* (1972), which deals with desire and its discontents from a frankly female point of view. More politically aware engagements, however, occur in *The Grimm Sisters* (1981) and in *Dreaming Frankenstein* (1984), both of which are shaped by second- wave feminism, dealing head-on with questions of authorship, agency and the scripting of femininity within patriarchal culture. *The Grimm Sisters* is popu- lated by marginalised female figures, from hags and harridans, to bawds, spin- sters and even frustrated fairytale heroines (the speaker of 'Rapunzstiltskin', for instance, is so enraged by the obtuseness of her princely rescuer that she tears herself in half). But Lochhead's critique is not solely directed towards men; she is also interested in addressing the damage women can inflict on themselves by uncritically absorbing and transmitting self-limiting ideals of femininity. 'The Grim Sisters', for instance, traces a young girl's fascination with the 'grown up girls next door' and their masochistic notions of female beauty. As the sisters alarmingly patch their bodies together from soap, spit and under-wired bras, fifties-style femininity emerges as a monstrous amalgam between armour and a strait-jacket. 'Wasp waist and cone breast, I see them yet', the now-adult speaker reflects: 'I hope, I hope / there's been a change of more than silhouette.'[6]

To break out of the 'silhouette', though, is no easy task (as the torn heroine of 'Rapunzstiltskin' could surely testify) and in Lochhead's work articulation itself is frequently figured as a kind of violent breaking. The trope is central to *The Grimm Sisters* and surfaces too in *Dreaming Frankenstein*, which is framed by two poems explicitly centred on representation. The first of these poems, 'What the Pool Said on Midsummer's Day', offers a powerfully seductive voice, a self-reflexive and somewhat threatening version of what used to be called the feminine mystique: 'What are you waiting for? / I lie here, inviting, winking you in.'[7] There's power of a sort here, but it is of a rather airless and self-dramatising kind; the image of the dangerous pool, as Christopher Whyte points out, depends upon essentialist stereotypes about femininity.[8] Still, the poem that ends the volume, 'Mirror's Song', would seem to deliberately counterpoint the problematic agency of 'What the Pool Said', suggesting that a far more radical solution – a revolutionary destruction of language – must be performed before women can authorise themselves. 'Smash me,' the mirror sings, 'for your daughters and dead / mothers', a process likened to a 'woman giving birth to herself'.[9]

The violent energies of female self-making are a constant in Lochhead's poetry, as well as her many celebrated plays. Interestingly, as her career has progressed, Lochhead has become absorbed too by the complexities of being female *and* Scottish, particularly as these identities relate to the nexus of language and power. Where her early work was typically written in standard English, Lochhead's later poetry often draws on parallels between the marginalised status of women and of the Scots language. 'Kidspoem/Bairnsang' from *The Colour of Black and White* (2003), with its parallel accounts in Scots and in English of the same event, presents a case in point.[10]

it wis January
and a gey dreich day
the first day Ah went to the school
so ma Mum happed me up in ma

good navy-blue napp coat wi the rid tartan hood
birled a scarf aroon ma neck
pu'ed oan ma pixie an' ma pawkies
it was that bitter
said *noo ye'll no starve*
gie'd me a wee kiss and kid-oan skelp oan the bum
and sent me aff across the playground
tae the place Ah'd learn to say
it was January
and a really dismal day
the first day I went to school . . .

Bluntly vivid in performance, 'Kidspoem/Bairnsang' enacts in miniature the marginalisation of Scots within 'standard', English-speaking culture, a process likened to the daughter's separation from the mother at the gates of the school. What's lost in the moment of splitting is not just a language, but, also, an intimate connection between women; the scene repeats and repeats, as if stuck in the loop of trauma. Much of Lochhead's work derives its energy from such unresolved divisions.

The notion of 'breaking into speech' appears too in the work of Carol Ann Duffy, which returns often to the subtle dislocations of memory and identity. Born in Glasgow, Duffy moved at the age of seven to Staffordshire and grew up in England, an early uprooting to which she has returned often in her poetry. A prolific, skilled and often political poet, Duffy is acutely sensitive to how power dynamics shape subjectivity, dynamics explored in poems that range easily between intimate reflections and dramatic monologues; Duffy, Daniel O'Rourke has written, is 'at once a *performing* and a *confiding* poet' a description that neatly conveys the slipperiness of subject positions in Duffy's poetry.[11] The effect is dazzling in its variety, subtly subversive of the unspoken assumptions implicit in the first person 'I' (male and heterosexual) of traditional lyric poetry.

Duffy's interest in subverting such assumptions appears from her first book *Standing Female Nude* (1985), the title poem of which presents the response of a female model to a male artist intent on creating her image on canvas, an act rendered as a form of sexual aggression. The model's sceptical assessment – 'It does not look like me' – may seem understated, yet, as the poem suggests, alienation is the necessary first step towards self-realisation (a topic which returns with a vengeance in the monologues of Duffy's wildly popular collection *The World's Wife* (1999)).[12] Still, not all of the speakers in Duffy's poetry can speak with such confidence and she frequently registers the real world forces – sexism, racism, homophobia – that police identity, at times through physical force, but also through language itself. Words like 'strange', 'homesick', 'exile', 'deportation', 'foreign' and 'translation' riddle, for example,

Selling Manhattan (1987), which is full of radically estranged and alienated speakers. 'Things get away from one,' the unhappy matron of 'Recognition' says, blaming herself for the gradual erasure of the aging woman from society, 'I've let myself go, I know.'[13] Similarly erased is the immigrant speaker of 'Yes, Officer' who is strong-armed into confessing to a crime of which he knows himself to be innocent. Meanwhile, in 'Foreign', Duffy directly asks the reader to '[i]magine living in a strange, dark city' where '[y]ou think / in a language of your own and talk in theirs'.[14]

Poems like these provide an important and very deliberate counterpoint to more personal treatments of estrangement in *Selling Manhattan* and the book that followed it, aptly titled *The Other Country* (1990). In each of these volumes, exilic loss is figured as painful and yet intrinsic to desire and imagination. Thus, in 'Homesick', the poet wonders whether 'when we love, when we tell ourselves we do / we are pining for first love, somewhen, / before we thought of wanting it' and in 'Strange Place', she considers how even the most exquisitely intimate moment – watching her lover undress by 'household candlelight' – will later became a distant, dislocated memory.[15] Most intriguing in this respect, then, are the several poems in which Duffy addresses her childhood move from Scotland to England. 'Originally', begins with a surreal vision of the Duffy family's removal 'from our own country' to England 'in a red room / which fell through the fields' as absurdly and terribly as Dorothy's house in *The Wizard of Oz*.[16] To find the security of ground, the poem suggests, the child emigrant has no option but to assimilate; the narrator recalls 'my tongue / shedding its skin like a snake, my voice / in the classroom sounding just like the rest'. Yet, below this new 'self' remains the resistant tug of the Scots word 'skelf' (meaning splinter), a discomfort that produces difficult feelings, like shame, but also a consciousness, an openness, to other ways of being, that may, in fact, be crucial to the creative imagination. 'I am homesick, free, in love' the speaker in 'The Way My Mother Speaks' says of listening to her mother's Glaswegian accent; in 'In Your Mind', imaginative exploration is likened to being 'lost but not lost'.[17] Perhaps appropriately, then, 'Originally' concludes, not with an assertion of origins, but with questions, a hesitation and a withheld response, that may in its own way offer a kind of gift to the poet: 'Now, *Where do you come from?* / strangers ask. *Originally?* And I hesitate.'[18]

To choose among identities may represent a kind of freedom, but it is a freedom hard-won, if it is achievable at all; what's more, the downside of indeterminacy may be the erasure of history. This is something Duffy is far from naïve about and which Jackie Kay, her former partner, is all too aware of. Born in 1961 to a Highland mother and Nigerian father, Kay was adopted at birth by a white Scottish couple and brought up in Glasgow in a household deeply committed to the Communist party. Like Lochhead and Duffy, Kay is interested in the use of dramatic technique in poetry; like several of the writers discussed here, she draws frequently on her own life for her subject matter. It is reductive, however, to read Kay's poetry as autobiography (and she herself has repeatedly warned readers against doing so); more accurately, writing her self is an opportunity to stage questions about identity.

Kay's first book, *The Adoption Papers* (1991), draws together the voices of three women – a birth mother, adoptive mother and the daughter of both – to braid a narrative about interracial adoption. It is an intriguing and ambitious book, as interested in pushing against the boundaries of the family (as conventionally construed) as it is in challenging the perimeters of genre. On the page, Kay uses three different kinds of typeface to distinguish the separate voices, a visual texture further enhanced by the collision of Glaswegian and standard English patterns of speech. Overall, the result is to suggest a script that is 'unified' only in so far as it is the product of different subjectivities, a process of knowing that cannot but complicate the adoptive daughter's efforts to piece together the story of her origins, highlighting the ambiguous relationships between language, identity and power. In one comic passage, for example, the adoptive mother tries to conceal her radical politics from a social worker's assumed disapproval: 'All the copies of the *Daily Worker* / I shoved under the sofa / the dove of peace I took down from the loo.'[19] The humour of this scene plays differently, however, in 'Black Bottom', which explicitly distinguishes between identities that are freely chosen and those that are imposed by others. Where the white communist can – if she chooses – conceal her politics by shoving *The Daily Worker* under the cushions, her black daughter has no choice but to confront openly a racist society that insistently defines her skin colour as a mark of inferiority. This is a perspective that is difficult, but necessary, for the white mother to grasp: 'colour matters to the nutters; / But she says my daughter says / It matters to her.'[20]

How and why '[i]t matters' is a *leitmotif* in Kay's work. *Off Colour* (1998) diagnoses the systemic effects of racism, sexism and homophobia, figured as viruses spread through society by language. 'Say the words came first. / Then the look followed. / Then it was the smell. / The fear of touch.'[21] Though Scotland often flatters itself as colour-blind, Kay finds the legacy of racism to be as Scottish as tattie scones – or, say, 'The Broons', a longstanding cartoon strip that portrays the day-to day activities of a 'representative' Scottish family. In a subversive little skipping rhyme towards the end of *Off Colour*, Kay gets to the heart of the Scottish disease, slyly upending one stereotype with another: 'Scotland is having a heart attack / Scotland is having a heart attack / The Broons' Bairn's Black.'[22] Yet if there is an argument being made here for the necessity of identity politics, subjectivity is never a simple issue in Kay's work. In 'Pride', the poem that rounds out *Off Colour*, a speaker meets a black man on a train who instantly identifies her as Ibo, a claiming of kinship at once pleasing and alienating to the speaker who finds her entire face turned into a map, in which the stranger locates 'even the name / of my village in Nigeria'.[23] Faced with a flood of flattering generalisations about her 'people', the speaker recognises a tribal pride she has also seen in Scotland too. 'And what,' she asks pointedly, 'are the Ibos faults?' The final image is as much one of self-recognition as it is of displacement: 'When I looked up, the black man had gone. / Only my own face startled me in the dark train window.'

Still, if language is the source of the problem, it may also represent the only possible cure; certainly, it is the medium within which the poet must work. *Life Mask* (2005) wrestles with this necessary contradiction, a contradiction magnified by the concept of art as 'self-expression'. At first glance, *Life Mask* looks, once again, to be strongly autobiographical; written during and after the break-up of Kay's fifteen-year relationship with Duffy, its overall narrative arc describes the gradual collapse of a long-term relationship; the image of the 'life mask' is drawn from Kay's real-life experience of having her face cast in clay by sculptor Michael Snowdon. Yet the life-mask is also a symbol, a means of exploring the various possibilities of an art derived from, and yet also distinct from, the life of the artist. Thus, while 'Clay=Freedom' describes the surrender to the mask as an almost liberating escape from the pain of selfhood, 'Gone with the Wind' considers the horror of imposed racial categories. Only in the hands of the poet does the clay-powdered life-mask offer a way of enduring and transforming experience so that life can begin again: 'I sat up with my pale face in my hands / and all of a sudden it was spring.'[24]

The troubled interrogations of identity explored in the work of Lochhead, Duffy and Kay take a somewhat different direction in the work of Janet Paisley. In a 1991 article in the poetry magazine *Chapman*, Paisley vividly attacked the elision of the words 'woman' and 'feminist' in literary criticism, before moving on to reject the usefulness of the term 'woman poet' altogether:

> The words *woman* and *feminist* have the precisely the same relationship to the word *poet* as have the words *man, girl, boy, pensioner, politician, soldier, housekeeper, golfer, wrestler*. If the poetry is truth it can have no option. A poem communicates experience by releasing the emotional impact of that experience within the reader. If not it fails. The gender, world or socio-political view of the poet has no bearing on the poem's success or failure. Nor does the subject matter.[25]

There's fair comment in this statement (Paisley rightly skewers the view that 'for "Scottish poets" read male'), as well as some rather unexamined assumptions (is poetry 'truth'? Whose 'truth'?). As Paisley herself goes on to say in defence of the notion that '[p]oetry that is universal is deeply feminist', 'we must be careful about how we use words . . . [O]nly fools, male and female, think being a boy is the same as being human.'[26]

In fact, an awareness of the trickiness of language infuses some of Paisley's most interesting poems. 'Conjugate', for example, (from the 1996 volume *Alien Crop*) plays on the root meaning of that word ('to join' or 'to unite') to riff on language, marriage and heterosexual love as a means of approaching a far less commonly discussed topic: the hormonal storm of sexual desire that can precede menstruation. '[L]ooping the full moon', the speaker finds herself in a state of apparent paradox, 'seriously / deranged' yet also 'in possession of / all my faculties'.[27] What's dismantled here is not just the stereotype of the premenstrual woman as mentally incompetent (this speaker has no trouble in being able to use her mind to think about the intensity of her bodily desires – she can even compose a poem on the subject), but also the notion of female desire as irrational and, therefore, dangerous, a problem in need of policing. The full implications of this bristling, clever poem, however, emerge in its second stanza:

Consumed by
feeling for you
biology stands on its head.
What is instead
consummate
in this desire is
I'm seriously
dispossessed.

'[B]iology stands on its head' because what's also undone in 'Conjugate' is the shackling of morality and reproduction in traditional Judeo-Christian thinking about female sexuality; the female speaker's desire is a phenomenon with a life outside of her physical ability to conceive. It is this realisation that prompts the serious recognition of dispossession in the final lines – for it is male-dominated language and culture, the canon long assumed to represent 'universal' experience, that has 'dispossessed' female desire.

Certainly, the writing of dispossessed feelings – sexual longing, but also, anger, love and sadness – is important to Paisley's work, which moves easily, and without self-consciousness, between English and Scots. 'I am awash with you, floundering / as flood breaches hull and stern,' she writes in 'Sinking the Ship'.[28] 'Be careful man / if you come in to this woman,' announces 'Storm Warning', 'you may never sleep / soundly in your silent bed / again.'[29] Meanwhile, the monologues of *Ye Cannae Win* (2000) feature a range of speakers – mostly, though not entirely female; mostly, though not entirely, Scots-speaking – who voice emotions and attitudes ('freedoms big and sma') hitherto unaccommodated within ruling social narratives.[30] The speakers of the fifty-six poems in this book include the shy, the aging, a rape victim, the mother of a rapist, an emotionally-bullied caregiver and in the section entitled 'Neighbourhood Hoodwatch' an

entire community of gossiping and aggrieved neighbours. What's most effective
about the collection is the sense that it aims to return the marginalised to the
centre, to expand the 'home' of Scottish culture.

Being at home with the female body in all its mess, absurdity and pleasure
is the central concern of Angela McSeveney's poetry, a poetry that dignifies
the domestic and quotidian with a precise, almost hyperreal, attention to
detail. 'My breasts / walk ahead of me,' McSeveney writes in Coming Out With
It (1992), as if surprised by the presence of a pair of strange, soft animals.[31]
Elsewhere, a starched blouse 'finds its backbone' and a ponytail in a plastic
bag functions as a curious, almost sacred, relic of childhood.[32] Celebrated,
memorialised – but, more often, simply looked at, the body in these poems
inspires a stir of feelings: anxiety accompanies a late period; the fear of being
considered ugly meets a confession of love; and, in 'The Fat Nymphomaniac's
Poem', desire is, at once, announced and mocked: 'Tall men turn me on,' the
'fat nymphomaniac' confesses, 'If there's more of him pound for pound / I can
lay me down not smothering anyone.'[33] This is funny, but also somewhat dis-
comfiting; is the reader really being invited to laugh at a confession of shame?
Perhaps, yes; McSeveney's uncomfortable humour resembles Duffy's s(k)elf. In
fact, what is bold about this poet's work is its unflinching willingness to explore
thoughts and feelings long considered unspeakable (at least, when presented
by a woman) within the more rarefied precincts of canonical literary culture.
McSeveney's abrasive language attacks, for instance, long-standing notions of
ideal femininity as flawless and compliant. Here, the body pregnant, scarred,
raped, sexual and, even, self-mutilated abruptly intrudes on the reader's attention. Where Paisley resorts, perhaps too often, to classic, aestheticised symbols
(woman as sea, flowering tree and so on), McSeveney recalls having lice as
a child or meditates on an unusually hairy acquaintance. Emotional experience, too, is frequently described in physical terms. 'He tore half my torso
from me when he left,' 'Exposure' records, 'My nerve-endings hung invisible
in the air.'[34] Even more striking is a group of poems about bi-polar illness that
strongly emphasise the biological origins of manic depression. In 'Vivisection',
for example, a psychiatric interview is likened to surgery without anaesthetic:
'[L]aid open', the speaker says, 'I spill my guts.'[35]

This is language that, like Paisley's, inverts mind/body dualism, dragging the physical and historical presence of the writer's own body – neither
normative nor transparent – firmly into the view of history. Thus, 'Stretch
Marks' describes 'the white lines' that show 'where my skin took the strain' of
puberty, while 'Breast Exam' tells of how

[o]n my left breast a faded scar
reminds me of the lesson I learned at fifteen.
It can't always happen to other people.[36]

In 'Ultrasonic Scan' 'invisible incisions' produce unreadable 'omens . . . on a black screen'.[37] It is this sense of the body as possessing a language not always understood, or openly articulated, that lends force to the collection's title poem, 'Coming Out With It', which tenderly traces a series of tragi-comic misrecognitions between a gay man and a straight woman. To come out with 'it' is not simply to admit the body, or even sexuality, but to articulate the self as it has rarely been spoken before.

Dilys Rose, like most of the poets above, confesses herself 'turned off by [poetry] that preaches its point . . . whether it's feminism, socialism or nationalism'.[38] Still, Rose's poetry hardly shrinks from issues of social injustice, often coolly documented in her work. *Madame Doubtfire's Dilemma* (1989), the collection that brought Rose to public notice, exemplifies this approach, opening with a poem, 'No Name Woman', that links poverty to sexism in the figure of an anonymous female worker in an unnamed developing country. For 'no name woman', linguistic exclusion is hardly an aesthetic issue; it has drastic, real-world consequences, not least the utter denial of her personhood. 'All day,' Rose writes, 'she feeds the drunken menfolk' as 'they gamble / Quarrel and groom their fighting cocks'.[39] The Western female observer is not off the hook, however, here or elsewhere in Rose's poetry; sisterhood is not to be simply assumed. What is the narrator's relationship anyway to the nameless woman she describes? Is the narrator, by virtue of her economic privilege, placed among the men served – or, aligned, because of her gender, with the server?

If the complexity here is typical of Rose's poetry, which is deeply alive – without 'preach[ing] its point' – to issues of power and language, 'No Name Woman' also provocatively counterpoints the monologues that form the core of *Madame Doubtfire's Dilemma*. In these poems – as in the similar monologues of Lochhead, Duffy, Kay and Paisley – a succession of female personae rail against their own oppression. Thus, in 'Sister Sirens', the archetypal seductresses of Greek myth 'bitch, squabble' and curse the gods '[w]ho blessed us, with the songbird's voice / The hawk's claw'.[40] 'Caryatid', stuck in place too, complains of the 'elegant pose' she must hold though its 'inbuilt twist of the hip / Is crippling'.[41] And in the much-anthologised 'Figurehead', a speaker describes her own gradual effacement:

I lumber on, grudging my status –
I'm purpose-built to dip and toss
My cleavage, crudely carved

To split waves
My hair caked with salt
My face flaking off.[42]

This is vivid and capable work, but, in its very skilfulness, it points ironically to the limitations implicit in this kind of writing. Rose's speakers, one
notices – like speakers in Duffy's *The World's Wife* – have meaning only in
relation to men (that's *why* they are sexist stereotypes in the first place).
Fixed in place, they speak primarily to lament, or rage against, their own
powerlessness; all are as 'tethered' to their roles as the Sirens are to their
rocks. Revisionary 'talk back' may feel good, but it offers limited rewards. The
challenge for the poet is how to move beyond a form that, without radical
innovation, threatens to become a dead end, as restrictive as the very forces
it seeks to resist.

Yet Rose is a nimble writer, as demonstrated by her latest collection,
Bodywork (2007). Here, she takes on the by-now well-travelled topic of the
body. This is not primarily autobiographical poetry and the absence of that
mode seems significant; Rose's interest does not lie, like that of McSeveney,
in personal experience, but in wide-ranging ideas about the body – delighted,
doubled, photographed, studied, gendered, martyred, working, aging, dying,
spectral, tattooed, mystical and commemorated – as described by an accom-
plished writer who is also a woman. In so doing, *Bodywork* gives a vibrant
assent to a way of knowing that Rose seems to feel has been so undervalued in
Scotland which, at first, it appears 'foreign', 'female' and perhaps impossible
to assimilate. In the wonderful 'Siguiriya in Scotland', Spanish flamenco and
Scottish culture are summoned together in a dance that begins wrong-footed,
but ends with a joyful affirmation.[43]

> the whisky the beer the soft-shoe stagger
> the shiv in the fist
>
>   aye
>
> sandstorm sirocco mirage
>
>   ay!
>
> smirr drizzle haar
>
>   aye
>
> the rose the thorn the hot bloom of blood
>
>   *ay!*
>
> the thistle   the thistle

aye
ay!

Questions of home and abroad figure prominently in the poetry of Kate Clanchy, which longs to move freely across borders, from the so-called 'centre' to the notional 'margin', much like the swallows that appear through-out her second book *Samarkand* (1999). Crossings of all sorts, in fact, are frequent in her work. Born in Glasgow in 1965 and educated in Edinburgh, Clanchy views herself as Anglo-Scots (her father is English and she lived for several years in England) and rejects monolithic nationalism in preference to a national identity formed somewhere in the middle. Clanchy's attitude to the role of gender in her work also assumes a position that is flexible; though she clearly sees herself as writing in distinction to a male tradition, she is less interested in openly opposing the canon than she is in occupying its tropes and habits and appropriating them for her own use. It is an approach that suits her cool and intelligent handling of heterosexual desire in *Slattern* (1995) and *Samarkand*; and in *Newborn* (2004) her treatment of the strange, and still barely represented, continent of motherhood.

Slattern begins with a catalogue poem, the speaker of which lists with a velvety irony her favorite kinds of men.

I like the simple sort, the soft white-collared ones
smelling of wash that someone else has done,
of apples, hard new wood. I like the thin-skinned,
outdoor, crinkled kind, the athletes, big-limbed,
who stoop to hear, the moneyed men, the unironic . . . [44]

'Men' could be a description of *Slattern* as a whole, given that the book itself features a large number of poems devoted to male figures: a haunted married man, a cuckold, a bar fly, a teenage busker, an aerialist in tights and lycra; even a grown man imagined 'as a lonely boy: / at the biscuit smelling, sour milk stage'.[45] But Clanchy is far from either mothering these strange fauna or being swept away by them: 'I put them all at sea. They peer at my dark land / as if through sun on dazzling waves, and laugh.'[46] '[D]azzling' irony is the mode of much of this book. Thus 'Tip' offers advice for a potential lover ('Get a hat, a homburg, keep / it on in bars, tipped / so just your profile shows'), patching together the male beloved in a blazon as stylised as that of any Renaissance sonnet.[47] This is masculinity as fancy dress, gender as a pose – and there's never really any question that the poet/tipper, with her total command of line breaks and rhythm, is completely in charge:

Be lean.
Be leaning on the bar I plan

to enter. Irony's the ice I keep
my dreams in. Drop
some in your whisky. Hold it there.

Samarkand extends the sexually transgressive material of *Slattern*, with
poems that again reverse standard dynamic between the male/writer/lover
and the female/muse/beloved who is written. The cleverly titled 'Spell',
for example, invites the male beloved to read the poem itself so that 'you
shall not know which one of us is reading / now, which writing, and which
written.'[48] 'Conquest' finds the female poet laying claim to the body of the
male beloved, a gesture repeated in a group of poetic border raids on the
canonical poetry of Yeats and Tennyson. Other border-crossings occur too,
from the migrations of multicultural Londoners to the far-flung travels of
Clanchy's extended family. Still, as 'To Travel' suggests, the difference
between the exotic and the familiar, the foreign and the domestic, may be
more in the eye of the beholder than one might expect: 'But staying,' the
poem asserts, 'is a kind of leaving.'[49]

Particularly interesting, then, is 'The Bridge Over the Border', which
deals with Clanchy's mixed feelings about her Scottish origins. The poem
begins with the speaker on a bridge between England and Scotland, in an
in-between place that makes her uncomfortably aware of the demands of
national narrative:

Here, I should surely think of home –
my country and the neat steep town
where I grew up . . . [50]

It is that 'should' that draws attention, registering as it does the sense of
an obligation that is, at once, recognised and resisted (a response further
underlined by the open-ended dash that accompanies the word 'home',
breaking the first and second lines). The kind of thing, it seems, a poet in
her position 'should surely think' is conveyed next in a pair of visual images:
the first is of wild Caledonia, with its 'winds and changing, stagy light'; the
second, of a busker picking out 'Scotland the Brave' in 'filmic golden light'.
Neither satisfies the speaker and the artifice of such claims to an 'essential'
Scotland is indicated by the use of the words 'stagy' and 'filmic'. Instead, a
personal memory comes to her mind, the memory of an unfinished relationship. Categories clash, dissolve and reform; Clanchy's country, it seems,
was a man.

It was October. I was running to meet a man
with whom things were not quite settled,

were not, in fact, ever to settle, and I stopped
halfway to gaze at birds – swallows
in their distant thousands, drawn
to Africa, or heat, or home, not knowing
which, but certain how.

CHAPTER THREE

Contemporary Poetry in Scots

Tom Hubbard

To kill a language is to kill a people. (Pearse Hutchinson, 'The Frost is All Over')[1]

The following survey takes as its starting point the continentally-convulsive year 1989–90, a time of serious moves towards bringing 'Europe', culturally speaking, to Scotland. The Scottish Poetry Library invited poets from post-Ceauşescu Romania to read at the Edinburgh International Festival. Peter France and Duncan Glen had brought out their *European Poetry in Scotland* (1989), an anthology of translations made by Scottish poets. Many of these versions had appeared over the years in magazines; those in Scots had been scattered throughout issues of outlets sympathetic to the language, such as *Akros, Chapman* and *Lallans*. It was a revelation to view this material within one set of covers. A counterpart volume of European poetry translations into Gaelic, edited by Derick Thomson, was refused funding by Glasgow City of Culture 1990 on the grounds of its 'irrelevance' to the city; happily the volume came out anyway, under Thomson's Gairm imprint.

Glasgow's confused attitudes to Scottish language and literature were not limited to Gaelic. From its very title, Philip Hobsbaum's essay, 'Speech Rather Than Lallans', exemplified an orthodoxy of the 1990s and beyond, pitting spoken Glaswegian against 'Lallans', a register which is better designated as Scots language *reintegrated* from its various dialects.[2] The trendified city ('Glitzgow') seemed to be looking after its own, at the expense of other parts of Scotland. Curiously, the Scots of Edwin Morgan, the city's national treasure, is not limited to Glaswegian 'speech' though it is built – fittingly – on a Glaswegian base; much the same could be said of the Scots of a later Glasgow poet David Kinloch (1959–). But the conventional wisdom was that Hugh MacDiarmid – the doyen of reintegrated Scots – was passé, a frightful male chauvinist to boot, and that the Scots Language Society (perceived as dogmatically pro-'Lallans') was comprised mostly of old duffers obsessed with spelling rather than spells. Relatively petty acrimonies were exaggerated to create ersatz controversy. (Duncan Glen's Scots poetry, based on a relaxed, conversational Lanarkshire idiom, was overlooked by both camps.)

Into this fetid atmosphere stepped two young men who were hell-bent on saving 'Scotland' from its supposed stay-at-home 'small-mindedness'. Bellshill-born, a promising Glasgow graduate before he proceeded to Oxford, Robert Crawford (1959–) and the Scots language did not detain each other for long: the reasons why occupy his sections of the collection *Sharawaggi* (1990), which he co-authored with the Dundonian W. N. Herbert (1961–). (Dundee became, to all intents and purposes, an honorary Glasgow.) Crawford celebrated himself as a 'ghetto-blastir' against the 'ghetto-makars'. With a scattering of f-words he alerted us to how tough he was, and in 'Bonnie Macho' he ticked off the requisite feminist boxes.

Herbert, his temporary accomplice, was less disposed towards politically correct gestures, and evolved a Scots idiom from the Dundonian speech which came naturally to him. Though he has not completely abandoned the sophomoric smart-assery of the *Sharawaggi* days, there has always been more to him than court jester to the Scottish literary establishment. By far the best poem from *Sharawaggi* was his 'The Hermitage'; here, one had the sense that the poet had more than a merely academic grasp of the relations of Scotland's past to its present and to possible futures. Edwin Muir had inveighed against 'sham bards of a sham nation': Herbert's target was James Macpherson, he who seduced all Europe with his fake 'Ossian' prose-poems. Herbert descends from the Hermitage, the folly erected atop a Perthshire gorge as a tribute to 'Ossian', to the flora and fauna of the surrounding woodland and to symbolic stirrings in the water: '*thi saumon loupin i thi firth, / shakkan sealice frae 'iz scales / fur thi push upstream*' [poet's italics].[3] Here both the landscape and the poem expand beyond the Hermitage, adjacent Black Linn Falls and River Braan, which later flows into the greater River Tay, which in turns meets the North Sea at Herbert's home city. Herbert's favoured fish – salmon here – is more usually the 'gairfish', a dolphin of these particular waters, and the poet's somewhat MacDiarmidian objective correlative for Scottish resurgence. At his best Herbert revives MacDiarmid's practice of a pliable, often playful Scots that reaches parts of the gairfishy fathoms of the unconscious that straight English cannot reach; the dictionary is starting-point rather than endgame, is the imagination's servant rather than its master. As long as the native-speak undercurrent is maintained, this is a poetry that even as it eschews 'nationalism', knows a local habitation and a name. If there's 'belonging', though, there's even more detachment. In 'First Fit', the historical palimpsest of the poet's city both draws him and repels him: 'There's nae solvendiness [trustworthiness] tae Dundee's screed; / uts anely alphabet is fisses and / a screel o limbs across thi pehvment's sklate.'[4] Herbert got out, and is now based in Newcastle, as a professor in creative writing.

A number of poets born in the mid–late 1950s and early 1960s, including Crawford and Herbert, designated themselves the 'Scottish Informationists'. An anthology that acted largely as the group's showcase, *Dream State* (1994), edited by Daniel O'Rourke, was rounded on by the robustly non-institutional poet and dramatist George Gunn:

> But their poetry does not inform, it obscures. Because information is power. With power you can control. & with control you can edit. & with editing goes publishing. With publishing goes status & so it goes on . . . It's as if there has been an intellectual surrender. Let us call a spade a spade: the means of production of contemporary Scottish poetry has fallen into the hands of a few ambitious academics whose terms of reference will kill off poetry in Scotland, if we let them. They are just another kind of English Department imperialism.[5]

Gunn's polemic appeared in a relatively little-known poetry magazine, and a potentially genuine controversy failed to materialise.

Dream State's editor, Daniel (aka Donny) O'Rourke has been oddly dismissive of the translations he made of Blaise Cendrars, and of other early twentieth-century Modernist poets. These appeared in an intriguing pamphlet which he co-authored with Richard Price, *Eftirs/Afters* (1996). O'Rourke's register draws on *both* Glaswegian-speech and reintegrated Scots. Cendrars, Swiss (and part-Scottish) *cosmopolite*, receives a make-over that situates him in one of his ancestral lands; Glasgow is convincingly asserted as a city of Europe:

> An thon's thi wey Ah stravaig Glesca ilka nicht,
> Frae Kelvinbrig tae thi Calton, corsin thi Andes
> Ablow the glister o brent new starn, gretter, mair kittlie:
> Soudren Rood mair bi ordinar wi ilka step ye tak towards it
> Clims oot o thi auld warld
> Aboon thi new continent.[6]

This was by no means the first attempt to create, via translation, a panoramic, quasi-Cubist cityscape in western-Scots: I reprinted a version of Apollinaire's 'Zone', by James Russell Grant (1924–2008), in *The New Makars* anthology.[7] John Manson's 'Toun Graveyaird' is a version of the Spanish poet Luis Cernuda's melancholy observations, in exile, of the Glasgow Necropolis. The city's European visitors are not always cheerleaders. But Manson's pamphlet collection of translations, *Frae Glesca til Manila* (2000), which includes his Cernuda, is a major marker of the international concerns of Scots-language poetry, as of its tendency to strong social conscience. Among the Latin-American poets rendered by Manson (1932–) is César Vallejo, who draws forth a particularly fine version of 'Piedra Negra sobre una Piedra Blanca'

('Black Stane on Tap o a White Stane').[8] *Lallans* editor John Law (1951–) commissioned radically-minded poets such as John McDonald (1939–) to produce Scots versions of the work of Pablo Neruda (who was, in turn, an admirer of Hugh MacDiarmid). Law's own contribution, published in pamphlet form as *The Heichts o Macchu Picchu* (2006), revives in the Andes the collective memory of markedly Scottish working people, as part of that of their counterparts everywhere:

I see the auld bodie, the bondsman, the sleeper
in the paurks, I see a cheil, a thousand cheils, a man, a thousand wemen
droukit in the bleck onding, brunt bleck wi rain an nicht
livid an staned wi statue's wecht
Johnnie mac a'Chlachair, son o Wiracocho
Johnnie Cauldwame, aff the green starn,
Johnnie Barfuit, graunwean til the turquoise
come rise wi me an be born aa, ma brithers

. . . Lat me staun lodesman for the deid.

Speak for yersels throu ma vyce, ma bluid.[9]

In an article mainly on recent Northern Irish poetry, I wrote that 'the target register [of Law's Neruda] was absolutely spot-on for a lament for lost community, with that countervailing hope in the capacity of human tenderness, of the generous gesture, to reclaim us somehow from the tragedy of transience'.[10]

John Corbett's *Written in the Language of the Scottish Nation: A History of Literary Translation into Scots* (1999) has established itself as a pioneering document of reclamation. Elsewhere he has remarked that

[w]here translators into Scots are distinct from their anglophone counterparts is purely on the issue of visibility, openness. Scots as a medium of translation is as inescapably foreignising as it is simultaneously domesticating . . . this is a necessary outcome of centuries of marginalising of Scots as a written medium. Translators into Scots are therefore always visible, their ideological hearts permanently displayed on their sleeves.[11]

In this article, Corbett is referring to a Scot's familiarity with spoken Scots, counterpointed by the relative strangeness of the language in written form.

Corbett's Irish colleague Michael Cronin has berated postcolonial literary critics for failing to include minority European languages in their deliberations, and thereby helping to consign such languages to the oblivion favoured by the imperia against which postcolonialism normally vents its righteous polemics. 'Minority languages,' claims Cronin, 'can be seen as the quintessential and emblematic expression of the local in the era of globalization.'[12] An Aberdeen-based (and Ayrshire-born) colleague of Corbett and Cronin is J. Derrick McClure, who seamlessly combines the roles of linguist and poet-translator. In a succession of studies published during our period, McClure has emphasised the historical pedigree of Scots as a medium for translation. Back in 1990 he argued that 'translation was . . . a means of demonstrating the continuity of the national literary tradition and buttressing the claims of the contemporary poets to be the heirs of the great mediaeval Makars.'[13] In making Scots versions of Gaelic poets such as Sorley MacLean, Aonghas MacNeacail and (most recently) Aonghas Pàdraig Caimbeul, McClure has demonstrated a solidarity between Scotland's two indigenous languages, so often pitted against each other by divide-and-rulers, but he also ranges well into Europe. Advised and assisted by the Austrian poet-scholar Heidelinde Prüger (who has herself translated Scots work into Austrian dialects), McClure has translated germanophone Austrians such as Alfred Kollerisch ('The Hous I Wes Born In' appeals to the elegiac strain in Scots) and Schoschana Rabinovici.[14] Rabinovici's originals are in an Austrian form of Yiddish. McClure's versions express a very Scottish intimacy with central European tragedy, not of course in the sense of a shared historical experience (though the Nazi bombings of Aberdeen and Clydebank were real enough), but as part of a general human compassion with the dead (and still living) victims of the Holocaust. As with John Law's Neruda, the capacity of Scots for simultaneous toughness and tenderness – all harsh consonants and sinuous vowels – is movingly displayed, as in 'A Bonnie Simmer's Day', when the young girl is told of her father's arrest:

> The pynes is beginnin nou for us Jews,
> the Germans hes come tae Vilnius nou,
> an brocht muckle ill aareadies tae you. . . .
>
> When he'll win hame, an whit's tae happen then,
> ye'll jalouse yourself aareadies, hen (translator's italics).[15]

Moreover, McClure's engagement with Yiddish reminds us of a time when there was such a register as Scots-Yiddish, as spoken by the Edinburgh Jewish community, and as documented by David Daiches in his memoir *Two Worlds* (1959).

McClure's 'continuity of the national literary tradition' accords with Hamish Henderson's 'the carrying stream' – the phrase that names the annual festival, held in Edinburgh during November, to celebrate his legacy. Henderson (1919–2002) was himself a fine poet in Scots but because of his main commitment to the oral tradition, it was for a long time difficult, though not completely impossible, to obtain his work in printed form: a prime example of the need for researchers to get out of the university library and undertake fieldwork – in accordance with Henderson's own practice and that of his School of Scottish Studies at Edinburgh University.

In recent years the most striking instance of 'the carrying stream' has been the Indian summer syndrome: the simultaneity of veteran poets' later work with first collections by younger figures. A case in point is Lillias Scott Forbes (1919–), whose earliest Scots poems were admired by Hugh MacDiarmid, the friend of her composer-father, Francis George Scott. She was approaching eighty when she brought out a new pamphlet collection, *Turning a Fresh Eye* (1998).

Her cousin, George Bruce (1909–2002), enjoyed the most remarkable of Indian summers. His late collection *Pursuit: Poems 1986–1998* (1999) charges forth with an energy rare in poets a third of his age. Bruce's locus in 'the carrying stream' is north-east Scotland, its sense of community (at least in the past) and of course its distinct forms of the Scots language. 'Mindin David Murison' is a fine tribute to a fellow north-easterner, the editor of the *Scottish National Dictionary*:

Sic a wecht o warlds tae cairry,
an that he did maist lichtly.
That deen hame, tween roarin seas
an Mormond Hill. Bit niver feenished.
He tripped alang, sma-boukit man,
gryte hertit, mair than ony meth unnerstan.[16]

In 'Weys o Self-Preservin Natur' the poet handles a clam-shell fossil:

Aince there stirred under this shall – life.
I thocht o the bearers o the chyne o life
that would gang on and on or lang deid this haund,
and yet the mair I vrocht at thocht
the mair I kent hoo peerie was the thocht.[17]

Introducing the collection, Bruce writes: 'The demand was for a wider, more accommodating integrity, a wholeness which would contain opposites. This is the impulse which underpins this book.'[18] That sums up the 'integrative vision' required for a Scots poetry that can achieve both expansiveness and dynamism.

Now that a substantial selection of the poems of T. S. Law (1916–97) is at last available – *At the Pynt o the Pick and Other Poems* (2008) – there is an opportunity to digest the corpus of a major but neglected makar of the mid–late twentieth century. A former Fife miner, Law found both pre-history (reminiscent of the time-span of George Bruce's clam-shell) and present tragedy within the underground seams of *Licht Attoore the Face*, perhaps the greatest of his longer poems, and, in the year before his death, wrote with dignity of the fatal shootings of schoolchildren at Dunblane. Law is concerned with an unequal and fragmented society, and his poetry engages in the search – indeed the struggle – for humane, healing values. Such social existentialism, as it were, drives the current of the carrying stream, and animates the work of later-generation Fife poets with family connections in the coalfields, such as Ian W. King (1955–), William Hershaw (1957–) and John Brewster (1957–). Hershaw records the Lakota Sioux who found himself in Cowdenbeath High Street: the oppressed of different cultures find common ground.[19] Another Fife-based poet, Harvey Holton (1947–), has explored contact points between Sioux and Scots language cultures. Both Holton and Hershaw respond to the craftsmanly ('makarlik') practice of their artistic elders; witness such a piece as Hershaw's 'Dysart Tide Sonnet', where perfect end-rhymes matter less than internal echoes and alliteration: this is true makarhood, as distinct from the look-at-me mechanics of a form-before-content virtuosity.[20]

In recent years Hershaw has been published by Duncan Glen (1933–2008), founder of Akros Publications and a poet who found his Indian summer voices first in Edinburgh, then in Fife, after his retirement in 1986. His return to Scotland, after decades as a lecturer south of the border, released fresh energies. He had previously lived in Fife during the 1950s, and though he was not a native of the county, it seemed like a homecoming: 'I have always thought that Fife's literary background has not been really recognised and I know Fife better than Lanarkshire though I was born there.'[21] Though he preferred Fife to Edinburgh, he found in the capital a means towards resolution of his long-term attempt to 'mak a unity' of Scotland. In their subject-matter the Edinburgh poems are generously inclusive of visual as well as verbal arts (Glen had lectured in graphic design, and he relished the opportunity to spend time in the city's galleries); Fergusson and Dante turn out their respective Scottish and 'Italian tricks'; football supporters 'fair owregilt oor speech' ('A Brig'); eighteenth-century luminaries such as Burns and Creech, together with MacDiarmid, are there in spirit: the past in the present ('From Edinburgh's High Street [For William Wolfe]'):

Aye leid! Aye a flag, fadit
but raised, moves like the thunnerstorm
agin the saftnin wund. A man doonby says, slawly
"It's faur oot the wey, but gey
haundy."[22]

William Neill (1922–) belongs to south-west Scotland, an especially rich area for poetry. Writing in Gaelic, Scots and English, he made his own 'unity' of Scotland. Approaching eighty and aware of increasing infirmity, he retired from writing, but not before making his last Scots translations (of the Swiss-German poet Conrad Ferdinand Meyer).[23] His versions of another nineteenth-century poet, G. G. Belli, who wrote in a dialect of working-class Rome, exemplify the irreverent 'coorseness' for which Scots can provide apt registers:

Ye'll say that I suid chynge ti ither wark –
guid coonsel yon! Or mebbe stey et hame?
Ay, fine the chance! But I maun airn ti eat.

I'll hae to thole it. Washin shift an sark –
whit ither wey for me ti keep a wean?
Eh, mistress? Tak ti hoorin on the street?[24]

It seems to me that Neill's natural successor/stream-carrier in the south-west is Rab Wilson (1960–), former miner and later psychiatric nurse. Wilson made his name with a sparkling Scots version of Omar Khayyam and his own original poems are collected in *Accent o the Mind* (2006). Here are sonnets growing out of the Miners' Strike of 1984–5, which he knew at first-hand; and, above all, the long 'Cormilligan', a highly-wrought symphony on a working family forced into emigration:

Dochters o dochters,
sons o sons o sons,
Whase enigmatic answer underscores,
The meaning o the cairn built at Glenore.[25]

Another south-westerner to have emerged since the early 1990s is Liz Niven (1952–), who has worked hard to promote Scots language and literature in schools. Her *Burning Whins* (2004) contains the remarkable dialogue 'Merrick tae Criffel', in Scots and English, between two personified hills that overlook the region which was devastated by the outbreak of foot and mouth disease in 2001:

As I gaed bi the Lunky Hole
a kent the parks wir bare
nae yowes wir sprauchlin throu the gap
nae lambs joukin rare.[26]

The echo of the ballads (not least 'The Twa Corbies') intensifies the sense of continuity across space and time.

It is the East Coast, however, from which most Scots-language poetry grows. As sense of place (both home and abroad) is strong in this tradition, W. N. Herbert as a Dundee poet shares space with Matthew Fitt (1968–), who was the youngest contributor to *The New Makars*. Fitt's retelling of an iconic Scottish narrative poem as 'Kate o Shanter's Tale' brought the house down when he first performed it at a ceilidh for Scottish expats in Luxembourg. Less populist but more profound is his sequence 'A Cauld Second at Bulovka', on the assassination of Reinhard Heydrich, Nazi over-lord of Bohemia and Moravia, and its terrible aftermath. Fitt, who is married to a Czech, demonstrates that there are no off-limits, in terms of subject matter, for the Scots language:

> this émigré,
> come hame in his echtieth year
> tae steer the shaddas o his first life
> grups ma elba
> havers alood in broken Canadian
> the names o the fechters'
> thirled tae the wa
> reid paper flouers
> sit skellie
> in a jar o bleared gless
> ablow the vent.[27]

It is not a case of trying to 'validate' Scots by taking a European theme: it is rather a recognition that Scotland is part of Europe and can revive its historic relationship with its continent, albeit with regard to twenty-first century realities and potentialities. Examples such as Fitt's, as also that process which we call translation, do not in themselves guarantee a renewed European sensibility for Scotland, but they are vital to that objective. We have sterling precedents in our literature: Robert Louis Stevenson and Allan Massie, for example, have shown that it is possible to write Scottishly on non-Scottish themes. Like MacDiarmid's drunk man, we can contemplate the thistle for its intrinsic merits but also in order to look beyond it.

Two further Dundonians, Ellie McDonald (1937–) and Lydia Robb, deploy the local speech with a female hard-headedness that allows their lyricism to emerge with greater force. Scots language poetry, by and large, remains true to its MacDiarmidian roots and is concerned with matters of class, region, nation and (as we have seen) inter-nation, rather than that prim concept 'gender'. McDonald and her *consœurs* are not easily and pat-ronisingly reduced to the label of 'women's voices'. Poets like McDonald resist trendy pieties in favour of a particular erotic charge belonging to women rather than men:

tulziesom tykes aye hirple hame
an fine I ken, at the hinner end,
I'll hae ye back – ye scunner.[28]

The poem's title is 'Smeddum', suggesting that the hormone-rampancy is part of something larger: the word means 'spirit, energy, drive, vigorous common-sense and resourcefulness'. McDonald's bawdy Scots version of Aristophanes' *Lysistrata*, transferred to 'the ancient world of Dundonia', was premièred in Dundee during October 2008.

The dramatic monologue is popular with female poets, and a more southerly counterpart of McDonald in this respect is Janet Paisley (1948–). Falkirk, where she lives, is hardly the sexiest town in Scotland but it is the site of rough sex enough. I find Paisley's monologues, spoken by her Sharleen, Maggie and Sandra, more darkly-hued than those of Liz Lochhead.[29]

Moving further up the East Coast, to the North (and also, in a sense, to the far South), we encounter Raymond Vettese (1950–), whose work has been neglected of late. Somewhat in the line of Robert Louis Stevenson, he is concerned with geocultural polarities, in his case because of his Scottish and Italian ancestries. If Rab Wilson is occupied with diaspora out of Scotland, Vettese affectionately records diaspora into it. He addresses his grandfather, once 'fresh aff the boat / at Leith', and whose own father was a Garibaldino, fighting for a union even as the poet seeks to 'brak' the British union in favour of a Scottish-European synthesis:

In your bags
there's us . . .
a generation seeded in twa earths
that gies us mebbe the richt mix o strengths:
a gless o warm South
laced wi North ice.[30]

Like George Bruce, Vettese celebrates a small community, without sentimentality but with mischievous humour, and within which he finds 'Edna', garrulously reeling off her extensive genealogy:

she's keeper o the web,
a priestess o the intricate bonds
that weave us aa thegither.[31]

An integrative vision is once again boldly but not piously asserted. Vettese's evocations of the coastscape between Arbroath and Aberdeen suggest a verbal equivalent of Joan Eardley, though much gentler.

Sheena Blackhall (1947–) is the most prolific poet writing in north-east Scots, or 'Doric' as it is less fussily designated. The unwary will assume that they are being taken on a couthy journey through 'Aiberdeen an twal mile roun' [Aberdeen and twelve miles around]'. She is certainly the bard-*chanteuse* of her 'Norlan neuk' – the phrase comes from her poem on the 'kirkyaird' of Aberdeen's St Machar's Cathedral,[32] and she was for some years the writer-in-residence at the university's Elphinstone Institute. Blackhall is her own woman and her own makar, however, and her strong identification with her native airt is counterpointed by a tart, grotesque wit. A favourite word of hers is 'stammygaster', defined as a nasty surprise or shock. Tenebrous eroticism is rarely far away; take the last stanza of her 'The Auldest Profession', to the tune of 'There Wis a Dundee Weaver':

> Sae aa ye hoors frae Lunnon ye should niver leave the Thames
> Wi dreams o connin ilemen tae pairt wi gifts an gems
> The siller in the granite toun's nae fur the likes o ye
> The locals winna pye a maik fur somethin they get free.[33]

The unwary will also assume that Blackhall is not a poet for the whole of Scotland, but she gives us rollicking pan-Scottish panoramic poems such as 'Scotch n' Watter', in spate 'frae Thurso tae the Royal Mile', and homes in on Dunfermline grannies and Loch Fyne-shampooed poodles.[34]

Poems from her travels are not mere postcards: she delves into the sinews of other cultures, and her love of the pictorial-tactile derives from her work as a visual artist. Her pamphlet of translations, *The Touer o Babel* (2004) is her counterpart to John Manson's *Frae Glesca ti Manila*, and is where she offers Scots versions of poems from Polish, Inuit, Slovene, Romanian and modern Greek. It might be objected that these are not 'translations' as she is not working directly from the languages concerned. She herself prefers the word 'owersetts', and an even better word might be 'transcreations', which was favoured by veteran poet Tom Scott (1918–95). Other Scots 'transcreators' from a brace of largely east-Scottish poets include James Reid Baxter (1954–), from Spanish; Alexander Hutchison (1943–), who ends a Catullus poem with lines that a more spirited Scotland would know by heart: 'Ony limmer glaums on t'that / quid easy sook plooks aff a / scaffie's backside';[35] Kate Armstrong (1944–) has worked with German originals; sometime editor of *Scots Glasnost* and *Lallans* Neil R. MacCallum (1954–2002), from Belgian-Dutch and Swiss-French; Donald Campbell (1940–), from the Gaelic of Rob Donn; James Robertson (1958–), whose Baudelaire in Scots led me to commission his versions of the post-Baudelairean Swiss-French poet Louis Duchosal. He remarked, when publicly reading them, 'If that's not Swiss Symbolism, I don't know what is.'[36] During Arthur Rimbaud's centenary year in 1991, the small press Scots Glasnost published a pamphlet of Scots versions, by various makars including Alastair Mackie (1925–95) and Tony

McManus (1953–2002).[37] Mackie's œuvre belongs to an earlier period than ours, and his Rimbaud features among the last of his many translations. As for a culture as remote from Scotland as one can imagine, David Purves (1924–) and Brian Holton (1947–; twin brother of Harvey) have addressed themselves to Chinese poetry, for which they find an appropriately laconic register.

My own work has focused on European myths and archetypes and has attempted to give them an east-of-Scotland makeover. *Isolde's Luve-Daith* (1998) transposes a Celtic legend to the coast of Fife; portions of the poem were set to music by Ronald Stevenson and premièred as such in 2003. *Scottish Faust* (2004) does pretty much what the title implies.

Magazines hospitable to work in Scots include Joy Hendry's veteran *Chapman*, the Dublin-based *Cyphers*, *Scots Glasnost*, *Zed20*, and above all *Lallans*, whose content is entirely in the language. *Lallans* serves as a barometer for the single-author collections of the future: one contributor, Maureen Sangster (1954–) offers earthily comic observations on the menopause; another, Elaine Morton, displays a craftsmanly economy of line. David C. Purdie, a joiner to trade, also knows how to knock a good poem together. In recent years *Lallans* has found a prolific contributor, in prose comment as well as poetry, in Robert Calder (1950–). Polemical and indeed combative, Calder distrusts what he sees as Scotland's mood of facile optimism, the PR blandness which has replaced dissent and debate. He is not interested in the poem 'sic as could win a prize', preferring (like his mentor, Edwin Muir) 'the things poetry can dae to some intelligent human purpose'.[38] This attitude underlies his 'Greenfield the Name o the Pit' which may owe much to another mentor, T. S. Law, on whose *Licht Attoore the Face* Calder has proved a sensitive commentator. Calder's poem ends not so much elegiacally as symphonically; this makar is indeed musically inclined, with a bass voice well-suited to his beloved Russian operatic roles:

Northern Lanarkshire wather's spittin curse
fits the glovit haunds on the haft to lunge
throu clayey thrawn ground wi a solid thrust;
guid yirdly vapours lift, worms turn and spill . . .
The graith's rhythm sweetens friable tilth.[39]

Calder's most recent work is the sequence 'Griencide', parts of which have been published recently.[40] 'Griencide' is a pun on 'Greenside', the area of Edinburgh which he feels has been devastated by the developers who are among the leading beneficiaries of the much happy-clapped 'new' Scotland. Calder sees rather the murder of yearning, according to the definition of the word 'grien': destruction, in other words, of 'intelligent human purpose'. When it is published in full, 'Griencide' may well prove a landmark in Scots-language poetry: watch this space.

The Bibliography of Scottish Literature in Translation (BOSLIT, at http://boslit.nls.uk) records well over 3,000 translations *from* Scots into other languages. Most of these items derive from earlier poetry; there is an urgent need to promote more recent Scots poetry overseas (deploying, of necessity, existing Scots-language learning materials). At its best, Scots-language poetry is based on speech, *but goes beyond it,* as do opera and song. Plain speech without poetry and song can be merely random and banal, but poetry and song lacking a speech-basis can be arid and effete. The rich resource of Scotsoun recordings, now being reissued on CD by the Scots Language Society, is evidence of a poetry that values musicality; but, despite current vigour, there is no room for complacency as long as official backing (that is, money) is unforthcoming. A few years back, a group of writers produced a report for the Scots Pairlament Cross Pairty Group on the Scots Leid (*Scots: A Statement o Principles,* 2003). It opened with this epigraph – 'Tak tent or it's tint': take heed or it's lost.

Note: I would like to thank Lizzie MacGregor of the Scottish Poetry Library for her help and advice during the research for this essay. For further reading, including much quality Scots-language poetry not mentioned in this essay, check the library's catalogue, INSPIRE, at http://www.spl.org.uk/search_spl/quicksearch.html

CHAPTER FOUR

Contemporary Gaelic Poetry

Niall O'Gallagher

Among the poets who have published collections in Scottish Gaelic since the start of the new millennium, Derick Thomson (1921–), or Ruaraidh MacThòmais, is a towering figure. His 1982 collected volume, *Creachadh na Clàrsaich/Plundering the Harp*, won the Saltire Book of the Year Award – the first Gaelic book to do so – and gathered together poems from Thomson's six previous collections, along with some twenty-three new poems. Thomson is a crucial figure in the development of contemporary Gaelic poetry, as well as the major voice of Gaelic poetry in the second half of the twentieth century. His poetry provides a link between the work of those poets writing in the years since *Creachadh na Clàrsaich* was published, and an earlier generation of Gaelic writers whose work did so much to establish Gaelic poetry as a modern, outward-looking literature with high intellectual and artistic ambitions, marked out by its engagement with the art and the politics of Europe and the wider world. The anthology *Nua-Bhàrdachd Gàidhlig/Modern Scottish Gaelic Poems* (1976) brought these writers together, featuring Thomson's work alongside that of Sorley MacLean (1911–96), George Campbell Hay (1915–84), Iain Crichton Smith (1928–98) and the editor Donald MacAulay (1930–), with English translations provided by the poets themselves. This pivotal anthology became the standard text of Scottish Gaelic Modernism and added to the growing interest among non-Gaelic speaking readers that had begun with the translation and partial republication of MacLean's poetry a few years earlier.[1] While MacLean's work achieved popularity among English-speaking readers, it was Thomson's poetry that set the tone for Gaelic verse in the years that followed. As a teacher and publisher, Thomson facilitated the emergence of many poets of the younger generation. His poetry also had a more direct influence on their work. Thomson was the first writer to develop free verse as a serious medium for Gaelic poetry, and the prevalence of free verse in the work of the poets that followed him marks a decisive move away from the work of Sorley MacLean and George Campbell Hay, whose preference for rhyme and regular metre connected their work more directly with that of their predecessors.

Aonghas MacNeacail (1942–) was one of the first writers to signal the arrival of a new generation of Gaelic poets after the publication of *Nua-Bhàrdachd Gàidhlig*. MacNeacail began publishing poetry in Gaelic in the 1970s after beginning his career as a poet in English. While Glasgow would become a focus for Derick Thomson's later poetry, the influence of Scotland's largest city on MacNeacail's work was much more formative. MacNeacail was one of the writers involved in Philip Hobsbaum's writers' group during the 1970s which included Alasdair Gray, James Kelman and Tom Leonard. Like the poetry of Hobsbaum's university colleague Edwin Morgan, MacNeacail's work owes a great deal to developments in modern American poetry, from William Carlos Williams to e.e. cummings. His third Gaelic collection, *an seachnadh agus dàin eile/the avoiding and other poems* (1986), opens with a short piece that introduces MacNeacail's poetic persona:

> do ghuth a' glaodhaich
> foillsich thu fhéin
>
> a charaid, is mise
> an t-amadan naomh
> am bàrd
> amhairc is èisd rium[2]
>
> (your voice crying
> *reveal yourself*
>
> friend i am
> the holy fool
> the bard
> observe and listen)

MacNeacail's Gaelic poetry is marked out by his preference, like cummings, for the lower case. He is a writer of free-verse poems that are highly rhythmical, in which the presence of the poet as a visionary, even shamanic figure is crucial. This persona is at the centre of Macneacail's work whether as a love poet, a poet of the natural world or as a writer of political verse. His poem, 'oideachadh ceart'/'a proper schooling', is representative of MacNeacail's technique of juxtaposing related but conflicting ideas:

> nuair a bha mi òg,
> cha b'eachdraidh ach cuimhne
>
> nuair a thàinig am bàilidh, air each
> air na mhathan a' tilleadh a-nuas

às na buailtean len eallaichean frainich
's a gheàrr e na ròpan on guailnean
a' sgaoileadh nan eallach gu làr,
a' dìteadh nam mnà, gun tug iad gun chead
an luibhe dhan iarradh e sgrios,
ach gum biodh na mnathan
ga ghearradh 's ga ghiùlan gu dachaigh,
connlach stàile, gu tàmh nam bò
(is gun deachadh e màl às)[3]

(when i was young
it wasn't history but memory

when the factor, on horseback, came
on the woman's descent from
the moorland grazings laden with bracken
he cut the ropes from their shoulders
spreading their loads to the ground,
alleging they took without permit
a weed he'd eliminate
were it not that women cut it and carried it home
for bedding to ease their cows' hard rest; and there was rent in that weed)

The opposition between 'eachdraidh' – the official history of scholars and book-learning – and 'cuimhne' – history as memory, as an oral record passed on through story and song – structures not just the argument but also the rhythm of the poem. One of the dangers MacNeacail faces when approaching political subjects is that his poetry risks appropriating the suffering of others, granting the poet legitimacy by claiming to stand for those who cannot speak for themselves. Despite these dangers MacNeacail prefers political commitment to ironic detachment. He is a poet of considerable range. At times, the poet moves to one side, as in 'dèanamh ime'/'making butter', from the 2007 collection *Laoidh an Daonais Òig Hymn to a Young Demon*:

chan eil a shamhla ann –
tionndadh 's a' tionndadh a' ghileid òraich
am broinn dòrcha na h-eanchainn
ag èisteachd ri suirghe is
dealachadh is pòsadh
nan lid luasganach leaghtach
ag èisteachd airson nam boinne
blàthaich a' sileadh air falbh o
ghramalas òrbhuidhe dàin[4]

(there's nothing like it –
turning and turning the golden whiteness
inside the darkness of the brain
listening to the wooings and
partings and weddings
of soluble tossed-about syllables
listening for the drops
of buttermilk trickling away from
the golden yellow firmness of a poem)

Here the emphasis is not on the poet, but on the precious, sustaining material of poetry itself, as MacNeacail's flowing, continuous lines echo the 'tionndadh 's a' tionndadh' ('turning and turning') his speaker describes.

Myles Campbell or Maoilios Caimbeul (1944–) began publishing poetry in Gaelic in 1970s. The influence of Derick Thomson's work on his early poetry is discernible both in his facility with free verse, and in his ability to be both a personal, introspective poet and a public, political writer. Like Thomson, the 1979 devolution referendum provided Campbell with material for polemical poetry. 'An Referendum air son Pàrlamaid na h-Alba 1/3/79' contrasts the speaker's hope on the day of the referendum itself with his disappointment following the result. The second part of the diptych deploys the long-standing, even hackneyed image of nation as woman to express the speaker's anger with the Scottish people for failing to support home rule in sufficient numbers:

A thruaghain!
'S tu nad òigh fhathast
gun saorsa, gun solas, gun ola.
Nach bochd nach tàirgneadh cuideigin thu!
Ach tha eagal orm gu fàs thu
nad sheann mhaighdeann, gearanach, crosta,
ag èisteachd ris a' ghaoith anns an t-simileir
agus anns na craobhan fàsail,
a' feitheamh ris a' phosta a' tighinn,
a' faicinn do thiormachd anns an sgàthan,
a' tarraing do shàilean an taigh d' athar –
thu na thaice gu h-iomlan –
a' smaoineachadh air na seòid
nach tig gu bràth gad iarraidh.[5]

(O wretch
you are a maiden still
without freedom, without light, without oil.
What a pity that no-one would nail you!

But I'm afraid that you will grow
to be an old maid, complaining, bad-tempered
listening to the wind in the chimney
and in the lonely trees
waiting for the postman to come
seeing your dryness in the mirror
dragging your heels in your father's house –
completely dependent on him –
thinking of the suitors
that will never come looking for you.)

Only a limited selection of Campbell's poetry has so far appeared in English translation, meaning that he is rarely mentioned in surveys of recent Scottish writing. The work gathered in *Breac-a'-Mhuiltein/Spéir Dhroim an Ronnaigh* (2006), Campbell's collected poems with Irish translations by Rody Gorman, nonetheless displays a commitment to Gaelic verse over a long period and a playful interest in language, as in the poem 'Rud a Thachair' ('Something that Happened'), which puns on the Gaelic word for 'nothing' or 'zero' and the woman's name, 'Nonnie':

B' ann mu dheidhinn neoni a bha na dàin 'to make a short song
out of nothing' agus a-rithist 'the thistle and the gorse
the kiss, the blessing, the curse

are built on nothing' agus bha Mòrag à Uibhist 's às an Eilean Dubh
a' bruidhinn ri boireannach à Tiriodh, agus b' e Nonnie a bh' oirre
agus bha i ag ràdh a h-ainm mar gun canadh tu neoni

agus dh'fhairich mi gaoir beag a' ruighinn mo spioraid,
no co-dhiù am pàirt ud a tha do-ruighinn. Agus airs bidh an e gòraich
no sar-ghliocas gun ainm a bh' ann

dh'fhairich mi gun robh e air leth neònach, Nonnie agus neoni
a' coinneachadh mar siud anns na fhalamhachd
agus ag èirigh gu chèile às an t-sruth do-sheachanta.[6]

('The poems were about nothing 'to make a short song
out of nothing' and again 'the thistle and the gorse
the kiss, the blessing, the curse

are built on nothing', and Morag from Uist and from the Black Isle was
speaking to a woman from Tiree, and Nonnie was her name
and she was saying her name in the way that you'd say neoni

and I felt a little cry reaching my spirit,
or at least that part that is unreachable. And whether it was stupidity
or nameless genius

I felt that it was very strange, Nonnie and neoni
meeting like that in the emptiness
and rising together from the unavoidable flow.)

Much of Campbell's most succesful poetry is in this quieter, contemplative style. His poems are lifted by his attention to sound, and, unusually among contemporary Gaelic poets, he seems equally at home in both free and regular verse.

In 1983 a group of translations from the modern Greek appeared in *Gairm*, the Gaelic journal edited by Thomson. These were the first published works in Gaelic by Christopher Whyte, or Crìsdean MacIlleBhàin (1952–).[7] The original poems which followed marked a significant departure for Gaelic poetry. A poem from Whyte's first collection, *Uirsgeul/Myth*, which won a Saltire Award in 1992, suggests something crucial about Whyte's poetry and the feeling of novelty it inspired:

Thusa, mo chànain
(is tha mi gun fhios
am fear no boireannach thu),
dè an sgeul seo, ràbhanach is daor,
san deach mo ribeadh?
Dè an rathad cagarach is càm
ris am bean do shàil cho aotrom
's gur gann gu lean mi thu?
Dhearbh iad orm gu robh thu aosd'
ach chuir t' òige fo gheasaibh mi.[8]

(You, my language
(and I don't know
if you are a man or a woman),
what's this dear and complicated story
you've mixed me up in?
what's this whispering, twisted road
your foot touches so lightly
I can scarcely follow you on it?
They told me you were old,
but your youth enchanted me.)

Whyte here plays with the fact that the Gaelic word for 'language' can be either masculine or feminine. He also replaces the usual image of Gaelic as a language of antiquity with one in which it is a new speech, one that allows the speaker a voice he would otherwise be denied. Speech and silence are important issues in Whyte's poetry.[9] His most important contribution to Gaelic verse in the early part of his career is the long poem, *Bho Leabhar-Latha Maria Malibran* (*From the Diary of Maria Malibran*).[10] It runs to 790 regular pentameter lines, divided into seventeen sections which are followed by an italicised envoi, in which the figure of the poet addresses the audience directly. The rest of the poem is in the voice of the historical Maria Malibran, a nineteenth-century opera singer and contemporary of the Italian composer Rossini. Whyte is also a novelist, and *Bho Leabhar-Latha Maria Malibran* is highly novelistic. Each of the poem's sections reads like a diary entry, in which the poet uses the events of the singer's day-to-day life to stage a debate about human relationships and the potential for art to redeem them. The tone is informal, even prosaic, disguising the absolute strictness of the underlying metre:

Thachair mi ri Maighstir Rossini 'n-diugh.
Bha mi tighinn a-mach bho bhùth nan ad,
searbhanta 'nam dhèidh, a gàirdeanan
làn de bhogsaichean 's de phacaidean.
Bha fonn math orm, an carbad a' feitheamh
aig oir na sràid, is dìreach air an stairsneach
thachair mi ri gnùis a dh'aithnich mi
gu furasda bho làithean m' òige anns
an Ròimhe 's sa' Chathair Nuadh.[11]

(I met Master Rossini today
I was coming out of the hat shop
the maid following me, her arms
full of boxes and packages.
I was in a good mood, the carriage waiting
at the edge of the street, and right at the threshold
I came across a face I recognised
easily from the days of my youth in
Rome and Naples.)

In the final envoi, the figure of the poet addresses the audience directly, engaging in a debate about the perceived limits of Gaelic poetry. After an ironic list of subjects considered fitting for a Gaelic poet, Whyte's speaker offers this defiant response to those who would doubt Gaelic poetry's capacity to explore as many aspects of human experience as poetry in any other language:

An àite sin, sgrìobh mi mu bhoireanach
nach robh facal Gàidhlig aice, nach robh
fhios aice, 's dòcha, gu robh cànain ann

den t-seòrsa. Mura bheil mi comasach
air dàintean fìor-Ghàidhealach a sgrìobhadh,

tha sin a chionns nach eil mi 'nam fhìor-Ghàidheal,
a-rèir coltais. Ach, a luchd-leughaidh chaoimh,
tilgidh mi na faclan seo air talamh
nàimhdeil, seasg, neo-mhothachail, is faodaidh
sibh a bhith gam chreidsinn, ged nach e

deudan a th' annta, air neo dèideagan,
aig a' cheann thall tòisichidh iad a' fàs,
cnàmhan is crè is craicean aig gach fear dhiubh
's an leabhar ùr fo chomhair nan sùl ùr ac',
a sgrìobh mi mu Maria Malibran.[12]

(Instead, I wrote about a woman
with not a word of Gaelic, who did not
know, perhaps, that such a language
existed. If I am unable
to write truly Gaelic poems,

that's because I am not a real Gael,
apparently. But, dear readers,
I will cast these words upon
hostile, barren and indifferent ground, and you
may believe me, although

they are not teeth or pebbles,
at last they will grow,
each one with bones and flesh and skin
and before their eyes the new book
I wrote about Maria Malibran.)

Whyte's poetry has continued to develop in the long form, and in particular, the elegy. The focus of Whyte's later poetry moves beyond Gaelic and Scotland, to a more philosophical meditation on the nature of poetry and language, and their place in a Europe scarred by conflict and prejudice. If his poetry is difficult, and it frequently is, it is because it anticipates an audience that may not exist yet, one for whom Gaelic's fitness to discuss such subjects is not in question.

Publishing poetry in Gaelic, particularly without English translations, is a less public act than publishing in a more widely spoken language. Something of the sense of Gaelic as a private language, of Gaelic poetry as intimate or even conspiratorial, survives in the debut collection by Meg Bateman (1959–),

Òrain Ghaoil/Amhráin Ghrá. This appeared in 1991 and featured Irish translations by Alex Osborne. Bateman's was a new voice, taking its musicality from the Gaelic song tradition while producing poetry with a distinctly personal, even confessional sensibility. The first poem in the collection uses song-like rhythms and a refrain to put forward a very modern kind of irony:

Thigeadh e thugam
nuair a bha e air mhisg
        a chionn 's gu robh mi measail air.

Dhèanainn tì dha
is dh'èisdinn ris
        a chionn 's gu robh mi measail air.

Sguir e a dh'òl
is rinn mi gàirdeachas leis
        a chionn 's gu robh mi measail air.

Nist cha tig e tuilleadh
is nì e tàir orm
        a chionn 's gu robh mi measail air.[13]

(He used to come to me
when he was drunk
because I was so fond of him.

I'd make him tea
and listen to him
because I was so fond of him.

He stopped the drink
and I was pleased for him
because I was so fond of him.

Now he comes no more,
indeed he despises me,
because I was so fond of him.)

The structure could be lifted from a traditional working song, associated with women rather than men, in which one singer would give a line followed by a refrain from the others. The tone, however, is highly personal, and not without bitterness. This poem sits on the border between public speech, or song, and something much more private. Perhaps it is this sense of being taken into the speaker's confidence, of being complicit in something half-public, half-private, that made Bateman's early poetry so appealing to many readers. The speaker addresses her lover directly in 'Aotromachd', or 'Lightness', the poem which provided the title of Bateman's 1997 collection, in which the poems from Òrain Ghaoil were reprinted with Bateman's own English translations:

B' e d' aotromachd a rinn mo thàladh,
aotromachd do chainnte 's do ghàire,
aotromachd do lethchinn nam làmhan,
d' aotromachd lurach ùr mhàlda;
agus 's e aotromachd do phòige
a tha a' cur trasg air mo bheòil-sa,
is 's e aotromachd do ghlaic mum chuairt-sa
a leigeas seachad leis an t-sruth mi.[14]

(It was your lightness that drew me,
the lightness of your talk and your laughter,
the lightness of your cheek in my hands,
your sweet gentle modest lightness;
and it is the lightness of your kiss
that is starving my mouth,
and the lightness of your embrace
that will let me go adrift.)

Each of Bateman's four-stressed lines ends lightly on an unstressed syllable, softening the chime of her rhyming couplets. While 'A chionn 's gu robh mi measail air' describes its object in the third person, here the informal second person 'do' ('your') lends the poem an intimacy which is undercut by ornamentation that asks to be admired. With her most recent collection, Soirbheas/Fair Wind (2007), Bateman has moved away from much of the intimacy of her earlier work, losing something of her earlier intensity in the process. 'Ceòl san Eaglais' ('Music in Church') reads like a defence of Bateman's shift from an art that laments the gap between idealised love and the reality of human relationships, towards one that finds humanity in that very difference:

Ach is annsa leam an coithional nach seinn ach meadhanach –
an seinneadair nach buail air na puingean àrda,
an tè a cheileireas os cionn nan uile,
an t-òrganaiche a thòisicheas air rann a bharrachd;

Oir 's ann an sin a thèid an gaol a dhùbhlanachadh,
eadar àilleasachd is dìomhanas is breòiteachd dhaonna,
's ann an sin ge b' oil leam a nochdas am beannachadh –
am fios nach eil lorg air ceòl nas binne.[15]

(But best I like indifferent singing, –
the soloist who gets the high notes flat,
the warbler who makes herself heard over all,
the organist who embarks on an extra verse;

For here is the greater challenge to love,
amid fastidiousness, vanity, human failing;
here, in spite of me appears the greater blessing, –
on finding love sweeter than any singing.)

The regular quatrains stand out from the poems in free verse that dominate
the collection. It seems ironic that in a poem defending artistic imperfection
Bateman deploys the same qualities of metre and assonance that made some
of her early poems so satisfying.

After publishing Aonghas MacNeacail's *Oideachadh Ceart* (1996) and
Meg Bateman's *Aotromachd agus Dàin Eile* (1997), Polygon brought out *Fax
and Other Poems* (1997), the debut collection from Rody Gorman (1960–), a
poet who also writes in Irish. The first poem, which gives the book its title,
contains much that is representative of the collection as a whole:

Tha am fax anns an oisean
Na thrèan-ri-thrèan anns a' chluain

No na mhuc a' griosail
Ann an guth ìosal

'S tha am printer taobh ris na eas
Agus duilleagan bàn' a' sruthadh às

'S tha seallaidhean gan sgrìobhadh
A chaidh a dhraghadh

A grunnd a' Chuain Siar
Air sgàilean mo chomputer

'S iad uile cur an cruth fhèin gu seòlta
Air saoghal an latha.[16]

(The fax in the corner
Is like a corncrake in the meadow

Or a pig grunting
In a low voice

And the printer beside it is a waterfall
with white pages gushing out of it

And scenes are being depicted
That were trawled

From the bed of the Atlantic
On the screen of my computer

And they all put their own form neatly
On today's world.)

In modern Gaelic poetics, rhyme ignores final consonants and is based only on the agreement of stressed vowel-sounds. Gorman diverges from this here, in eight couplets in all with consonantal half-rhymes and lines of uneven length. While the poem has absorbed a formal structure from outside of the Scottish Gaelic tradition itself, it finds modern technology resistant to such absorption. The words 'fax', 'printer' and 'computer' are all left in their English forms, stubbornly resisting the Gaelicisation implicit in Gorman's choice of naturalist metaphors. The poem seems to suggest that Gaelic is part of the natural world, not the modern world of fax machines and computers. It tries to convert the material of that modern world into terms that it can assimilate, using the Gaelic form 'na', meaning literally 'in its', implying that one term is identical to another. Yet the poem dramatises the failure of this process, as the speaker fumbles around for an appropriate metaphor; the fax is first a 'trèan-ri-thrèan' ('corncrake') and then a 'muc' ('pig'). It remains however, a 'fax', fundamentally unchanged by the poem's attempt at naturalisation – both its use of natural metaphors and its attempt to make the fax natural to the Gaelic language. The poem is therefore double-edged, being at once an ironic commentary on Gaelic poetry's failure to accommodate modernity, and an enactment of that failure, suggesting that Gaelic verse can only approach the modern world indirectly, through a process of metaphor that leaves the stuff of that world still foreign to Gaelic experience. Gorman has been a highly prolific poet in the decade since his first Gaelic collection, particularly in Irish, and as a translator between Gaelic and Irish. His Irish-language poetry will have to wait for another essay. In Gaelic, Gorman has developed an epigrammatic style, in which he builds short, crisp, free-verse poems around striking individual images. He has become known for poems in which lines are shorn of clutter in an attempt to form clear, crystalline images from the simplest of colloquial diction.

The last few years have seen the publication of the first full-length collections from Angus Peter Campbell or Aonghas Pàdraig Caimbeul and Martin

MacIntyre or Màrtainn Mac an t-Saor (1965–). Both poets emerged in the early years of the twenty-first century as writers of prose, publishing novels and short stories through the Ùr-Sgeul initiative. Their collections include self-authored English translations, though in Campbell's collection these are supplemented by Scots versions by J. Derrick McClure.[17] Making an assessment of a poet's work based on their debut collection is a risky business, but perhaps less so than passing over these writers without comment. Campbell's poetry in *Meas air Chrannaibh/Fruit on Braunches/Fruit on Branches* (2007) tends towards free verse. In common with the style of his three novels, 'Ceàrd na Bàrdachd Gàidhlig' ('The Gaelic Poetry Tinker'), is built from a series of lists:[18]

A' dìreach a' bhealaich
a' gliogadaich 's a' glagadaich,
mo phoitean 's mo phanaichean,
mo bhiorain 's mo phrìnean,
mo theanta canabhais
mum ghuailnean

's làn fhios a'm g'eil mi air chall
ann an tìm
a dh'fhalbh

gun duine beò ag iarraidh mo chuid
trealaich,
mo chiofainnean,
mo luideagan
dathach staoin
a nì feum dhut
dìreach ann am fìor staing
nuair a bhristeas an dealan sìos 's a dh'fheumas tu poit a chur air an teine.[19]

(Climbing the brae,
clinking and clanking,
my pots and pans,
my pegs and pins,
my canvas tent
on my shoulders

fully aware that I'm lost
in an age
that's gone

with not a living soul wanting
my rubbish,

my shreds
my rags
of coloured tin
that are used
only in real emergencies
when the electricity fails and and you need to put a pot on the open fire.)

Campbell's poetic persona seeks to position him as the representative Gaelic poet. His adoption of this role leaves little room for other voices, and his association of Gaelic with a world that is past is at odds with the insistence of MacLean and Thomson that Gaelic poetry engage with the modern world, however fraught that engagement might be.

Martin MacIntyre is unusual among his contemporaries in that his poetry has a strong relationship with the conventions of Gaelic song. 'Dannsam led Fhaileas' ('Let Me-Dance with Your Shadow'), exemplifies his poetry's musicality:

Dannsam led fhaileas 'n Dùn Èideann
cluinneam do chòmradh thar Chluaidh
drochaidean, eaglaisean, òrdugh
bu nòs air feadh bhailtean mo luaidh.

Cuiream mo ghàirdean mud cholainn
pasgan do cheann na mo ghruaidh
anail is fàileadh an dùsgaidh
bu thus do gach madainn lem luaidh.[20]

(Let me dance with your shadow in Edinburgh
let me hear your chatter across the Clyde
bridges, churches, orderliness
familiar through my darling's cities.

Let me put my arm around your body
let me parcel your head in my cheek
breath and the smell of waking
the start of each morning my darling.)

The tenderness of the poem is mirrored by the gentle echoes and assonances that complement MacIntyre's full rhymes. Though he is often experimental in his prose fiction, many of the poems in MacIntyre's first collection are metrically conservative and draw their strength from his knowledge of traditional music and from the poetic possibilities of rhyme and regular metre. His poems seem to suffer more than those of his contemporaries when he translates them into English. Neither his technical skill in Gaelic verse nor his ear for the music of his lines is suggested in his English versions, which make no attempt to reproduce those elements that make some of his Gaelic poems so attractive.

Since the appearance of *Creachadh na Clàrsaich* in 1982, Derick Thomson has published a further three collections of verse. *Smeur an Dòchais/The Bramble of Hope* (1991) was followed by *Meall Garbh/The Rugged Mountain* (1995) and most recently *Sùil air Fàire/Surveying the Horizon* (2007). In Thomson's later work Gaelic poetry moves decisively to deal with the city of Glasgow, where the poet himself has lived for many years. With the sequence, 'Air Sràidean Ghlaschu' ('On Glasgow Streets'), the city moves to the very centre of Thomson's poetic world, and with it the variety of the city's inhabitants:

Cainnt bhlàth Eadailteach gam shuaineadh
faisg air cridhe a' bhaile mhòir seo,
foghairean Barolo,
co-fhoghairean Valpolicella:
tè dhe na h-Eadailtean Nuadha
is opera beò innt' fhathast;
chan eil mi 'g ràdh
nach eil Caruso ac' ann Taverna air choireigin;
's ma tha Dante fhathast ann
chan eil fad aige ri dhol
gus a lorg e inferno
ach tha mo Pharadiso-sa caillte
am badeigin an Glaschu.[21]

(Warm Italian talk surrounding me
close to the heart of this city,
Barolo vowels,
Valpolicella consonants:
one of the New Italies
where opera still lives;
I daresay
there's a Caruso in some Taverna or other;
and if a Dante survives
he doesn't have far to go
to find an Inferno; but my Paradise is lost
somewhere in Glasgow.)

Like his Glasgow contemporaries, Alasdair Gray and Edwin Morgan, Thomson sees Glasgow here as a place where both heaven and hell can be found together. His position as an incomer also informs Thomson's Glasgow poetry. In a later poem, 'Glaschu-an', he sees the city not as a place of exile, as earlier Gaelic writing did, but the place where Scotland's future will be seen first:

> Saoghal ag atharrachadh gun fhaochadh
> is Glaschu 'na chabhaig
> ga ath-chruthachadh fhèin.
>
> Is sinne a' coiseachd nan sràidean,
> an dòchas gu ruig sinn ceann-uidhe ùr
> ann an saoghal ùr 'na h-Alba.[22]
>
> (A world changing non-stop
> and Glasgow hurrying
> to recreate itself.
>
> While we walk the streets,
> hoping to reach a new destination
> in the new world of Scotland.)

One of the remarkable things about Thomson's later poetry is its openness to change. Thomson is too thoughtful and too honest a poet for any facile optimism. At the end of a long career, however, his poetry seems to look forward to the future he will not see.

The middle years of the twentieth century were a remarkable period for Gaelic poetry. The writers collected in *Nua-Bhàrdachd Gàidhlig* were innovators both aesthetically and technically, and in the extent of their engagement with the wider world. Much of the poetry that has followed has consolidated the development of modern Gaelic verse, rather than taking that process further. Sometimes the focus of contemporary poets on Scotland and their activism on behalf of the language itself can seem self-defeating when compared to the work of the *Nua-Bhàrdachd Gàidhlig* writers. Their engagement with the art and politics of Europe was at the same time an insistence that the Gaelic language be accorded a position of equality in the mainstream of European culture. Gaelic poetry has faced practical difficulties in recent years, not least the limited opportunities to publish collections, particularly where a poet is unwilling to provide translations. Yet there are signs that this is changing and that a space is developing where writers and critics can discuss Gaelic verse openly and frankly. Remarkable, original poetry has been written in Gaelic since the seventies and continues to be written, poetry that should be much better known both in Scotland and further afield. As one surveys the horizon, it is clear that there are poets committed to taking Gaelic verse forward in the twenty-first century. What direction they take is a question for the future.

CHAPTER FIVE

A Democracy of Voices

Kirsten Matthews

This chapter offers a thematic survey of a number of poets whose work sits awkwardly alongside narrow or prescriptive expectations about what Scottish poets are and what they choose to write about. We begin with the work of Ron Butlin (1949–), Roddy Lumsden (1966–), Maud Sulter (1960–2008) and Elizabeth Burns (1957–), focusing on their interest in personal identity over more familiar designations of class, gender and ethnicity. Through the work of Tom Pow (1950–), Valerie Gillies (1948–) and Brian McCabe (1951–) we examine the way in which the local and familiar is rendered exotic by poetic imagination. The final section of this essay will introduce another much understudied area of Scottish writing and translation, and in doing so will consider the work of Donny O'Rourke (1959–), David Kinloch (1959–) and Alan Riach (1957–).

Over half of these writers have been affiliated, as academics, creative writing tutors or writers in residence, either to universities or to Scottish regional or city councils: Ron Butlin was Writer in Residence at both the Universities of Edinburgh and St Andrews; Tom Pow is a senior lecturer in Creative Writing at Glasgow University's Crichton Campus; David Kinloch teaches Creative Writing at the University of Strathclyde; Alan Riach is Professor of Scottish Literature at Glasgow University; and Brian McCabe is Writer in Residence at Edinburgh University. In many cases institutional support remains vital to the sustainability of contemporary Scottish poetry. Despite their affiliation within educational institutions of Scotland, this study concentrates on the way in which these writers deliberately eschew pre-occupation with the national question in their poetry. The fact that they look to transcend national boundaries, to speak to a global audience, could be read as a crucial component of any successful work of art. This chapter examines their conscious efforts to expand the existing debate and to reset the parameters for the analysis and interpretation of contemporary Scottish poetry.

In *Modern Scottish Poetry* (2004), Christopher Whyte comments: '[T]he national is not the only, or necessarily the primary totality, within which the lives of individuals, real or fictive, can be placed, in order to be endowed with meaning.'[1] Poetic depictions of individual experience interrupt the kind of communal identities offered by a more nation-centred poetry. They foreground a host of other affiliations premised on issues of gender, sexuality, class, age, religion, race and so on. Elizabeth Burns, in the prefatory notes to her poems in the anthology *Dream State* writes that she is 'interested in writing about invisible, unrecorded lives in history, particularly those of women'.[2] The experience of individual women, much maligned within male- and nation-centred formulations of history, offers a point of departure in much of Burns's poetry. As the title of her collection, *Ophelia and Other Poems* (1991), demonstrates, she is also interested in recovering the voices of women that have been subordinated, silenced and sidelined within patriarchal constructions of the literary canon. Burns's writing confronts the exclusively male nature of Alexander Moffat's painting *Poets' Pub*, and in doing so situates itself alongside the blossoming of writing by Scottish women poets outlined by Fiona Wilson's contribution to the current *Companion*. The male dominated world of Scottish poetry comes under sustained scrutiny in 'Valda's Poem / Sleevenotes'. The Valda of the title is, of course, Valda Grieve, wife of Christopher Grieve/Hugh MacDiarmid. The poem describes a scene that appears as a footnote on *Whaur Extremes Meet*, a recording made of MacDiarmid reading his poems in 1978. The epigraph reads:

Recorded at Brownsbank . . . Chris, in his chair by the window, talking with his friend, the poet Norman MacCaig, a wee dram in every glass. Valda in swimsuit, working in the garden, or keeping the soft-coated Wheaten and Border Terrier quiet for the recording.[3]

Valda is off the record, both literally and metaphorically. Burns's poem challenges the marginal status of this sleevenote, shifting the focus and bringing Valda's experience centre stage. The latent vitality of Valda, outdoors in her swimsuit, is juxtaposed with the relative staidness of the men, sitting inside and talking over their whisky. Burns compounds the sensuality of the swimsuit by imagining Valda luxuriating in the touch of the sun on her body. In flipping this scene on its head Burns asks us to reconsider where life is being realised to its fullest intensity. We hear the two poets through Valda: 'I hear their talk and laughter, his and Norman's / I hear the rise and fall of Chris's voice.'[4] Her use of the two poets' Christian names makes them more familiar, less formal; Valda's experience invokes our sympathy in its own right, but it also shortens the distance between us and these imposing figures of Scottish poetic tradition. We are asked to see them as individuals, rather than literary giants. In 'Work and Art / We Are Building a Civilisation' Burns attacks the conventional appreciation of Ancient Greece through its statues and monuments. She focuses her attention instead on the contribution women made to the longevity of Greek civilisation, through their domestic and agricultural chores, their sewing and their handicrafts. She concludes:

it is more important
that we have a record of the olive-oil harvest
than that we know what the oracles once spoke

This is how we will be known
We are making our own history.[5]

The 'we' of this last phrase represents a female collective identity which, again, seeks to challenge male-dominated narratives of history. It also, in more general terms, rejects the exclusivity of such artistic heritage, breaking down the boundary between art and life. As Burns puts it in her poem, 'there is art, / and folk art'.[6] Her emphasis is firmly on the latter.

Ron Butlin similarly explores the tension between overtly literary experience and the reality of everyday life. A focus on personal experience and an autobiographical mode characterise his work, where a self is often self-estranged and looking for a stabilising sense of meaning and purpose. We see this in the collection *Ragtime in Unfamiliar Bars* (1985) and particularly in poems like 'Inheritance', 'Claiming my Inheritance' and 'My Inheritance'. The interior record of a personal life, experienced as dislocation, and the lack of rootedness relate to the fact that although he was born in Edinburgh, Butlin grew up in the Dumfriesshire village of Annan. When he was eleven years old the family moved to Dumfries, and at the age of sixteen he left home for London. Whatever personal experiences intensify Butlin's feelings of division and self-division, a shift from the country to the city adds a wider context. In 'Inheritance' an older speaker addresses a younger self in terms of loss, and its last line, which has the child's fist clutching 'on fragments of an unfamiliar tense' suggests an uneasy entry into an adult awareness of time.[7] Similarly, 'Claiming my Inheritance' ends with a sense that 'the present tense' is 'happening too soon' for a speaker who feels that

an empty sky above me blue,
gave definition to
my isolation.
Only this completed world remained.

Interior disorientation and absence of direction is foregrounded:

The older I become the more
I am aware of exile, of longing for –

I clench my fist on nothing and hold on.[8]

To find ways out of his existential dilemma, Butlin examines his relationship with a father whose recurrent presence in the verse compensates for
his seeming absence in life. 'Poem for my Father' includes the lines 'I haunt
myself since childhood', and 'Time and again his dead hand reaches for mine',
which leads a disoriented speaker to 'forget the laws of love and territory'.[9] In
'Two Landscapes: Father and Son' a speaker waits expectantly for a sense of
definition that might help him

> to become other than what's here
> between the shadow and the sun,
>
> resolving whatever accident I am.[10]

The elusiveness of self-definition and a consequent self-estrangement is finely
caught in 'Strangers', which begins 'I am being lived in: / strangers enter and
depart, the rest perishes', and ends

> Lest they depart forever
> I fashion them day by day to resemble me:
>
> and whoever most resembles me most perishes.[11]

In 'My Inheritance', the tenth anniversary of a father's death reminds a
speaker of the time Odysseus spent away from home. But given his repeated
attempts to weave self-definition out of absence, ghosts and shadows, this
speaker crosses gender to record his feeling 'like Penelope':

> forced to stay behind, I weave each hated thread
> into its rightful place then tear the tapestry
> apart dreaming I cancel out my grief.[12]

'My Inheritance' finds a precarious resolution in personal love, reminding
us that Butlin is also a sensitive love-poet. But it was not until the publication of The Exquisite Instrument in 1982, with poems adapted from classical
Chinese, that Butlin began to situate and extend his existential quandary. If
'This Embroidery' remembers a past love 'part-dream / and part-imaginary'
it nonetheless achieves a calm of distance and reflection.[13] A use of poetry
as the self's reconstruction frames loss and separation and extends a sense of
personality and place, in a technique developed in Histories of Desire (1995).
The poem 'Three Biographies' depicts three passengers on a bus – the narrator, a man and a girl. There is no interaction between these characters,
no dialogue, and they are not named. It would appear that there is little on

which to build an interesting narrative, and yet as the title suggests, their lives are being offered as the stuff of biography:

> Three biographies all up to date:
> we turn the page, read on (our dreams alone
> our own responsibility).[14]

There is a haunting, almost Beckettian aspect, to Butlin's phrase 'our dreams alone'. As an image of modern alienation it suggests that even at our most lucid and fanciful we cannot escape the existential cell that is the self. We are trapped by our inevitable distance from others. Butlin's evocation of biography, as a form of writing with implicit assumptions about the import and significance of its subject matter, casts a sidelight on the anonymity – 'a man', 'a girl', and 'me' – of the characters in the poem. The reflections of these characters in the glass deepens the poem's estrangement, giving them a ghost-like quality, suggesting we only half inhabit the world.

> There are spirits trapped outside us;
> we keep them at arms length or
> beyond. Their image caught on glass:
> a spell conjuring who we are
> as if from nothing; and our lives
> the small enchantment that remains.[15]

The depiction of such ephemeral identities challenges the assumptions of a verifiable and substantiated existence, implicit in biography as a form of writing. The poem concludes: 'our histories continue out of sight'. Echoing the title of the collection, Butlin is preoccupied with the past, with recording and testifying to the transient and fleeting experiences of modern life. As in Burns's verse there is a democratic spirit in such poetry, a commitment to the stories that remain outwith the official sanctioned narrative. Individual iden-tity, however tenuous, is irreducibly important to both poets. Its amplification in Butlin's poem deliberately subverts the validity of mainstream history and its claims toward authenticity and authority. Jon Corelis, in his assessment of contemporary British poetry in *Chapman* in 1997 states that *Histories of Desire*: 'suggest[s] that we can derive from various types of personal relationships, and from the poetry written about them, a sense of significance equal to that which we could gain from meaningfully affecting the historical process'.[16]

Roddy Lumsden is originally from St Andrews but like many Scots over the years, has relocated and now lives in London. His work connects with Butlin's 'Three Biographies' in terms of its interest in the anonymous nature of so much contemporary urban experience. For Lumsden it seems that even our most intimate encounters are habitually characterised by a failure to contact and connect with each other. From *The Book of Love* (2000), the poem 'Marmalade' draws on the title of the collection to interrogate the complicity of literature in some of our most misleading perceptions of human relationships. 'Marmalade' depicts an anonymous sexual encounter with a male narrator pondering why such missed connections are so regularly played out:

> Face facts, I could be anyone.
> So, toss a coin on which will happen next
>
> from all the oldest stories in The Book
> of Love . . . [17]

The image of 'The Book / of Love' echoes the title of the book in which the poem was included; as it appears in 'Marmalade', the 'Book / of Love' fits a long tradition of the literary representation of love; it also reminds us that the narratives of this collection offer an addition to, and commentary on, that tradition. In 'Marmalade', the echo of great love stories contained in 'The Book / of Love' is set against the less romantic, and more contemporary sexuality of the reference earlier in the poem to the girl's 'well-thumbed copy of The Joy of Sex'. The poem oscillates between the esoteric and the more physical realisations of intimacy. The enjambment of 'The Book / of Love' underlines the notion of books in general and the ways in which convention courts and creates romantic love as the ultimate fulfilment of human existence. Like Butlin, Lumsden searches out a solution to the problem of alienation in our capacity to imagine and dream. The poem's final stanza warns: 'Sweet dreams. By which I mean, beware; / best know just who and where you are and why'. This echoes not only the Oracle at Delphi with its command to 'Know Thyself', but also Shakespeare, and Polonius's advice to his son Laertes at the beginning of *Hamlet*:

> This above all: to thine own self be true,
> And it must follow as the night the day
> Thou canst not then be false to any man.[18]

In the play the strength and self-knowledge advocated by Polonius provides a contrast with Hamlet's own instability and uncertainty. In Butlin's 'Marmalade' such assurance is offered as a foil to the kind of anonymous encounters that are our everyday experience.

In contrast to the mistimings of modern love, Maud Sulter's *Zabat: Poetics of a Family Tree* (1989) presents the gradual process of loving another as part of a deeply affirming journey toward self-knowledge. Understanding one's self, she posits, can be attained only through a concerted and sincere attempt to know someone else:

Whispering stories
our secrets
histories
sharing
a ritual fire
for in knowing
you I know
myself.[19]

The confident self-aware voice in Sulter's poem is remarkably different from
the masculine insecurities evident in both Lumsden and Butlin. For Sulter
'histories' are personal, authenticating, affirming. Both the speaker and the
addressee are identified as artists. The intimacy of 'whispering' and 'secrets'
is compared with the public status of an artwork which in the end detaches
itself from its creator:

as artists
our ultimate creation
is independent of we.

Unlike Butlin's 'biographies' and Lumsden's 'Book of Love', Sulter makes a
careful distinction here between personal experience and the limited capacity of the work of art to communicate this. If each of these writers interprets
the conflict between public and private in different ways, this fundamental
question fascinates them all and is interwoven throughout all their work.
Sulter, although born and brought up in Glasgow, is connected through her
family to the village of Ano in Ghana. Like Jackie Kay, she is careful to define
her stance as a black woman in the predominantly white world of Scottish literature. The identity Sulter presents, however, is far more overtly politicised
than that developed in Kay's poetry. The poem 'As a Blackwoman', which
was also the title of her debut collection in 1985, states:

As a blackwoman
every act is a personal act
every act is a political act[20]

To focus on the individual is not to elide the big political issues. It is a
process of reframing, of translating the abstract rhetoric of theory into
a more personal narrative, one that brings home the deeply charged
and emotionally intense nature of such issues. Sulter aligns herself with
a tendency within a strand of feminist thought in which issues of personal identity cannot be separated from questions of power and freedom
from subordination.

Before her untimely death in 2008 Sulter also worked as a visual artist and photographer. This expansive repertoire is also an important part of the work of Valerie Gillies who has published six volumes of poetry, as well as several books which combine poetry, prose and visual art. Gillies was appointed Edinburgh Makar in 2005, but despite her affiliation to the city, her work remains characterised by a close and very visual relationship with Scottish landscapes, from the Borders to the north-west Highlands. In Gillies' earlier poetry, though, the scenery of India provides a point of fascination, alongside the images of Scotland. Gillies studied at the University of Mysore in South India (in conjunction with studies at the University of Edinburgh); her travels reflect the increasingly globalised nature of contemporary experience, a phenomenon which resonates elsewhere in Scottish poetry, for example Kathleen Jamie's writings about Pakistan and Tibet. In reviewing Gillies' first collection of poems, *Each Bright Eye* (1977), Robert Garioch commented: '[T]he richness of Mrs Gillies' language may hold its own in a northern latitude; one wonders how it might have developed without the benefit of the tropics.'[21] The collection draws extensively on the poet's experience of Mysore (now officially Mysuru). Many of the poems invoke specific people and places experienced on her travels. The poem 'Sangam, Mysore State' depicts a confluence of two branches of the Cauvery river in what is now Karnataka state in south-west India. Through recognisably Scottish metaphors Gillies brings the waters to life, constructing an image in which their currents

> Run high and up against each other,
> link arms in a reel of whirlpools.
> They course for fleeing rocks,
> rain bowstrung splinters of light
> on their retreating stone flanks.[22]

The 'reel of whirlpools' echoes with the birling energy of a ceilidh, while 'bowstrung' works as an image of the rainbow's curve but also reverberates the Celtic tone of Gillies' vision. This is India, but one that is refracted through a peculiarly Scottish lens. The poet may leave home physically, but she cannot completely leave behind the ways she imagines and re-imagines her experience. In a similar vein the poet Tom Pow established himself as a travel writer with the publication of *In the Palace of Serpents* (1992), which describes his journey to Peru, via the Caribbean, in 1989. And like Gillies, Pow's interrogation of place, including Scotland, is unmistakably inflected by a sense of the exotic. In *Rough Seas* (1987) the poem 'The River' imagines

> pensions in foreign towns
> with the shutters open wide and, as here,
> lights strung out along the river.[23]

Similarly 'The Ship' describes three drunken men boarding a foreign boat docked in a Scottish town. This simple act of harmless trespass has a profound effect on their vision and they suddenly recognise their own river as part of a global network, a pathway to the exotic lands of 'Nile, Amazon, [and] Limpopo'.[24] Pow concludes the poem with the men's determination:

> to dissolve what we'd become, to hold
> onto this profligate world
> of dreams and possibilities.[25]

The river becomes a conduit to another world, an imaginative and potentially real escape from the everyday social reality of Scottish coastal life.

The transformative power of poetic vision is a recurrent motif in the work of Brian McCabe, whose work takes the most quotidian of objects and submits them to alternative scrutiny. In contrast to Pow and Gillies, it is not exotic places that interest McCabe so much as rendering strange the minutiae and marginalia of everyday life. His collection *Body Parts* (1999) offers a series of snapshots featuring animals, assorted objects and, as the title intimates, parts of the human body. The status of these objects is continually played on; at one moment they are part of a political critique, the next they lay bare the frailty of human experience alongside our capacity for wonder and joy. The poem 'Object' explores seeing, not as a discrete event, but rather as a process, a slowly realised act of revelation. The concrete world reaches out to us:

> we are offered the savage object
> of the senses:
>
> what we are given;
> what we have forgotten;
> what longs to find a voice.[26]

The 'savage object', the inert world, is refracted through the prism of the poetic imagination. In order to 'draw [its] contours / faithfully, as far as I can follow', 'The Cartographer' looks for ways 'to map the imaginary country / where distance between us is dissembling', and its speaker claims to be 'working on a scale of one to one'.[27] For the realist and representational elements in McCabe's verse 'the chords / and cadence of our daily talk' become an important resource.[28]

He grew up in a coal-mining village south-west of Edinburgh, where his father was a lifelong communist and trade-union organiser. 'Coal' sets up a dialogue with the resurrected voice of a father looking back at a life-time's labour, contrasting the solidarity of Monktonhall miners during the strike of

1984–5 with a subsequent derelict sociality, and the ravaged communities left to cope with de-industrialisation:

> And what is there to show for it?
> Flattened sites, non-places, absences
> Surrounded by meaningless villages.
> The bars look like air-raid shelters.[29]

This responsive son, who has been out to the coal-shed for night-time fuel, stumbles back into the house

> to light a fire,
> to watch the flames rise and flare
> into eloquent tongues.

McCabe does not usually express a politics as directly as this, more usually developing empathy through the angle of perception appropriate to a situated speaker. There is, at any rate, a down-to-earth element in his writing, a refreshingly 'let's be clear about this' aspect that is a recurrent tactic for initially engaging the reader's attention.

'To Make' serves as a kind of credo for McCabe's use of a simple vocabulary, while including the provisional element in any quest for linguistic clarity. 'To Make' delivers its provisionality through an absence of punctuation, leaving each line to reach out and explore relationship, so that the syntax seems developmental on the page:

> To sift the trash of the word
> to use our impure senses
> to find the elements
> to make
>
> Something pure maybe this time
> it will be pure as pure
> as chaos was before
> we made our order of it[30]

Since detecting the mood of a poem depends upon catching its trick of speech, the specifics of voice lie at the centre of McCabe's poems. Admiration for the hawking and spitting speaker of Garioch's 'Heard in the Cougate', as well as his fluent handling of Edinburgh demotic come together in the five conversationally idiomatic sonnets that make up 'The Rat Catcher'.[31] There's a shared sense of politics, too, in the rat catcher's insider knowledge of 'rats in high places' on the local council. In another poem McCabe personifies a kite and in giving it a voice achieves an unexpected level of pathos. The poem concludes:

> I say play with me, play me.
> I say hold me, let me go.
> Hold me – .[32]

The rhythm of the sentence enacts the tension, then release, then more tension of the wind tugging at the kite. The childish simplicity of this request carries both joyful innocence and a sense of fragility. The string could snap. Things could go wrong. And we have the deeply adult question of how one relates to one's children and allows them to grow up – holding them, letting them go, holding them again. The metaphysical ambition of the poem is figured through giving the kite a task: 'to gather the open sky / into your mind's shuttered room'.[33] 'The Kite' is a useful way to approach McCabe's poetry. His work asks us to look at the world we know and to look again.

The act of translation seems ever more important in a globalised world where cultural collision and interaction is a regular facet of everyday life. Literary allusion and translation are key aspects of the 'cosmopolitanism' laid claim to by the group of poets termed 'Informationists' by Richard Price and W. N. Herbert in their anthology *Contraflow on the Superhighway* (1994). Along with Herbert and Price the group included Robert Crawford, Alan Riach, David Kinloch and Peter McCarey. Donny O'Rourke comments briefly on the label in his Introduction to *Dream State* describing: 'an intellectual breadth, confident absorption and redeployment of poetic source material' and 'capacity for cosmopolitan sophistication'.[34] Cosmopolitan literally, of course, designates a citizen of the world. Such a definition might equally be applied to each of the poets mentioned in this chapter as they are all extensively influenced by other places and the unavoidable internationalism of modern Western experience. The term, 'Informationists', is not universally accepted as a helpful way of categorising these poets, but it represents an attempt to place emphasis on the role of poets in the international, information-driven society that is the developed world. Amongst many attributes, Informationist poetry might be identified by a degree of self-conscious intellectualism and a willingness to transverse the boundaries of language and culture. The use of translation and literary allusion in this way is indebted to the Modernist erudition of T. S. Eliot, Ezra Pound and Hugh MacDiarmid. Notably, Alan Riach, W. N. Herbert and Peter McCarey all wrote PhD theses on MacDiarmid's poetry.

Alan Riach's work is notable for its enduring concern with the nature of individual thought and experience. His continual use of the anecdotal, the conversational and the autobiographical imbues his work with a sense of intimacy, a closeness to the lived reality of human experience. It echoes the preoccupations with narrating individual lives that we saw in the work of Butlin and Lumsden earlier. However, as Carol Gow in her review of *First and Last Songs* (1995) comments: '[Riach's poetry shows a] recognition that the act of recording frames experience – autobiography is art, not life.'[35] *First and Last Songs* contains two poems adapted from work by the Peruvian poet César Vallejo (1892–1938). Riach also contributed four loose translations of Vallejo's poems to *César Vallejo: Translations, Transformations and Tributes* (1998), edited by Richard Price and Stephen Watts. Richard Price, besides his work as a poet, was particularly influential in the 1990s as founder of the Vennel Press, which published much of the work by the Informationist poets.

César Vallejo's poetry is syntactically and linguistically complex. The density of his style, however, is frequently counterbalanced by the highly emotive and personal nature of its subject matter. Riach's adaptations from Vallejo are far more accessible than the original; but they are also very different poems. Arguably they are not translations; they follow in the interpretative tradition of Robert Lowell's *Imitations* (1958), which Lowell introduced with the proviso: 'I have been almost as free as the authors themselves in making [the poems] ring right for me'.[36] Riach is freer still. 'Going Under the Bridge' from *First and Last Songs* differs so much from the original that without Riach's explanatory note pointing us in the direction of Vallejo's 'Intensidad y Altura' I do not think it would be possible to make a connection between the two works.[37] By referring to Vallejo's poem, Riach highlights the process of composition, drawing attention to the influence of other work in the production of his own, and in doing so situating his own work in a demonstratively international context. The poem – both in Vallejo's original and in Riach's reworking – is about a struggle for articulacy in writing; in this it reflects a concern that is common to poets writing in all languages. Both poems deal with the frustrations involved in attempting to formulate the welter of thoughts and emotions that constitute daily experience. Vallejo's 'Intensidad y Altura' begins: 'Quiero escribir, pero me sale espuma, / quiero decir muchísimo y me atollo' ('I want to write, but produce only froth, / I want to say so much and I stumble').[38] Vallejo's poem is a strictly formed Petrarchan sonnet with the technical perfection of the poem standing in marked contrast to the poet's own claim to be lost for words. Riach chooses to interpret the poem's theme in a different way, beginning:

> the words connect before they are real words
> I gather what I think I need to guide them then and wait
> I feel as though I'd want to write and want to write and wait[39]

Riach's use of free verse, with no punctuation in the first stanza, lends the poem a sense of immediacy; it has become a glimpse of the speaker's consciousness, at once more open and more cryptic than Vallejo's abstruseness.

Donny O'Rourke, editor of the much discussed anthology *Dream State*, is a poet in his own right, who has also experimented with translation. Mirroring the Auld Alliance, O'Rourke takes France as the point of cultural contact in translating from French into Scots. His translation of Valéry Larbaud's 'Musique après une lecture', entitled 'Musick Eftir A Readin', explores the relationship between the semantic and sonorous qualities of language. The translation begins with the exclamation: 'Eneugh wurds, eneugh sentences! O rael lif, / Ertless an wioot metaphor be mine.'[40] Unlike Riach, O'Rourke stays very close to the original in his choice of words. The French of Larbaud's original gives us 'Assez de mots, assez de phrases! Ô vie réelle, / Sans art et sans metaphors, sois à moi ('Enough words, enough phrases! Oh real life, / without art and without metaphors, be mine').[41] O'Rourke maintains Larbaud's word-choice as far as is possible, and sticks to Larbaud's lineation; but by choosing to write in Scots, O'Rourke conveys a tone very different from that of the *academie* French of the original text. Riach makes Vallejo's poem his own by reinterpreting the sense; O'Rourke by his choice of idiom. O'Rourke's translation of Larbaud, like Riach's borrowing from Vallejo, explores a theme of universal significance among poets and authors. A poet writing of a desire to escape language may do so with frustration, but such declarations are inevitably accompanied by a self-conscious sense of irony. The poem oscillates between the aesthetic and a more immediate version of lived experience. The next line presents a metaphor for an artless life as a girl, whom the poet begs, not only 'come intil ma hert', but also 'come intil ma lines'. The smell and taste, the texture of everyday life, is not reduced but enriched by place in poetry. Playfully the poem brings together the two worlds, the literary and the lived, and exiles the poet from both, concluding with his misanthropic and anti-literary wish to go 'whaur naebody bides, far frae books'.[42]

The process of translation offers unique insights into the various meanings that reside in a particular piece of literature. The task challenges the translator to realise and reconfigure a variety of technical, musical and syntactic energies harnessed in the original verse. It questions the very process of cultural signification, often with the soundscape of the original being compromised by the journey into another language. The Glasgow poet Frank Kuppner, who has been Writer in Residence at the Universities of Glasgow and Strathclyde, invokes in the long poem 'West Åland', a similarly ambiguous correlation between music and words. Whereas O'Rourke's 'Musick Eftir A Readin' looks for a simplicity of experience outwith language, Kuppner offers music as a source of reprieve, filling in the gaps and elisions of a purely semantic understanding of language:

and thus it is that melody, that the verbal music
can fill out in gorgeous tones the poor fallible thinking
the absence of clarity, the absence of mere exact meaning[43]

Kuppner's poem stresses the sensuous beauty of music ever present within spoken language. It draws us back to one of the fundamental, yet often forgotten, differences between poetry and prose, namely the added emphasis on the sonorous qualities of language present in the former. Donny O'Rourke describes 'thi soun o streengs an wuid, mair douce nor slaff itsel' where 'slaff' or sleep suggests not only peace and comfort but a withdrawal of the conscious grasping after meaning.[44] Kuppner is sceptical of separating meaning in this way, of distinguishing between the semantic and sonorous qualities of language which he maintains are inevitably intertwined. While his poem recognises the limitations of our ability to articulate the highly abstract, it does not advocate a wanton retreat into a soundscape bereft of verbal signification.

David Kinloch, originally from Glasgow and now a lecturer in Creative Writing at the University of Strathclyde, worked for many years as a French teacher. His poetry, like O'Rourke's, is frequently built on an exchange between Scotland and other parts of the world. From the collection, *Un Tour d'Ecosse* (2001), 'Lorca on Morar' imagines the Spaniard visiting rugged terrain on the West Coast of Scotland, opening with the attempted pronunciation of local placenames:

'Areesaig', 'Morrarr . . . '
the beach stands up
in little whirlwinds of ash
in my Hispanic mouth[45]

This playful misreading, the collision of cultures, echoes the crossover of Indian and Scottish landscape in Valerie Gillies's writing, or Tom Pow's juxtaposition of the local and the exotic. The intimate relationship between language and place is brought into focus by the poem's interest in place-names and the fact that the foreigner struggles to accommodate them. Indeed, just as Gillies and Pow invigorate their images of Scotland by reference to foreign landscapes, it is the foreignness of Lorca's pronunciation in Kinloch's poem that brings the sands of Morar to life in the reader's imagination, as Lorca's mispronunciations construct his own identity for the reader and render his foreignness in a gentle and understated way. It is the way in which words are spoken, the very texture and tone of language, that Kinloch's poetry seeks to remind us of.

Many of the poets discussed here are actively involved in the teaching and criticism of Scottish literature. However, what emerges from their work as writers is their deep commitment to their craft and its ability to take us beyond the categories and codifications of criticism. Kinloch in his reference to Lorca does more than simply forge a poetic link between Scotland and Spain; he transcends the confines of both nations by invoking a morality, an indignation at injustice, that connects political and cultural identities. Maud Sulter's stance 'As a Blackwoman' is a search for similar ground. The exploration of individual lives and the anonymous nature of modernity we saw in Butlin and Lumsden; the imaginative escape from the particulars of a Scottish landscape in the work of Pow and Gillies; the cultural interchange of allusion and translation in Riach and O'Rourke: all these demonstrate the richness with which these poets look both through and beyond any easily digestible Scottish context. Without belittling the importance of a Scottish literary tradition, these poets attempt to forge a place for their work in the world at large, and in doing so they invite their critics to do the same.

CHAPTER SIX

Nomadic Subjects in Recent Poetry

Colin Nicholson

That sense of place people bang on about is absolutely crucial. And there is something about trying to get back to that beach where I walked. (Robin Robertson, 'Love and Loss') [1]

In August 2008 the *London Review of Books* carried a poem by a leading editor for a metropolitan publisher. 'At Roane Head' is dedicated to John Burnside (1955–), the Dunfermline-born poet and novelist who lived in the English Home Counties and Gloucestershire before returning to Fife, where he teaches at St Andrews University. Burnside's novel of the same year, *The Devil's Footprints*, transfers to the fictional Scottish village of Coldhaven a mid-nineteenth-century South Devon superstition that grew up around the appearance of mysterious tracks in the snow; and then develops it as a convincingly realist narrative of contemporary East-Coast schoolboy experience. Robin Robertson (1955–) sets his poem for Burnside in Ireland, where conversational familiarity – 'You'd know her house by the drawn blinds' – and Scoto-Irish idiom – 'It would put the heart across you, all that grief' – personalise an encounter with the folk-lore, fairy tale and popular beliefs that Edwin Muir had warned all Scottish writers against.[2] In *Scottish Journey* (1935) Muir presented his appraisal as a matter of 'no choice' for poets looking to make their mark, emphasising instead the need for a 'more individual and less local' voice.[3] Robertson, who was born in Scone, Perthshire, brought up on the coast of north-east Scotland, and has since spent much of his professional life in London where he now lives, exercises a different take on both the folk impulse and local orientation, while amply fulfilling Muir's requirement.

Known as 'selkies' in Scotland, 'roanes' are the Irish version of 'seal-people' who put seal-skins on their natural human form (or vice-versa) to pass through water from one region or state to another. 'At Roane Head' extends Robertson's fascination with the shape-changing customary in myth and legend; and poetry, he has suggested, 'like myth or spirituality or religion' offers 'similar ways of making sense of our lives'.[4] Raised in Aberdeen, where his father was Church of Scotland university chaplain, Robertson grew up familiar with lore and legend because Aberdeenshire, with its many standing stones, is a place where 'history, legend and myth merged cohesively in the landscape'.[5] Though Robertson's approach to myth and associated beliefs is distinctive, we begin to understand something of his interest in work by the English-born, Welsh-descended poet David Jones (1895–1974) that invests legendary figures and a redemptive environment in sacralising mystique. But whereas the conservation of archaism is important to Jones's design, Robertson's turn to originating script radically foreshortens the distance travelled from founding figuration to contemporary redaction. He was, for example, drawn to translate *Medea* (2008) because he saw Euripides giving an 'utterly modern' feeling to an age-old tale of marital betrayal and revenge by presenting his protagonists as 'ordinary people in extraordinary situations'. Classical past speaks compellingly in the present when 'our recognition that not much has changed in two and a half thousand years' intensifies the contact.[6] In this light, and with due allowance that 'nothing is ever quite so extreme as it is in Greece', exchanges between the estranged Jason and Medea struck Robertson as 'dialogue you might hear in any house on a Friday night': he could think of their conflict as 'a domestic' partly because the personal resonance of a failed marriage lay behind the project: '[I]t was fresh in my mind and I wanted to bring my own experience to this one-line dialogue exchange between Jason and Medea.'[7] Present reference typifies Robertson's method of working with classical text; from 'The Flaying of Marsyas' in his first collection to 'Asterion and the God' in his second, and 'The Death of Actaeon', 'Actaeon: the Early Years' and 'Holding Proteus' in the third.

Not Greek but Gaelic otherworlds provide structures of motive and intention for 'At Roane Head', and a useful resource for redesigning temporal connection with and across storied space. Its fable of murder, revenge and loving devotion to the memory of the dead moves from folk-lore and superstition into an unnerving present and back into the realm of folk-tale through the medium of a grounded and recognisably real-world speaker who traverses both: 'Then she gave me the sealskin, and I put it on.' Given the prime function of words to navigate distances real and imagined, to travel and connect speaker with hearer, page to reader, 'At Roane Head' mobilises for its permeable territory an interstitial but seamlessly connective lexis. Generally obsolete, 'quicken' for rowan tree survives in Northern Irish usage; 'whicker' for wingbeat is dialectal; 'hirpling' is current Scots; 'beglamoured' for spell-bound (leading to weakness of sight where objects appear other than they are) is literary Scots; and 'smoor', for smother, is still in places conversational. 'Chittering' is an older English variant of chatter, and the OED cites both a sixteenth-century Scots usage of 'relax' as a freeing from restraint and a nineteenth-century example of the word in relation to execution. This latter helps to contextualise without lessening the impact of a returning husband's drunken violence to the four web-footed sons 'born blind' at Roane Head he claims 'couldn't be his'; and so 'made them stand / in a row by their beds' while he

> went along the line
> relaxing them
> one after another
> with a small knife.

All we know of the wife's revenge is the speaker's evidence that she 'gave me / her husband's head in a wooden box'. With liminality as topic and theme, 'At Roane Head' centres the structuring of our relationship to a poem that dramatises historical and linguistic crossovers between various communities and localised beliefs; and with a poet 'trying / to hazard the heart's meridian'[8] in contexts that reconfigure customary value. Typically combining effective image-making with oblique narrative, the poem enacts a moral requirement for attentiveness to the choices made on the page and in any communicative group or society where language organises priorities and responsibility.

Slow Air (2002) was written in memory of the poet's father: 'A gifted, wise and generous man,' he told Nicholas Wroe, explaining why 'a sense of grief after his death gave that collection its unity':

> But it's not a question of saying, 'Today I'm going to write about grief'. Coleridge talked about a well of the unconscious into which everything is dropped, and the act of creation is lowering the bucket and pulling up images and words that, hopefully, have undergone some metamorphosis.[9]

A transforming figure of absence seems also to signify the co-vanishing of the faith that sustained his father in life. In homage to that paternal thought-world and in memory of its valued sensibility, a recurrent, crafted oblation of observation and experience produces images of unusual concretion that impressed the American poet Billy Collins: '[E]ach poem comes to us so cleansed of excess, so concentrated and perfectly pared down to its essence we can only wonder at the adamantine sharpness of its edges.'[10] Beyond the warning against vanity in Ecclesiastes, and Petrarch's caution that 'the fruit of my vanity is shame, and repentance, and the clear knowledge that whatever the world finds pleasing, is but a brief dream' which together open *Slow Air*, a secularised reverence is part of this writing from the beginning. 'Three Ways of Looking at God' in *A Painted Field* (1997) is an early example;[11] and the inclination is memorable in the elegiac 'These Days'.[12] It is inflected in the thought that 'even a god can't stop the light / that finds us, annealed'; heard in the sea's 'slow worship of erosion', and is more tremulously caught in the 'jealous screech' of covetous resentment that sends 'The Flamingos' 'striding into paradise'.[13] The figure left 'not praying, just on my knees in the dark' at the end of 'Entropy', like the one who hears 'that petitionary, leaden / litany of the sea', existentialises the postlapsarian poetics that informs this work:

> In the walled garden
> form is imposed on this fugitive green,
> this rinsing light; to enclose is to make sacred,
> to frame life's chaos for a slow repair,
> to make an art of healing, of release,
> an amnesty against despair.[14]

As he tests the ability of language to set a viable speaking voice anywhere in space and time, tracing formations of selfhood in both remembered and remembering subjectivity, Robertson's rhythms can be unsettling and his eloquence sometimes austere because the issues he raises will not go away. Nonetheless his way with words, together with the residual optimism of formal accomplishment, repeatedly satisfy a stated intention to deliver 'the refreshed world and, through a language thick with sound and connotation and metaphor, make some sense: some new connection between what is seen and felt and what is understood'.[15]

'We are drawn to edges,' the opening poem of *Slow Air* begins, 'to our own parapets and sea-walls', and continues 'we have forgotten how to walk':[16] risk-taking on the edge, at or near the limits of mental/emotional or linguistic tolerance, is something Robertson both courts and excels at. 'I sometimes think poets create their own subjects', he has suggested, and a characteristic intimacy of exchange between lived experience, reconstructed event and remembering writer, puts disclosure at the service of self-formation. 'I don't know if it's true', he went on to say, 'but [poets] do seem to put themselves in peril.'[17] There is angst enough in writing where a hankering for fidelity to experience can read like a hunger for faith beyond the ineluctable modality of the visible. Perhaps that is why the city speaker of 'The Thermal Image' seeks out the 'ghosts of radiation' left as trace after love-making:

> I track and root out heat,
> its absorption and emission,
> the white bed's infra-red, the bright
> spoor of the soul's transmission.[18]

Both the definition Robertson can achieve and the liminal contexts he devises and occupies are effectively displayed in the sonnet 'Wedding the Locksmith's Daughter', where the sound of phrasal music slotting and clicking into a persuasive clarity both distances and delivers the erotic proximity

of love and death that is the poem's theme. A 'chime of sound / on sound' is
fleeting enough, and a sung note fades instantly; but it is 'the way the sung
note snibs on meaning // and holds' across the stanza break that enables a
rhythm of movement to 'engage and marry now' the mechanism of syntax
with formal transmission: artful articulation locks signifier to signified before
the imminent dispersal of the poem's closing line.[19]

The otherwise celebratory 'In Memoriam David Jones' closes on a sense
that the seeming permanence of an observable world, our compulsion to bear
witness to it, and the acknowledged transience of that impulse, all constitute
the transitoriness of things where:

> a grey seal surfaces, astonished,
> on a scene that stays the same;
> sinks back phantom and is towed under –
> has never tired,
> will never tire of this.[20]

'By the time you look you've missed it' is deceptive in 'First Winter' because
words on the page delay – however momentarily – the vanishing of a flown
bird: 'the snow-shy cardinal / newly gone'.[21] In a liminal space discerned subsequently as 'The Gift of Tantalus', sense impression lingers fleetingly as an
after-image 'still troubling the light' when:

> what we came to find
> is fading, leaching away,
> while the place mocks us,
> flashing up our mortality,
> our young ghosts,
> in a time-lapse film
> of flowers and rotting fruit.[22]

A senior editor in a major publishing house knows how cultural markets
produce and reproduce representations for the shaping of preferred perception, and this is part of Robertson's engagement with the difficult music of
what happens in the world: difficult because remembering for him is often
triggered by 'luminous ghosts' that 'let in the past with a stabbing spear'. The
variety of setting he devises for 'these . . . strange stigmata, the memories
that bleed'[23] includes memory merging with history and autobiography with
alterity in the life Robertson documents and invents for David Octavius
Hill (1802–70), the Perth-born painter and pioneer of photography. Hill
moved to Edinburgh in 1818 and was there in 1843, when his partner Robert
Adamson (1821–48) set up an experimental studio; and when the 'Great
Disruption' marked the secession of some 400 ministers – about a third of the

established Church – and the founding of the Free Church of Scotland. This led directly to the idea of photographing participating ministers, from which Hill would then produce the massive painting that hangs in Edinburgh's Free Presbytery Hall. Dedicated to Robertson's father, 'Camera Obscura' makes lucid representations of present love, grief and loss by weaving private with public moments in a nineteenth-century life.[24]

If poetry maps a nation's imaginative cognitions, then we need appropriate ways of charting the mobility of nomadic subjects that characterises recent Scottish writing; as when the sixteen sections of Robertson's 'Actaeon: The Early Years' adapt Ovid to existential effect, so that classical metamorphosis is reterritorialised to generate local impact and contemporary resonance. Violently rejected by his mother, when young Actaeon takes to 'hiding in the trees for hours' he comes to realise that:

> desire for intimacy
> was a transgression, and that
> the resulting fear of intimacy,
> which was also now a fear of disclosure,
> was understandable, even natural,
> in this place, among these people.[25]

Self-disclosure predicates a continuing process of becoming, where the elaboration of Scottish senses of being in the world calls for serviceable compass-bearings on a never-ending journey; and it seems likely that Robertson was among those who learned from Douglas Dunn (1942–), in his *Elegies* (1985) and elsewhere, how intimate disclosure can achieve expressive form.

Secular reconstructions of the shaping agency of Scottish circumstance also include a childhood playground on a 1940s Ayrshire farm vividly recalled by Stewart Conn (1936–), who is aware that writing a vanished past into the living present inevitably transforms known into imagined community. But 'for all that', he insists, 'no matter how mythologised my memories have become, or how fanciful they may have been in the first place, they remain related to real people – a sturdy people who belonged to a specific soil, as it belonged (for a while) to them'.[26] The farm has gone, the landscape of memory permanently altered, and so personal recollection involves a social history of uneven development. This is made more interesting by a progress – from Glasgow to Kilmarnock where his father was Church of Scotland parish minister; back to Glasgow where he would become head of BBC Radio Scotland's Drama Department, then to Edinburgh in 1976 where Conn has lived ever since – that crosses several of Scotland's internal fault lines; of social class and class prejudice, of religious sensibility, of regional and urban identification. Although he develops multicultural fields of reference,

anxieties about rootedness, transience and elusive senses of belonging characterise his verse, notwithstanding his appointment from 2002 to 2005 as the
first modern poet laureate of the capital, the Edinburgh Makar; where discovery of a family connection in the Old Town helped him 'feel less an inter-
loper, / than one who has been long away'.[27] It becomes understandable that
as name, figure and shadowy presence, ghosts both spooky and seemingly real
appear in Conn's poetry early and late. 'Makar' signifies invention, and self-
making fictions reinforce fiction-making selves: for his newly-minted position
Conn devises a possible precursor for the office of Edinburgh Laureate by
fleshing out a ghostly renaissance figure whose name but nothing else survives
in the historical record. A sometimes ventriloquised 'Roull of Costorphine'
sequence extends imagined selfhood into uncharted relationship where past
and present speaking subjects change places.[28]

Selfhood and relationships past and present – and enough journeys to
last a lifetime – also characterise work by the founder of the Scottish Poetry
Library. Tessa Ransford (1938–), who traces Scottish lineage through her
paternal grandmother, was born in India, educated in Scotland and has lived
all her adult life in Scotland, apart from eight years working in Pakistan in
the 1960s, married to a Church of Scotland missionary. The marriage did
not survive, but speculative, religious structures of feeling ranging from Sufi
to Quaker did, alongside an imaginative dialectic where India and Scotland
function as complementary opposites in an East–West synthesis of her own
making. Because it is a relationship Ransford sees in different ways at different times, memory and experience come into sharp relief. In terms of street-
level natural climate the East–West contrast is total, so that the lines:

> To have first found the world
> in abundant India
> is my life's greatest privilege

nicely counterpoint an historically perceived 'frosty forenoon' when,

> Singing a cold cadence Fergusson
> the poet
> shivered down the Canongate with rhythm in his feet.[29]

'My Indian Self' includes the contraries out of which Ransford makes her own
progression through comparative experience of interior landscapes shaped by
radically different cultural climates:

> Let me wear the silks,
> the sandals and the gold.
> Let me dip my fingers

in the bowl of desire
even here in the puritan
corners of my dwelling

Let me reclaim
myself. I cannot
be curtailed;
extravagance is my form
not my style;
intensity is how
my pulse is rated. [30]

When the collection *Shadows from the Greater Hill* came out in 1987, it was
evident that she had found a way of framing experiential intensity through
her living-room window perspective onto the immediate parkland edge of the
hill around which Edinburgh is built. By recording in diary form its changing
scenes and seasons, Ransford builds a mutable relationship in which her

wispy, slender, Scottish
Asian, aching, striding,
enduring, joyous, anxious, hopeful
woman-shape

is variously exercised across a range of moods and reflections. 'February 14th'
uses the contours of Arthur's Seat to reignite the extinct volcano in city sun-
light and associate it with cross-gendered Indian mythology: 'an elephant-god
/ fat, sleek, pregnant' now seen as 'detached from predicaments / of weather or
winter', and a figure who:

laughingly knows of desire's flame
never quenched to nirvana,
but lit anew in rock and sinew
year by year.[31]

Seven years later Ransford produced what might still be her strongest sequence,
thirteen poems called 'Medusa Dozen' that grew out of a failed relationship to
become an effective rehabilitation for the feminine intelligence of an ancient
symbol of sacred wisdom. To accommodate the energies of a serpent-goddess
figured only as vengeful and destructive in male-coded myth, a prefatory note
suggests that 'William Blake's maxim informs the whole: "Without contraries is no progression. Attraction and repulsion, reason and energy, love and
hate are necessary to human existence."[32] Subdued to form, there is passion
enough in the sequence, as well as the resilient solidarity of sisterhood:

In our poverty and bondage
we have our special orders
and grow our own gods.[33]

But in her search for

> this unemphatic,
> non-expectant, poised
> detachment
> I have worked for,

Ransford's commitment to a 'poetry of persons' remains tenuously hopeful:[34]

Perhaps we can recreate for each other a memory.
relive for each other, dramatise and share,
restore the person, who otherwise slowly fades:
for lack of a past the present floating away.[35]

Subjectivity and circumstance in Scottish recorded life as in any other are inseparable from the writing that makes them accessible; continuing re-inventions of both selfhood and context open the field of possibility, and Benedict Anderson's suggestion that communities are distinguished by the styles in which they are imagined plays out on Scottish turf as a plural diversity, and a sometimes fierce argument, with which its poets invest and associate their senses of identity and affiliation. Hugh MacDiarmid condemned Ian Hamilton Finlay's early forays into Glasgow demotic as the 'language of the gutter':[36] in the first of his 'Unrelated Incidents' Tom Leonard (1944–) picks up the charge and runs with 'thi / langwij a / thi guhtr' that is deemed

awright fur
funny stuff
ur
Stanley Bax-
ter ur but
luv n science
n thaht naw.[37]

Orality antedates literacy by a lot more than a country mile, so questing subjectivity as a process of continuing invention is older than the more recent practice of writing, a practice and technology where memory precedes inscription and contextualises perception as Mnemosyne the mother of remembering does her daughter Clio, the muse of history. In recognition of this order of succession the front cover of Leonard's *Intimate Voices* carries a poem that subjects its canonically scripted first line 'In the beginning was the word' to a series of phonetic reconstructions that legitimise its concluding utterance: 'in the beginning was the sound'.

A locally determined and seemingly class-bound contouring of expression generates wider resonance because dominance and subjection are as much worldwide phenomena as the experience of growing up in the sound world of localised groups or communities. Given the regional specifications of Scottish culture, Leonard's conviction that 'dialogue between one human being and another . . . is all that Literature is', confirms his sense of poetry as the drama of persons in relation. [38] That this drama is marked by conflict and resistance is made clear by Leonard's recurrent attention to intersections between linguistic and political systems of permission and exclusion. 'Putting it another way,' he writes in one of his prose pieces: 'if a piece of writing can't comfortably be read aloud in a "correct" (Received Pronunciation) voice, then there must be something wrong with it. It's not valid.' In these circumstances:

> prescriptive grammar . . . becomes the sound made flesh of prescriptive pronunciation. The tawdry little syllogism goes something like this:
>
> 1. In speaking of reality, there is a standard correct mode of pronunciation.
> 2. In writing of reality, there is a standard correct mode of spelling and of syntax.
> ∴ 3. In reality, correct spelling and correct syntax are synonymous with correct pronunciation.[39]

When the second 'Unrelated Incident' explores the power relations contingent on acceptance and refusal based on voice and speech, it includes linguistically-informed advice against casual approaches to this poet's work:

> fyi stull
> huvny
> thoata lang
> wij izza
> sound-system;
> fyi huvny
> hudda thingk
> aboot thi dif-
> frince tween
> sound
> n object n
> symbol; well,
> ma innocent
> wee
> friend – iz
> god said ti

adam:
a doant kerr
fyi caw it
an apple
ur
an aippl—
jist leeit
alane!⁴⁰

The last (untitled) poem in Leonard's *Situations Theoretical and Contemporary* (1986) advertises as established practice overlaps between diction, lexis and validating systems of power where 'their judges spoke with one dialect, / but the condemned spoke with many voices':

> And the prisons were full of many voices,
> but never the dialect of the judges.
>
> And the judges said:
>   'No-one is above the Law.'⁴¹

For a common grounding defined by a persistently variable acoustic, the working-class utterance Leonard energises is both indelibly realised and symbolically representative of a situated and self-aware voice subversively confirming while radically interrogating an overarching political state. His riveting of speech to place projects a class-conscious federal imagination secure in its allegiance to ideas of Scottishness where distinctive utterance in particularised environment constitutes the individual and local substance of that larger association. In circumstances where media saturation threatens a homogenising uniformity, Leonard's

          this
   is me tokn yir
   right way a
   spellin. this
   is ma trooth

becomes fitting as the badge of all our tribes, and one that Alison Flett might readily wear.⁴² Born in Edinburgh where she grew up, and moving to Orkney in 2006 where she now lives, Flett (1965–) took with her *Whit Lassyz Ur Inty* (2004), a striking first collection that relocates to Edinburgh and regenders the demotically edgy phonetics Leonard transcribes to capture the oral sound-world of an upbringing. From a different place and a later generation Flett has her own perceptions of class politics in a capital city, where as 'ikariss' suggests, any notion of the 'polis' as participatory community decays into a heavily policed subjection:

it wiz hardur tay buleev in
upwurd mobility
when thay pit barbed wire
oan taoppy thi lectric fens
thit ran roond thi skeem.[43]

In his anthology of largely forgotten nineteenth-century west-of-Scotland writers Leonard extends his sense of speech as the birthplace of intersubjectivity, the grounding of community and the origin of history. As it exercises the contemporary relevance of cultural retrieval, *Radical Renfrew* (1990) rescues local voices from the condescension of posterity partly because 'the sound of nothingness' that A. L. Kennedy called 'the huge, invisible, silent roar of all the people who are too small to record', was for Leonard a family experience.[44] 'Fathers and Sons', the closing poem of *Intimate Voices*, begins

I remember being ashamed of my father
when he whispered the words out loud
reading the newspaper,

and then switches to:

'Don't you find
The use of phonetic urban dialect
Rather restrictive?'
asks a member of the audience

before ending:

The poetry reading is over
I will go home to my children.[45]

When poetry readings were over for Mick Imlah (1956–2009), he went home to London where he worked at the *Times Literary Supplement* from 1992. Born in Aberdeen, brought up near Glasgow and in Kent, and educated at Magdalen College, Oxford, where he subsequently taught as a junior fellow, Imlah's epigraph for *The Lost Leader* (2008) is Edwin Muir's advice referenced above(Note 3):

[N]o poet in Scotland now can take as his inspiration the folk impulse that created the ballads, the people's songs, and the legends of Mary Stuart and Prince Charlie. He has no choice but to be at once more individual and less local.

As a dedicated desacraliser, Imlah makes a permissive charter out of this: his title poem quotes from an old song, is precisely localised in witness to the last betrayal of his supporters by the legendary Prince Charlie himself – and it focalises an individual speaker. On the day after the Battle of Culloden finally broke clan power, 'Sixteen hundred far-gone / Followers' of Jacobite insurgency retreated south to Ruthven barracks to prepare for further combat. But Charles, bent on saving his own hide, was already fleeing the country, having left as parting advice: 'Let every man seek his own safety in the best way he can.' Not very happy with this, the surviving clansmen torched the barracks and melted away, hoping to avoid capture and worse by the redcoats. As the ironic despatch of his final rhyme shows, any 'fire of belonging' has guttered out for the rain-soaked speaker of 'The Lost Leader', a leader already making good his escape

> west down channels
> of last ditch loyalty;
> To France at last, your safety,
> Prince, Your Highness,
> Your brandy, gout and syphilis.[46]

The Lost Leader's opening poem dates itself simply as AD, sets a twenty-first century voice in the enchanted twilight of Hiberno-Scottish saints, and has fun with myths of origin in a whirligig of time where riotous anachronism mobilises dead-pan satire on evangelical subjectivity then and now:

> before
> MacBrayne and the broken ice; before
> Colum and Camelot, whose annals skate
> over our failed attempt on Muck.

These Ulstermen heading east reconfigure the westward flow of conversion that shaped a minority faith-based region in the North of Ireland; and their discovery of 'a sham temple' on a Hebridean island discloses totems and trappings of pagany as well as the shared symbol of the fish. A two-way traffic in belief systems is already ironising subsequent history, and when 'blessed Kevin' our proselytising man in charge cries 'Back to the boats!' because 'we brought the word of God / to those in hiding here, and they don't want it!', we hear that for those who do the rowing he too is a lost leader, though not for reasons he would tolerate. The voice that speaks the poem emerges from a group sense of religious ideology internalised; coded as right or wrong for unthinking assumption by conscripted adherents who here refuse consent. Their absence in conventional accounts constitutes the historical silence that proves the code's general effectiveness, giving point to this speaker's subversive intervention:

> we sounded in reply the child's note
> of feigned frustration, masking the relief

our code forbids us to have felt, or
having felt, express.

Muted, because his sentiments are proscribed, there seems nothing feigned in the paganism of his closing toast to 'the gay goddess / Asarté – mother of false starts'; except for the joke it may be playing on the poem's own verac-ity and positioning.[47] The next piece, 'The Prophecies', foregrounds origin myths about Celtic monasticism but assumes instead a shared and functional awareness that legend derives from what is read (and therefore scripted). The story goes that Baithene, an Irish monk selected by St Columba as one of the sixth-century band of missionaries who landed on Iona, was the scribe who succeeded him as leader. In Imlah's version of events Baithene prophesies the book by Adamnàn that would preserve Columba's memory for future genera-tions, and so brings us into the present ken of a remembering speaker:

The Life of St Columba, Founder of Hy
by Adam something – many an abbot later –
in Penguin Classics, nineteen ninety-nine.
And now as he shared the vision he felt, he said,
a warm, delicious tingle and flush of the veins
as if he had been ravished by who knows whom.[48]

From these beginnings, The Lost Leader trawls widely over Scottish and related cultural territory, designing points of entry and angles of vision for a highly entertaining series of different takes on memories and events it finds there, some well-known, others retrieved from forgotten byways. As we move through its pages, discovery and self-discovery proceed in tandem; an auto-biographical thread that connects a sense of personality and place, including friends and relations; and a bracingly alternative range of responses to the historical ownership and control of acceptable or privileged narrative. In the warmly conversational elegy to 'Steven Boyd' Imlah tells us that

years of a Southern education since
Had trimmed my Scottishness to a tartan phrase
Brought out on match days and Remembrance Days,

making all the more unlikely the closeness he feels for the poem's addressee in their shared passion for rugby.[49] That upbringing helps to explain Angus Calder's reminder, cited at the beginning of 'Namely' that 'few people thought Mick Imlah, who teaches at Oxford, was a "Scottish Poet"'.[50] There can't be any doubters now. A bravura display of formal variety and techni-cal finesse enables Imlah to engineer innovative ways of seeing and saying for real and invented identities and actual and imagined relationship. In the process Scottish incident and event are revisited and reconstructed, the record re-adjusted, archetypes and stereotypes interrogated and revised, national pastimes and passions re-examined, and sacred cows rumbled: all of them subjected to a probing, witty and pragmatic sense of what is not normally said, not customarily included. *The Lost Leader* closes with 'Afterlives of the Poets', two mini-sequences about Tennyson and about James ('BV') Thomson that stretch and determine connections in ways that typify Imlah's ability to generate insight by refracting perspective.

In conjunction with 'dimensions of the sentient' that Douglas Dunn brought into play,[51] such refraction became newly available to Scottish verse over the last half-century largely through Edwin Morgan's use of technical variation for encyclopaedic discovery. Elliptical and time-travelling autobiography in *The New Divan* (1977), cosmic sightings and recognisable settings in *From the Video Box* (1986), political geographies at risk in *Hold Hands among the Atoms* (1991), 'our longing for the plenum of the weal' in the holographic and digitised worlds of *Virtual and Other Realities*;[52] each collection develops and extends the space for Scottish self-making. Written in response to the failure of the 1979 referendum on devolution, *Sonnets from Scotland* (1984) sets a bench-mark for imaginative independence liberated from conventional restraints of time and space – and varies traditional form too, in that Morgan invents a rhyme-scheme for the purpose. 'Deviation is as good as law' in *Cathures*, an assembly of historic personalities and events related to the city that in 1999 made Morgan its Poet Laureate.[53] *Cathures* is the ancient name for Morgan's home city, and the inclusion of poems not connected to Glasgow is part of the collection's political aesthetic because, a prefatory note explains, '[A]s Lucretius pointed out, it does not matter in what part of the universe you live.' The three lines Morgan then quotes from the free-thinking Roman's *De Rerum Natura* translate as: 'Nor does it matter in which of its regions you stand; so true is it, that whatever place anyone occupies, he leaves the whole equally infinite in every direction.'[54] A radically open conspectus with 'no barriers in subject matter or style' continues in *A Book of Lives* (2007): 'If it's any good,' Morgan has commented, 'the collection must be more than just a book of lives. The title is meant to set you off thinking, off on a course of ideas'; a prospect to gladden the hearts of adventuring travellers wherever they are situated.[55]

The situation in Orkney and Shetland is both typical and unique for regions with self-identifying culture facing the relentless processes of globalising anglophone incorporation. While for mainland writers the lexicon this makes available can expand opportunities, for Shetlanders it can as readily constitute 'a dilemma'.[56] Robert Alan Jamieson (1958–) thought of his first collection, *Shoormal* (1986), as 'an exorcism of youthful ghosts, through the use of certain sounds . . . I no longer use day to day', and suggested that 'in its symbolic movement from ebb to flow, it parallels my own from dialect speaker to English speaker.' While the flood-tide of English 'must never be allowed to break the thread of belonging', in terms of personal choice he shows how long and flexible that thread can be.[57] Now that 'the oil boom has exploded myths / of timelessness', creative argument about the proper form of dialect inscription is evidence of continuing attention to the preservation and promotion of a local sound world and its recorded speech.[58] Christine de Luca (1947–), born in Shetland where she grew up, now lives in Edinburgh, and a backward glance is traced in her work. The title poem of her first collection *Wast wi da Valkyries* (1994) marks the intrusion of metropolitan phrasing – 'veiled paradise', 'effortless / rollerbladers' – into dialect verse where 'Time is mizzered . . . bi da sea's favours.' Now, the poem concludes, is 'a time ta tak':

> ta pick owre
> gaets wir taen, or no taen,
> on dis wir langest vaege.[59]

The path taken by Jamieson measures the distance from a coastal crofting community in Shetland where he was born to Edinburgh where he lives and works, teaching creative writing at the university. The voyage he imagines and the self he invents as voyager in *Nort Atlantik Drift: Poyims ati'Shaetlin* (2007) shift from 'pure autobiography' in the opening poem to 'pure fiction' in the last, with the body of the collection 'developing as a kind of "life-I-might-have-led", had the nine-year-old boy I was gone to sea as he thought he might'. Parallel English texts and photographic images accommodate and compensate for the difficulty and Scandinavian strangeness of the Shætlin versions that 'linguists call "Modern Shetlandic Scots"'. [60]

Orkney is not Shetland, but both are busy places generating lively senses of who and how people living there are. Against the odds Orcadians have kept local publishing outlets in play, most recently the Hansel Cooperative Press, and its writers maintain self-aware dialogue between credible past, viable present and possible futures. Interesting in this respect is the experiential and dialectal sound-world that Morag MacInnes (1950–) recreates for a nineteenth-century Orcadian woman's improbable but true travels. Dressed as a man Isobel Gunn left Orkney for Canada and a labouring job with the Hudson Bay Company, maintaining the male disguise during a pregnancy throughout which she worked, including an epic 1,800 mile canoe trek supplying company outposts. In the sequence of twenty poems that comprises *Alias Isobel: An Orkney Narrative* (2008) MacInnes, who has lived in Shetland, Germany and Lincolnshire and is now back home on Orkney, develops a convincing and effective register for a sharply drawn historical character who became the first white woman to work in north-west Canada:

clingin tae the edge
in this new place: the map's
a blank.[61]

There are other versions of Gunn's story; this one crafts a persuasive sense
of how she might have spoken. Since past is prologue, we hear a fable of our
times in what MacInnes calls the 'mixter maxter of voices' found at any of
the Canadian trading bases, where 'there were many Orknies, as they were
called, [and] also a hundred other voices':

There as many words here
as trees.
They mak the skyline hard tae read, mak hid
hard tae mind whar yur fae.

The gutter girls, I mind the skirl o their
tongues, cuttan
under yur ear, hittan bone lik
their knives, here then gone.[62]

Because Isobel Gunn was posing as a man her dislocation was a double one,
in which 'she had to learn to accommodate more than just new dialects.'[63]
So must we all.

CHAPTER SEVEN

Edwin Morgan

Matt McGuire and Colin Nicholson

In 1983 Umberto Eco called the term 'postmodernism' 'bon à tout faire', since when the intellectual and categorical incoherence of this loosest and baggiest of monsters has been exhaustively demonstrated.[1] But recent recalibrations of Modernism, intended to develop a different take on postmodernity, rekindle interest by examining instead Modernist evolutions into the contemporary. These relate cultural practice to material context in ways that lead us into Edwin Morgan's interventions across a wide variety of movements and tendencies over his long writing career. T. J. Clark's 'Origins of the Present Crisis' adopts the title of Perry Anderson's celebrated 1964 essay, but takes as its springboard Anderson's *The Origins of Postmodernity*, published thirty-four years later, which itself outgrew its original purpose as Preface to Fredric Jameson's writings on postmodernism called *The Cultural Turn*, also published in 1998.[2] Clark is concerned to reinforce Anderson's emphasis on continuities between Modernism and postmodernism:

> Plenty of previous commentators . . . have pointed out that descriptions of postmodernism almost invariably thrive on a kind of blindness to the presence within *modernism* of the very features that are supposed to make postmodernism what it is. 'Virtually every aesthetic device or feature attributed to postmodernism – *bricolage* of tradition, play with the popular, reflexivity, hybridity, pastiche, figurality, decentring of the subject – could be found', as Anderson puts it, in the previous regime of representation. 'No critical break was discernible'.[3]

Yet the Introduction to this *Companion* proposed that the death of Hugh MacDiarmid in 1978 marked the end of an era. The old men in Moffat's painting *The Poets Pub* had had their day, history had moved on. This change of gears also coincided with the 1979 failure of the devolution referendum and the advent of Thatcherism with all its emotive consequences. The synthetic nature of such divisions, of course, runs the risk of distorting the record for the sake of a neat and compact story. Reality is always more complex than its models will allow and Morgan routinely interrupts and exceeds any cosy and convenient narrative with his own subversions and continuities. The young-est character of the central grouping in Moffat's painting, he was thirty years MacDiarmid's junior and belonged to a different generation. If MacDiarmid's star was beginning to wane by the mid-1960s, Morgan's was on its incandes-cent rise. The younger poet had not been attracted by the privileged modes of Modernist practice he came back to in 1946 after wartime service with the Royal Army Medical Corps in the Middle East. The current championing of verse in Scots did not compel Morgan's allegiance because he had places to take the language he was born into (a significantly Scottish and Surrealist-inspired Apocalypse movement that might have offered alternative perspec-tives would prove short-lived). That cultural argument stimulated a creative response that with hindsight has every appearance of a willed and determined construction by Morgan of a (post)modernism within which he could more congenially trace his own succession. MacDiarmid's preference for a Celtic mythopoeia as carapace for innovation and recognition threatened to close off perspectives that Morgan found useful. 'We Scottish poets,' MacDiarmid had announced in the Introduction to his *Golden Treasury* anthology (1940, reprinted 1946), 'must needs travel back . . . into Scots and Gaelic. Anglo-Saxon is not for us.'[4] Morgan admired Anglo-Saxon poetry, and part of his early search for a voice included translating, between May and June of 1947, 'The Seafarer' and 'The Wanderer' into modern English. On his way to becoming the admired and widely successful transcreator of *Beowulf*, he was already developing a genealogy of sister languages in what he later called the 'ur-historical sense that the Scots tongue developed originally out of the Northumbrian dialect of Anglo-Saxon'.[5]

At the same time Morgan was instinctively hostile to the right-wing poli-tics associated with a still-influential Eliot–Pound axis. To escape from rocks and hard places by extending the field of choice, he opted to speak his alterna-tive versions through the Glasgow-inflected voice of Vladimir Mayakovsky's revolutionary figure (1893–1930). In the early 1950s, when Communist politics were an active presence in cultures across Europe, Morgan was often an engaged if lower-case sympathiser. But he also had clear ideas about Stalinism at home and abroad when he began working with Russian texts by the poet whom Trotsky called the troubadour of the revolution. Together they sing interesting songs and tell choice tales, while the energetic Scots of Morgan's translations effectively subverts the repression of history Fredric Jameson finds in 'the perfected poetic apparatus' of early twentieth-century Anglo-American practice; where the political, 'no longer visible in the high modernist text, any more than in the everyday world of appearance of bour-geois life' becomes 'a genuine Unconscious'.[6] As *Wi the Haill Voice* (1972) shifts Russian futurism into sometimes-surreal Scots verse, the political is evident, refreshing and recurrently satirical. Facing the challenge of whether

Scots could match 'the mixture of racy colloquialism and verbal inventiveness in Mayakovsky's Russian', Morgan found reinforcement in what he called medieval Scots poetry's 'vein of fantastic satire'.[7] Additionally, the discovery of Mayakovsky was part of a life-long fascination with the arts and echoes of translation, to the extent that for its range alone Morgan's *Collected Translations* (1996) identify him as the most important Scottish translator of other people's verse in living memory.

If MacDiarmid's artistic agenda failed to capture Morgan's imagination, he soon became increasingly frustrated with what he saw as a residual parochialism in Scotland's literary culture. His essay 'The Beatnik in the Kailyard' (1962) sets out an agenda by which poetry might begin to break out of its cultural restraints:

> Scottish literature is being held back, and young writers are slow to appear, not only because of publishing difficulties but also because of a prevailing intellectual mood of indifferentism and conservatism, a desperate unwillingness to move out into the world with which every child now at school is becoming familiar – the world of television and sputniks, automation and LPs, electronic music and multi-story flats, rebuilt city centres and new towns, coffee bars and bookable cinemas, air travel and transistor radios, colour photography and open-plan houses, paperbacks and water-skiing, early marriage and large families: a world that will be more fast, more clean, more 'cool' than the one it leaves behind.[8]

In Morgan's concrete poems of the 1960s, and in collections like *The Second Life* (1968) and *From Glasgow to Saturn* (1973) he would place the material transformations of this new world at the heart of his poetic endeavours. The computer sent its first Christmas card, the Mercurians gave lessons in diplomacy and Marilyn Monroe died: all suitable subjects for a revitalised and forward-looking poetry, as Morgan redefines the terrain and sets new parameters for verse in Scotland. Whether relating to Hi-Tech, Hollywood or the distant heavens, the framework of reference for Scottish writing expands exponentially in the slipstream of Morgan's imagination. His is a riotous, kaleidoscopic and unremittingly playful poetry. Hungarian snakes, Chinese cats and Loch Ness monsters all sing out: new voices for a poetry moving toward the twenty-first century.

Experimental adaptability continues to enable Morgan's global reach for innovation and difference, past, present and future. His appetite for language is gargantuan and his range, like his sense of humour, is commensurate to that appetite to the extent that he seems repeatedly to be providing material on which critical theories proclaiming the shock of the new are then subsequently honed. His sometimes historical, sometimes autobiographical, sometimes futuristic and generally interactive sequence called 'The New Divan' (1977) produces effects that Salman Rushdie over a decade after

the completed poem's appearance would describe as constitutive of narrative itself in the new dispensations of postmodernity: 'hybridity, impurity,
intermingling, the transformation that comes of new and unexpected com-
binations of human beings, cultures, ideas, politics, movies, songs'.[9] Nearly
twenty years later, in 1996, Andrew Gibson's *Towards a Postmodern Theory of
Narrative* is citing Paul Virilio's film-based comment on what was now being
called the 'current crisis of "whole" dimensions . . . in which our traditional
notions of surface, of limit and separation, have decayed, and given way to
those of interface, commutation, intermittence and interruption'.[10] It seems
worth remembering that Morgan, a long-time aficionado of cinema, wrote
the first of his interactive 'New Divan' poems in December 1973, just after his
Instamatic Poems (1972) had played their distinctive games with apparently
documentary image projection.[11]

Donny O'Rourke singles out Morgan as the voice which made possible
the work of so many subsequent Scottish poets: 'In the verve and variety
of his verse, the insight and generosity of his teaching and in the copious
modernity of his imagination, Morgan is very much this anthology's presiding
spirit.'[12] For over four decades he has remained a gravitational centre within
Scottish poetry: as such he makes significant contributions and interventions concerning several of the themes addressed elsewhere in the current
Companion; including nationalism, the poetry of place, the use of Scots and
the role of translation in recent writing. Since the publication of his first collection *Vision of Cathkin Braes* in 1952 Morgan has been a prolific writer. The
Catalogue at the National Library of Scotland returns over a hundred different titles under Morgans's name including volumes of poetry, verse translations and collections of essays.

A crucial strand in Morgan's poetic development stems from his interest in
Scotland. Where 'The Beatnik in the Kailyard' lambasts an inward-looking
and antiquated cultural nationalism, rather than abandon the project Morgan
takes this as an invitation to recalibrate and reconstitute the numerous ways
poetry asks us to think about national and ontological identity. As we saw
in Alan Riach's chapter, his work sits at either end of the journey toward
devolution, at the centre of both the frustrations of 1979 and the official
celebrations of 1999. Writing in 1979 Morgan commented:

> Normally it ought to be enough to be called a poet, *tout court*, but I feel the
> present moment of Scottish history very strongly and want to acknowledge it,
> despite the fact that my interests extend to languages, genres, and disciplines
> outwith Scotland or its traditions. . . . If Scotland became independent tomor-
> row, there is no guarantee that it would enter a golden age of literary expression.
> Yet I am sure I am not mistaken in sensing, even among those who are less than
> sympathetic to devolutionary or wider political change, an awareness of such

change which in subtle ways affects creative endeavour, suggesting a gathering of forces, a desire to 'show' what can be done.[13]

The desire to show what could be done would manifest itself in fifty-one *Sonnets from Scotland* (1984), depicting the country from a number of perspectives including the prehistoric, the Neolithic, the biblical, the Enlightenment, the Victorian and the futuristic. Morgan's is a poetry of liberation, expanding the vocabulary and pushing at the ideological limits of cultural debate; rendering inadequate the familiar litany of terms (Stirling Bridge, Bannockburn, Culloden) and dates (1314, 1603, 1707) because for Morgan the story is infinitely richer, more complex and as a result inevitably more compelling than conventional history has allowed. In his Scottish *Sonnets* Morgan demonstrates that if his concrete and sound poems sought deliberately to transgress the formal rules for poetry, he is equally at home with the templates of more traditional verse and metre. Whereas ten 'Glasgow Sonnets' rub pure Petrarchan form in the gutter of urban dereliction and then raise it high, the *Sonnets from Scotland* are written in a rhyme-scheme of Morgan's own devising.

Since the decisive technical environment of the postmodern is provided by what has been called the 'whole flow' of continuous television production, and less neutrally a 'Niagara of visual babble', no engagement can avoid it.[14] Two years after Morgan's *Sonnets from Scotland* imagines a free-flowing time-scale from first development on the earth's crust to future political republic, *From the Video Box* (1986) is reworking both the conditions of production of the image and their associated strategies of transmission to examine what have become everyday practices of epistemology, subjectivity and representation. Morgan figures unusual contexts for twenty-seven characters to interrogate an electronically mediated colonisation of everyday life that has also been theorised in ways relevant to his technique. Guy Debord's perception that audiences in thrall to image-management and spectacular projection are participating in a structured intention 'to promote reconciliation with a dominant state of things from which all communication has been triumphantly declared absent' is one to which the *Video* poems respond with many alternatives.[15]

As they filter a complex, volatile and often hilarious critique into forms of utterance addressed to a recording lens about a broadcasting medium, the poems personalise oral encounters with the centring instrument of television in a globalising order of multi-media transmission. Together they enact a series of responses to Jean Baudrillard's sense that by virtue of its omnipresence television has largely become the social medium in itself, making obsolete George Orwell's projection of state control through the silver screen: '[T]he situation as it stands is more efficient than that: it is the *certainty that people are no longer speaking to each other*, that they are definitively isolated in the face of a speech without response.'[16] Interchangeably sequenced, the voices in Morgan's video poems fill their pages with responsive speech: if ever there were voluble universes, it seems that this poet has been there. He also raises domain-specific issues such that Jameson's comment about self-evident but usually forgotten time-management in film sequence – that fictive scenes and conversations on screen are never coterminous with the time such moments take in real life – connects with Morgan's management of structure, syntax and image. This includes 'the construction of just such fictive or foreshortened temporalities (whether of film or reading), which are then substituted for a real time we are thereby enabled to forget'.[17] But not quite forget.

By vocalising scripted difference, a non-sequential series both defies and enacts the technological assimilation of subjectivity that Jameson sees as contingent on the compelling immediacy of film. Yet where dialogic subjectivity is both medium and message, and 'insofar as speech is pre-eminently social', as Jameson was saying at the time 'From the Video Box' was in preparation, 'the intersubjective objects which are works of literature underscore the psychic function of narrative and fantasy in the attempts of the subject to reintegrate his or her alienated image.'[18] While some of Morgan's video voices engage a notion of ideology as 'the representation of the subject's *Imaginary* relationship to his or her *Real* conditions of existence', others recognise ideology as at the same time a possibility of knowledge.[19] In a related sense of connectedness, as they theorise ways of understanding postmodernism, both Lyotard and Jameson continue to prize narrative. For the former, 'the little narrative remains the quintessential form of imaginative invention, most particularly in science'; while for the latter 'story-telling [is] the supreme function of the human mind.'[20] Fine by Morgan: 'As a poet, of course, I am by definition a storyteller, whatever else I may be.'[21]

Given that his election as Glasgow's first Poet Laureate (1999–2004) signalled official recognition for his life-long fascination with the city of his birth, Morgan's poetry might be read as an implicit rebuke to the claim in Alasdair Gray's *Lanark* (1981) when Duncan Thaw laments the city's exclusion from the pages of Western cultural history:

'Glasgow is a magnificent city,' said McAlpin. 'Why do we hardly ever notice that?' 'Because nobody imagines living here,' said Thaw. McAlpin lit a cigarette and said, 'If you want to explain that I'll certainly listen.'

'Then think of Florence, Paris, London, New York. Nobody visiting them for the first time is a stranger because he's already visited them in paintings, novels, history books and films. But if a city hasn't been used by an artist not even the inhabitants live there imaginatively . . . Imaginatively Glasgow exists as a music hall song and a few bad novels. That's all we've given to the world outside. It's all we've given to ourselves.'[22]

Beyond Gray's satirical excess, Morgan's poetry has consistently sought to
challenge that historical neglect and in this context it is fitting that part of the
draft manuscripts for *Lanark*, held at the Mitchell Library in Glasgow, features
Morgan's own annotations and comments on Gray's novel. An early example
of Morgan's fascination with Glasgow appeared in the title poem from his
1968 collection *The Second Life* (1968), which evokes the high rise towers that
rose throughout Glasgow during the sixties as Modernist architecture sought
to eradicate some of the worst slum housing in Europe. There is a breathy
excitement and a palpable invigoration in the opening lines of the poem:

> But does every man feel like this at forty –
> I mean it's like Thomas Wolfe's New York, his
> heady light, the stunning plunging canyons, beauty – [23]

Glasgow and New York, the vertiginous cityscapes, reconfigure the Dear
Green Place and give it in Morgan's poem a place amidst the shiny optimism
of the space-race and a developing world. It is a poem of rebirth, but with
a radically different inflection from its earlier incarnations in twentieth-
century Scottish writing. Whatever else might be implicated by asking: 'Is
it true that we come alive / not once, but many times?' Morgan invites us to
consider the past as not always something to be embraced and held close, but
also as a skin to be shed. Beyond any personal resonance the poem calls the
city and its inhabitants forward, out of the darkness and into the light of the
here and now:

> The caked layers of grime
> Grow warm, like homely coats.
> But yet they will be dislodged
> And men will still be warm.
> The old coats are discarded.
> The old ice is loosed.
> The old seeds are awake.
>
> Slip out of darkness, it is time.[24]

In instamatic poems, sonnet sequences and *From Glasgow to Saturn* (1973)
the city becomes richer and more varied than had previously been imagined.
  Morgan returns to Glasgow with his 2002 volume *Cathures*, which takes
its title from the city's ancient name. He borrows a logical-seeming leaf from
the Roman poet and philosopher Lucretius to justify the functional spaces he
realises for his speakers in this collection: 'Now since we must confess that
there is nothing beyond the sum of things, it has no extremity, and therefore it
is without end or limit.'[25] Lucretius sought to free his readers from superstition

and the fear of death, and his extending horizons are familiar to Morgan, who begins with a story by and about his name and namesake 'Pelagius'; the possibly Scottish fourth-century theologian who challenged and condemned Augustine of Hippo for deciding that everyone is inescapably tainted with Original Sin. Over and above the happy accident that Pelagius translates his own name, Morgan is a time-served dissenter well-seasoned in the arts of prophetic posture. Speaking for open doors of perception against premature closure in the distant past generates pressing relevance in our immediate present. Born-again fundamentalism has a long history; witness the weary, resigned conscientious objector situated in one of Glasgow's ancient precursor communities, and feeling his age, who is Morgan's battle-scarred but not broken Pelagius. He remembers Augustine as a 'Christian pistoned by new-found fervour' who exercised considerable powers of damnation and exclusion:

> Bishop in Hippo branding anathemas,
> Bristling with intelligence not my intelligence,
> Black-hearted and indefatigable.

Pelagius knows he has lost the struggle for alternative values, and has become vividly aware that when rival belief systems commit to full spectrum dominance, 'Text and anti-text / Crush the light.' He is still persevering, though, making sure he has his say and remaining hopeful that a time must come when:

> No one will believe without a splash from font
> Their baby will howl in eternal cold, or fire,
> And no one will ever suffer the elect without merit
> To lord it over a cringing flock, and no one
> Is doomed by Adam's sin to sin for ever,
> And who says Adam's action was a sin,
> Or Eve's, when they let history in.[26]

Though few are aware of it, St Enoch's Square in Glasgow is named after Thennoch, mother of Kentigern the city's first bishop, and the woman who speaks third in the series of dramatic monologues called 'Nine in Glasgow'. Morgan has commented:

> I'm interested in that kind of semi-real, semi-legendary figure, where we don't have the full facts but would like to know more; so you can apply your imagination to it. I've always thought it a great pity Thennoch's name has disappeared, especially since St Enoch's Square is a very settled bit of central Glasgow. But no-one knows that St Enoch is a woman. Who is St Enoch? No such person. It was St Thennoch.[27]

This worldly-wise mother tells a lively tale of brutality and benediction that leads her to call Glasgow home. Eighth to speak in Morgan's laureate sequence is Louis Kossuth (1802–94), the Hungarian patriot whose visit to Glasgow in 1856 is a matter of historical record. But his meeting with the pedlar-poet James Macfarlan (1832–64), who asks 'What is the use of independence / If you are living on potatoes and black bread', is Morgan's invention and characteristic of the uses he makes of the past.[28] As he subsequently explained, the relevance of such an encounter to our ongoing present derives from the fact that 'Scotland has unfinished political business, with a devolved parliament that pleases some but not others. Neither socialist nor nationalist aspirations can be ruled out.'[29]

The Glasgow film-maker who speaks last in the sequence opens windows onto differently historicised political imperatives. 'Enrico Cocozza' connects the fugitive experiences of gay cinema-goers during Glasgow's 'fifties forbiddenness' with the 'abused sinews' of people Dante was compelled to place in hell. 'Hell Song 14' of *The Divine Comedy* condemns a gay bishop whose work as rhetorician had profoundly influenced the young poet, and Morgan develops that context of regret. 'Section 28', however, makes clear that there's nothing apologetic about Morgan's spirited resistance to repressive orthodoxy wherever it operates; and the 'Merlin' he imagines for his favoured republic gives effective voice to time and change. This magician now shares his experiments with a sister to the extent that theirs have become cross-gendered explorations: 'With our double vision we untwist binary stars.'[30] A preferred deity for Morgan's transhistorical community of unbelievers came ironically into view as a 'Professorial Trinity' when Alistair Gray, Tom Leonard and James Kelman were appointed to promote creative writing at Glasgow University. Here was a 'toga'd and tooled triumvirate' who could be relied upon to 'Invigorate the written state' and continue the work of Pelagius at the doors of perception by 'guard[ing] with grins the ganting [wide open] gate'.[31]

Since being diagnosed with terminal cancer in 1999, Morgan has turned his predicament to account on several occasions. Shortly after he learned about his condition, 'A Hearse Reborn' appeared outside his front door where it sat in the courtyard 'for a week', while Morgan noticed that 'its curtains twitch but no one dies'; so that for a diagnosed observer 'All is omen and surmise.' Truth turns strange as fiction when this speaker learns that:

> A happy grafter
> With a bob or two, and imagination,
> Has bought the thing for transformation
> Into a keen stretch limousine
> Where he can thread the urban scene
> With long canoe, so safely stowed
> He glides a river, not a road.[32]

Local event and personal context connect with mythic narrative as the figure of Charon, ferryman to Hades, survives in altered usage. But if Morgan found the appearance of the hearse initially alarming, it was a slight unsettling compared to the day 'A Gull' stood on his window-ledge, 'said nothing, but had a good look inside.' His own pending transformation into food for birds – 'That was a cold inspection I can tell you' – leads this speaker to figure the gull as

> a visitation
> which only used that tight firm forward body
> to bring the waste and dread of open waters,
> foundered voyages, matchless predators,
> into a dry room.[33]

In sometimes eerie, sometimes comic and repeatedly effective ways Morgan uses his illness to strike moving resonance out of unusual context; transferring concern for his own survival, for example, onto the disused 'Gasometer' that has become a piece of industrial archaeology he could see from his kitchen window. For this speaker, the gasometer is 'Constructivist to the core':

> Yours is the art of use.
> You could be painted, floodlit, archaeologised,
> but I prefer the unremitting stance
> of what you were in what you are, no more.

The poem ends on a rueful hope that in the 'Day of tearing down, day of recycling':

> Let the wind whistle
> through those defenceless arms and the moon bend
> a modicum of its glamorous light upon
> you, my familiar, my stranded hulk – a while![34]

While there are bits and pieces of a personal biography scattered across Morgan's work from the beginning, the history he lets into fifty lyrics he wrote during September and November of the year *Cathures* came out, and published as *Love and a Life* in 2003, was a departure even for him. Naming names and giving details of relationships he had alluded to in earlier work, he brings elements of his story up to date in a stanza form he first tried out in *Cathures*, linking formal structure with free-flowing speech by combining a long, Whitmanesque free verse line with six rhymes along the same sound. While that is challenging enough, a reflective feel to some of the poems fits their autumnal occasion. But Morgan's re-examined memories of earlier relationships are various; some of them updating autobiographical elements in *The New Divan* (1977), others inviting refraction through earlier versions. 'Freeze-Frame', second poem in *Love and a Life*, personalises to chilly effect the snapshot tactic of *Instamatic Poems* (1972), by situating vivid memory of precise context in the 'Frame of a moment made for friendless friendly time / to freeze'.[35] If there is only cold comfort there, the next poem asks encouragingly 'What use is a picture when the universe is up and running?' 'The Top' goes on to figure a 'ghostly file of memories' as medieval mummers 'mopping and mowing' while they try to keep a spinning top in motion:

> But soon it must fall back
> Into silence, attack
> As you will, take the lash as you will, to stave off the mundane numbing and
> dumbing.[36]

In compensation for its recognition that 'Memory is not a top that stops', 'Tracks and Crops' reminds us of another one that keeps going; a 'top of the tops / Call it a world'. The survival of desire in that world is sequence theme for a range of speakers about love in its many modes and manners. Morgan's poetics of resistance caters so successfully to a wide readership partly because the forms of power it addresses, and the terms of his address, make us all willing conscripts in any proposed extension of liberty. If 'Deviance is as good as law' in *Cathures*, those who practise it are historically aware of a harvesting power that has been erasing forms of bonding since time began. From 'the first faint stirring of / earthly unearthly crops', 'cosmic harvesters' have been 'scouring the universe': 'For sheafs and tracks of love left well by all from lucky you to luckless but once-loved horny veggie triceratops'.[37]

An unobtrusive sequencing continues in the next poem's 'Love laid the [dinosaur's] egg' that is now fossilised in Morgan's cupboard, 'hard, heavy, / fused to the rock it haunts', and promised to a friend. Here as elsewhere the survival of desire is in focus, with Morgan tilting at the prohibition that for so long condemned the existence, let alone satisfaction, of his own sexual nature. Here as elsewhere too, he approaches extinction with a studied refusal of any faith-based, post-mortem comfort, raising instead the possibility that the death of the dinosaurs was brought about because:

> Some malice surely must
> Have sent the deadly dust
> That smothers what the pregnant earth gigantically flags up and flaunts.[38]

The following poem, 'Crocodiles', invites us to 'communicate far back and down', both within ourselves and along the evolutionary chain, 'then further back and further down, eras, miles', where we might find unexpected 'ports of ingress', and learn 'how quickly the / esteemed veneer resiles'.[39] Stripping away socially constructed veneer is something Morgan has been doing for many a year; and since in any loving relationship 'Touch is everything or nearly everything or it is / nothing', tactile effect becomes a base from which he launches a lively assault on faith-based gender constructions and their associated hostility to unlicensed forms of pleasure. Blacksmiths know the swedger as a tool they use when shoeing horses: in 'Touch' it signifies the devil's phallus; with Morgan transporting Satan from hell-fire to the ice-cap for his speaker's uncompromising parody of sermons against the body:

> The Devil's swedger at minus a hundred is as cold and
> 	as ruthless as the Pole
> And only the most despairing and abandoned, female
> 	or male, could take in their hole
> Or so we were told, or so they were told, when
> 	wretched creatures were taught of the Fall
>
> Of Man instead of the Rise of Man[.]

To orchestrate their rising against the dirge of scriptural damnation, a thirteen-line sentence finds warmer space outdoors for people 'crying, to be free'; and a sense of natural release where 'our dearest soul' can

> 	use its body to be
> The means of greatest grace, frolicking and fucking
> 	in the tropical throbbing unstoppable waterfall.[40]

As part of this collection's 'surrealistic metamorphosis of love and lust' several gardens of both innocence and experience are reconstructed; [41] and a sometimes rollicking celebration of sexual variety combines with a persistent note of regret for opportunities not taken and chances missed. While these sometimes relate to a personal life and are sometimes borrowed from books, there is clear autobiographical reference in an angry refusal to forget the pain that started coming his way in 1938 on account of the love he felt for

> 	the first of men
> In that impossible dimension of love which now
> 	with unspoken groans and even secret tears
> 	I was approaching and discerning.[42]

So it is to the point that *Love and a Life* finds Christian ecstasy worth examining; and when 'Spanish Night' opens to inspection the passions of John of the Cross, who 'sank onto the breast / Of one whom he loved best', the poem scouts the possibility of an earthly lover.[43]

Meanwhile an intensified perception of the precariousness of life makes itself felt, such that an imagined survival against the odds for people ship-wrecked on 'Cape Found' constitutes a brave performance in its own right. Beethoven (1770–1827) wrote his 'Holy Song of Thanks' for a string quartet, composed when serious illness had forced on him a lengthy interruption to his work. It enters Morgan's poem first as a fragment of dialogue then as public offering:

'Do you remember the *Heilige Dankesang?*' 'Bits.'
    'Sing some.' The frail notes rose and crowned
        Our passage back to men,
        To women, to children,
To ships and sails of health, to the whale's road,
    the gull's acres, brilliant, bonded and sound.[44]

Morgan develops poignancy out of rival senses that while a return to active social life is no longer an option, advances in medical treatment enable him to keep on scoring his secular songs. The courage and resourcefulness with which he continues to husband and direct the energies of his commitment is nothing less than extraordinary – as is the survival he manages to engineer for expansive vision in cramped quarters. Computerised tomography (CT) tells it like it is in 'Scan Day':

    There are no chimeras
    Under the cameras.
You are laid out as you are, imperfect, waiting,
    wondering, approximately free.[45]

In 'Skeleton Day' a 'well-injected, clothed but / motionless man' exercises that limited mobility as continuing real time imaginative journey when he watches 'the benedictions of the bone scan' unroll 'a little / skeleton, a blue-print, a plan' on a screen monitor:

That plan is you! Skull, ribs, hips emerge
    from the dark like a caravan
        Bound for who knows where
        Stepping through earth or air
Still of a piece and still en route, beating
    out the music of tongs and bones while it can.[46]

Not surprisingly in a collection rampant with memory, some of the poems read like redactions of earlier Morgan incarnations, so that 'The Last Dragon' feels like Grendel come back to haunt *Beowulf*'s first modern speaker. In common with Pelagius, Merlin and Thennock from *Cathures*, the last dragon looks back over a 'memory trail' marked by conflict and stress. The Anglo-Saxon lines quoted here translate in Morgan's 1952 version a fighter whose 'breast is vexed within him, while the crowding / memories came down to him from many winters'. Half a century and many winters further down the trail Morgan scouts uncertain horizons, still successfully guarding his 'word-hoard' against the day when 'the dragon with / his flailing tail':

> Sweeps everything away
> Leaves nothing to say
> Either in turmoil or in peace, and neither poetry
> nor song nor all their longing can avail.[47]

CHAPTER EIGHT

Kenneth White and John Burnside

Marco Fazzini

Edward Said (1935–2003) tells us that the exile is an outcast who is 'inconsolable about the past, bitter about the present and the future'. This statement suggests a strong sense of nostalgia for the abandoned patria, a sense of discomfort in the present, and a gloominess about the future. According to Said the exile exists in a 'median state', neither fully integrated in the new system or society nor totally relieved of his or her burden of cultural and personal memories. The ambiguity of the border gives such a figure a dual position which can afford stimulating advantages. One of the most remarkable figures whom Said chooses to illustrate the point is the philosopher Theodor Adorno (1903–69), whose *Minima Moralia: Reflections from Damaged Life* (1951) Said takes as his representative work in this context. Adorno's life produces a 'destabilizing effect' which manifests itself in a series of 'discontinuous performances', and his work must necessarily be

> fragmentary first of all, jerky, discontinuous; there is no plot or predetermined order to follow. It represents the intellectual's consciousness as unable to be at rest anywhere, constantly on guard against the blandishments of success, which, for the perversely inclined Adorno, means trying consciously not to be understood easily and immediately.[1]

We will see in this chapter how both Kenneth White (1936–) and John Burnside (1955–) attract and transcend these characteristics, in different ways showing their enjoyment of knowledge and freedom, so that their personal, transcultural creative positions move from the local to the international through a spaciousness of voyaging and extended horizons.

Kenneth White

> I emerged from the Glasgow proletariat. They're a mixed bunch, the Glasgow proletariat. A lot of them came down from the North. On my maternal grandmother's side, there were Downies, on my maternal grandfather's side, Camerons. On my paternal grandmother's side, there were Mackenzies from Inverness. On

my paternal grandfather's side, it's folk from what used to be MacGregor country. In the old days, I might have been Coinneach ban Macgregor – Kenneth the White of the Gregor clan. But the MacGregors, as you know, being notorious rebels, were deprived of everything, including their patronymic: 'Children of the mist', they were known as.

My paternal grandfather, John Dewar White, was professional piper, strolling actor, soldier (whenever he could, so as to see the world), factory worker and bartender. To say the least, he'd been around.

My father, Willie White, a bright pupil at school, and always a great reader, worked on the railway, and was a strong trade-unionist, active in politics: he was a left-wing socialist, while my uncle, Archie Cameron, was one of Glasgow's staunchest Communists.

As to my mother, she was less socially inclined, more secretive, with all the contradictions of Scottish culture bundled inside her. [2]

Though he never lost touch with Scotland, in the early 1960s White moved to Germany and France for long periods before choosing to become a French citizen. He took a lot of Scotland with him, including an extensive Scottish library in his various places of residence (Paris, the Pyrenees, Brittany), and was often back in the home country, 'incognito' as it were, moving through cities, towns and villages, along the coasts, into the mountain areas, on the islands. Always with senses wide open and mind alert, he travelled over Scotland more than most people resident in the country. Yet, this Scottish nomad has kept outside:

> with the calling of the navigator-wanderer, the terrain of the difficult territory, and a sense of ongoing itinerary. The intellectual nomad (the term used, in passing, by Spengler in his *Decline of the West* [1918], and whose scope I was to develop) is engaged, outside the glitzy or glaury compound of late modernity, in an area of complex co-ordinates. He is trying to move out of pathological psycho-history, along uncoded paths, into fresh existential, intellectual, poetic space.[3]

As shown in the following short fragment from 'Walking the Coast', the intellectual nomad feels the strength of a gathering force within chaos, without surrendering to the attraction of any hegemonic 'target' or 'centre' to be reached or any meaning to be prescribed. The speaker here seems to lose not only control over a geographic itinerary, but also, and mainly, over some of the canonised or otherwise assumed speculative, epistemological and political horizons:

> living and writing at random
> but knowing
>   that
> though living at random

there is a tendency to stress
the essential in the random [4]

White's intellectual nomad is compelled to touch and cross traditions and cultures which he feels to be 'marginal' to the 'auto-route' of the Western world and its Western history.[5] It is a widely shared perception that nomads, 'clochards', homeless people and wanderers represent a mode of travelling that is often dangerous, amounting in some cases to a real pathology. Yet, what Michel Butor said about nomadism and wandering gives a new and dynamic status to this ontological process which may often acquire all the main characteristics of 'travelling' in a fuller sense, or at least some of its qualities.[6] Nomadism, together with its founding function in any social collective, translates the plurality contained in each individual, highlighting the interactive complexity of existence. At the same time, it can express the violent or discrete opposition against a fixed order, allowing us both to read the latent rebellious feeling of younger generations and to break the obligations linked to residency. In White's context, terms like 'erratic travel' or 'erratic path' are not only the anti-conformist choice for a geographical move from one place to another, but a clear reference to what the Scottish poet decided for himself and his writing when he moved to France for good in the late 1960s. From Paris, and later from Pau and the Breton coast, White has elaborated an intricate and fascinating series of prose books and poetry sequences in which his personas experience an alternative and enriching path through existence.

Any conventional journey can be easily transformed into an erratic path by a banal or fortuitous accident: a storm can delay or divert a ship from her route; the sight of a huge deer can lead the hunter astray or into a dark wood where he has to face unexpected experiences; or the lack of a detailed map can force the traveller to accept an occasional guide who changes routes and diversifies planned experiences. This happens, for example, in *The Blue Road* ([1983] 1990) when the narrator agrees to be guided by fortuitous acquaintances met on the way to Labrador; or, again, when 'By a stroke of good luck that morning I'd come across a taxi-driver who'd offered to take me to a hill-tribe village off the normal circuit.'[7] So, even though we have still to distinguish between a traditional journey which, by accident, may be transformed into an erratic one and an intentionally pathless itinerary, the two dimensions, like some of the differences between the exile and the immigrant seem to blur when one admits the presence of 'unexpected' or 'strange' events. But what is the relation between literature and travel? What's the rationale for transforming a poem or a prose book (a *way-book*, in White's case) into a kind of travelling amulet, or of transforming a repeated journey or a definite move (like exile) into an imaginative attitude to experiential life? White's refusal of every sort of classification or category that customarily defines literary genres, as well as the intimate essentiality of East and West, underlines once again the median condition of this new 'intellectual nomad':

> walking in the stillness
> half-way between the Old World and the New
> trying to move in deeper
> ever deeper
> into a white world
> neither old nor new[8]

Much of the attraction of White's writing derives from his determination to experience wilderness on his own terms. His prose writings, but especially his poems, chronicle his emancipation from the category of macho tourism or solitary travelling:

> [T]he pilgrim trip has an aim, the sacred spot. But beyond the sacred, there's emptiness. I'm not out to cover kilometres, or to reach a particular place, I'm out for a kind of spatial poetics, with emptiness at its centre. And you begin again, for the pleasure, to get at an even finer sense of emptiness-plenitude.[9]

This represents a fine and personal introduction to the final part of one of White's best-known poems, 'The Residence of Solitude and Light':

> Thinking
> of Khalil's definition of reality:
> $A + A - A - A + A - A + A \ldots$
> maybe that's what I've been working at
> these last nine years
> the result being:

> – a pleasant sensation of nothingness-potential
> a breathing space
> the beautiful breast of emptiness[10]

White described this as 'one of a series of "Pyrenean meditations"':

> For nine years I worked away down there in the Pyrenees, in distance and in silence. If Descartes composed *Meditationes de prima philosophia*, maybe what concerned me were *Meditationes de prima poetica* – a new mental cartography in general. The poem presents the situation and the elements I was working with, as well as the horizon I had my eyes on.[11]

One of the significant features of poetry is its 'sacral' quality. Christopher Whyte observes:

> While it is important to be extraordinarily tentative in ascribing a therapeutic function to poetry, there can be no doubt that, in moments of acute tension, whether this be the first experience of sexual love, a major bereavement, or dizzying ontological uncertainty, again and again isolated individuals have encountered, in a poem, normally within the space of a few lines or even in one single line, a formula, a spell almost, which helped them survive, a sort of talisman.[12]

This is the spell the reader often experiences when reading White's books. This is the spell contemporary men and women need because of the devalued relationship between 'human' and 'non-human' in our society. This is the talisman which can recall for us ancestral reminiscences and insights, serving as both a walking and linguistic yoga: writer and reader together become the field of experimentation where the internal landscape coincides with and faces an external one for an eternal resymbolisation of *being* in the world, so exchanging flux and energy, steps and passages, 'limites et marges':

> Now I have burnt all my knowledge
> and am learning to live with the whiteness naked
>
> what I call art now is nothing made
> but the pure pathology of my body and mind
>
> at the heart of a terrible and joyous world[13]

He has described this as a 'poem of the radicalisation process':

> presenting the attempt to get beyond knowledge *about* things into knowledge with and in things. If it passes through a stage of pathos (*pathos, logos*), it moves over into a synthesis of *eros, logos* and *cosmos*. Art, then, is no longer simply artefact, more or less attractive, more or less interesting. It comes from a deeper source, opens a larger space.[14]

Within a space where we have been spectators of the decline of philosophical, ethical, and historical fundamentals, as Lyotard has observed, it is no longer possible to start a new system of values: only a creative crossing can be accepted, a crossing where poetic erudition and an erratic route mingle and support each other. This is the only way to free our geographical landscape of all its lines encrusted by power and corruption: White's non-linear and non-logically-sequenced language-itinerary tries to redeem us in the world, transforming us into active presences whose culture finally interacts with nature, and whose agility of movement and thought manages to become the burning knot of a new congregation of illuminating trajectories. Gary Snyder (1930–), one of White's chosen 'companions' since his university years in Paris, wrote in 1984:

> We can all agree: there is a problem with the chaotic, self-seeking human ego. Is it a mirror of the wild and of nature? I think not: for civilization itself is ego gone to seed and institutionalized in the form of the State, both Eastern and Western. It is not nature-as-chaos which threatens us (for nature is orderly) but ignorance of the natural world, the myth of progress, and the presumption of the State that it has created order. That sort of 'order' is an elaborate rationalization of the greed of a few.[15]

Of his own experience, White has observed:

> . . . I am not suggesting that we celebrate any mountain goddess. I am suggesting that we try and get back an earth-sense, a ground sense, and a freshness of the world such as those men, those Finn-men, knew when they moved over an earth from which the ice had just recently receded. This is the dawn of geopoetics.[16]

It seems that moving from America to Europe, and from Europe to Africa, more than one 'eccentric' writer has decided not to treat nature as a guest in our world, or to act as nature's superior. Instead, he (always a 'he' in White's case, allowing us to identify the author more directly with his poetical voices) has focused on how it can improve the human standard of living. Kenneth White's persona loves the mountains and the deserted areas and feels he must go and live there for shorter or longer periods. The journey can be difficult (as in *The Blue Road*), where White's protagonist travels through Labrador, slowly moving out of civilisation and the urban areas of an industrialised society; many efforts are often tinged with a certain ascetic quality (as in *The Wild Swans* (1990) where the protagonist gradually moves towards an epiphanic moment of illumination and extended horizons); or an ironic intent is used to guide the reader towards a deeper understanding of our urban Western environment, as happens in many of the stories in *Travels in the Drifting Dawn* (1989). White's persona seeks in wilderness not only a denial of the weakness of the self but also emotional experiences and extended vistas which become a reward for his attempts to get far enough away from cities and settlements so as to experience nature alone. He is often found in nature where he comes to a better understanding of his place in the world, while seeking transcendental experience in contemplation of a cosmic total-ity. Yet, as an urbanite travelling through wilderness, he takes no pleasure in being a frontier traveller partaking of the commodity development in the West, or the destruction of the geological and biological landscape. His work can be readily studied according to an earth-centred approach, showing that the Scoto-French poet's 'world' must necessarily include the entire ecosphere where any theoretical discourse built upon it must dismantle surviving remnants of ecological imperialism for a negotiation between the human and the non-human:

> [T]hat's what I called 'white world'. But maybe I'd formulate the thing differently: I wouldn't say 'communication between writing and the universe, between literature and the world', but communication between the self and the world. For a great part of the work goes on *outside* writing, outside literature. You have to worldify the self, littoralise (if I may say so) being. Otherwise you remain in the pathetic, the illusory – in 'literature' (or 'poetry').[17]

White's favourite literary 'persona', the so-called 'intellectual nomad', walks the path that leads away from the Motorway of Western Civilisation. Along this path he looks for a power of synthesis which European culture has forgotten since the building of that 'auto-route' directed by Platonic idealism, Aristotelian classification, Christianity, Renaissance humanism, Cartesian and Hegelian historicism, and so on.[18] What Anne McClintock says in her study on race, gender and sexuality in the colonial context has some relevance to the kind of refusal White has maintained during his literary career. She notes that all the terminology which uses the prefix 'post' in contemporary intellectual life (post-colonialism, post-modernism, post-feminism, post-Marxism, post-structuralism, post-national, even post-history) is a symptom of a 'global crisis in ideologies of the future, particularly the ideology of progress'.[19] Discussing US Third World policies, the New World Bank projects adopted after the decolonisation of Africa, the collapse of the Soviet Union and its master narratives, and the failure of alternative forms of capitalist or communist progress, McClintock questions the value of the metaphor that has represented Western progress as a 'Motorway' or 'auto-route' able to guarantee security and development to certain human civilisations. Her desire for a new intellectual era includes the birth and the growth of innovative theories of history and popular memory, something which could replace all the words prefixed by 'post' with a multiplicity of intents and powers. Similarly, White likes to speak about his creative purposes in this way:

> and when a Japanese literatus
> > speaks of the series of *waka* poems
> > (sometimes as many as 100 in a sequence)
> > > written in the Kamakura period
> > > > (13th and 14th centuries)
> > saying 'the result
> > > was often a kind of kaleidoscopic beauty
> > > > with infinite variety

> revealed to the reader
>> in a slowly evolving movement'
> I recognize my aim[20]

There is no doubt that the 'auto-route' White speaks about in many of his books and articles signifies the violence or debasing values of so-called civilisation. There is also no doubt that in recent decades the attention that has been paid to travel and to the literature produced around and about it has been significantly enlarged. Obviously, such a phenomenon has been partly produced by both the recent accessibility of travelling, its regular banal uses, and in the politics and economics of mass tourism. This has often caused an impoverishment of the value given to travelling, especially to travelling as a means of acquiring and transferring knowledge. Yet, since the years in which White produced one of his core reflections on the 'nomade intellectuel' (encapsulated in *L'Esprit nomade*) he has given this figure the power to transform his exile into a soul-searching investigation through meditation. The aim is to attain a heightened illumination where emptiness ('blankness') and 'whiteness' are reconciled through their etymologies. This opens the possibility of a final (postmodern?) discourse where the sign, in its larger signification, generates an 'atlantic' and 'hyperborean' poetics which contours the world in the circle of an immortalising cosmology, the white shimmering world of

> Pelagian discourse
> atlantic poetics
>
> from first to last.[21]

John Burnside

John Burnside, who moved from Scotland to England when still a boy, felt 'angry, just being there, and wasted huge amounts of energy and time giving expression to that anger'.[22] Yet, exile for Burnside seems to be not only a personal and geographic trauma, but also something related to the loss of a kind of prelapsarian state, a condition longed for and idealised especially when he feels frustrated by the industrial/capitalist erasure of the possibility of 'being' in the world:

> I think exile – from the land, from other animals, from the sensual and truly erotic, from a lived sense of justice, from his/her true nature – is *the* fundamental experience in industrial/capitalist society. I believe that my writing (and the work of those writers who tend to interest me) is an essentially ecological pursuit: ecological in the sense of being a study of the art and science of

dwelling meaningfully in the world – or, in a piece of shorthand I have adopted, of 'living as a spirit'.[23]

This kind of exile involves moving from no specific state, no specific nation, so that even though Scotland is always in the background, it is an imagined and unspoilt world which has given up to business and corruption, being owned by polluting companies and corporations exploiting and destroying lands, and keeping many people in poverty. Burnside has written about all of this from his very first book *The Hoop* (1988), where he started listening to 'the song of the earth' in order to attain a re-attunement to the 'continuum of objects and weather and other lives that we inhabit'.[24] This discipline of the imagination, defined by Burnside himself as a kind of 'religious' enterprise, aims at reconquering a oneness, 'a renewal of the connection to the continuum of the real, a discipline for happiness'.[25] In an early poem called 'Out of Exile', which Burnside excluded from his *Selected Poems* (2006), the poet is inventing things 'as they might have been' if that dream-desire for 'home' had finally turned into something real:

Driving early, through the border towns,
THE DARK STONE HOUSES CLANGING AT OUR WHEELS,
AND WE INVENT THINGS AS THEY MIGHT HAVE BEEN:
A LIGHT SWITCHED ON, SOME NIGHT, AGAINST THE COLD,
AND CHILDREN AT THE DOOR, WITH BAGS AND COATS,
Telling stories, laughing, coming home. [26]

The 'exile's return' instead counterbalances that mythical idealisation of land and time. The poem that follows 'Out of Exile' in *The Hoop* collection is much more realistic and ironic: here, the idealised 'home' has been turned into something like a clichéd attraction for tourists who drive through hills or into a fake Scottish identity linked to some combination of colours in a tartan:

Hard to imagine it, lying intact,
folded into books: identity
to be assumed like tartan,
or spelt out on museum clocks
from heretic stones and peat-blacked pots,
history by strip light. Do we know
where we are in these tourist hills?[27]

Burnside's prose experiment, 'Suburbs', from his second collection *Common Knowledge* (1991), opened the ground to a personal way of presenting problematic issues, which he would later include in *Feast Days* (1992) in properly structured sequences. Two of these sequences, called 'Aphasia in Childhood' and 'Urphänomen', insist on the gap between two worlds, symbolised in a series of dichotomies such as childhood and mature age, or reality and dream or, better still, here and there, being and non-being. This is a kind of revisitation of the technique Geoffrey Hill used for his *Mercian Hymns* in 1971, with the addition of strong personal and autobiographical elements:

> Maybe you could say that the *general* trend in twenty century poetry has been towards this secular/ agnostic sacrality. Perhaps we could even say that there was a similar trend in the wider range of twentieth century thinking – in Bergson, in phenomenology, in 'Lebenphilosophie'; in Merleau-Ponty, in Heidegger, even in some of Wittgenstein; in the emergence of eco- and eco-feminist political thought, and in a growing appreciation of the knowledge, skills and insights of 'indigenous' people; in literary criticism and commentary (from Gary Snyder, say, through Mary Oliver, to Jonathan Bate); in the work of musicians such as Michael Tippett, Arvo Part, John Adams, and the increasing recognition of music created outside the 'Western classical' mainstream (Adams, for example, has cited Nusrat Fateh Ali Khan as a significant influence). In the visual arts, one looks to the painter Agnes Martin, or the photographer Raymond Moore, in film to Terence Mallick, Andrei Tarkovsky and others – the list could go on and on.[28]

It is by using the form of the religious prose hymn style that Burnside questions issues such as identity and place, framing them into a mock-religious structure which is his particular way of giving sacrality to a series of philosophical and existential questions:

> The questions I asked ... all the time, but never aloud: where is the soul? WHAT does it most resemble? I had an image of something transparent, a fine yet indestructible tissue of buttermilk or chitin . . .

> That one day I spent in the woods, digging leaf-mould: I kept finding thin silvery threads of mildew that dissolved in the air, and I was sure, if I dug a few inches deeper, I would find a being which resembled me in every way, except that it would be white and etiolated, like a finger of bindweed growing under stone.[29]

Memory (mainly of childhood years) holds the ground in these prose sequences, creating a hinterland where personal recall of past details mixes with dream fantasies. The mixture emerges from a mysterious darkness or a half-waking state, where memories 'form in my skin like a tumour: a quiet, untenable life surfacing through coffee and after-shave when I lock up the house of summer nights, and linger at the door to taste the distance'.[30] These are the 'mystery years' where long-past vistas and half-remembered details can be contemplated 'far in light and silence', and everything lives through a half-perceived distance from a personal time which enlarges together with the awareness of a threshold space, a liminal space, through which we can conjure up the dead and our pursued truths. This 'other country' is not only the terrain of difficult territories inhabited by animal presences, but also the unbridgeable distance between living and dead, self and other, religious values and human doubt, a responsibility to all living things.

It is relevant here to remember what André Gorz (1923–2007) proposes in his *Critique of Economic Reason* (1989) because it will be particularly important for Burnside's writing after 1992. Gorz says that we need to re-evaluate what he defines as the post-Marxist force in the Western conceptualisation of politics and philosophy, and abandon the trite praxis leading to the consideration of the Other as another human being or, worse, as a subject to be subjugated. Instead of insisting on the re-evaluation of the Other as a sensitive subject, Gorz longs for the equation the Other = the external environment, replacing the power relationships between two conflicting human beings or social classes with the relationship between human and non-human.[31] So, in order to annul the power of the *malin génie* that Jean Baudrillard (1929–2007) speaks about – a kind of central scrutiniser of all the simulations of the external world – and fill the gap between Self and Other, it is necessary to attract and destroy what lies at the very base of that prevaricative mode of perception.[32] This is exactly what Burnside himself has recently stated about the relationship between humans and the rest of the world:

> I am very much affected by Levinas's philosophy, especially with regard to our responsibility to 'The Other'. But this other, I would read not just as the human, but as the 'more than human' other, i.e. all living things. Our responsibility is to respect and protect all living things. To honour this vast 'Other', however, we must also respect all habitat: for we cannot honour other living things if we damage or destroy their sources of shelter, nourishment and play. Thus we must honour all things, from the air, to rocks and soil, to trees, to all waterways, to the ocean, to the wind, to pond life, to Arctic mosses, to temperate forest, to silt, to reedbeds, to glaciers – everything that is, is a habitat. At the same time, this demand that we honour The Other is also a call to enlightened self interest. For the truth is, we are not separate from The Other, we do not, and cannot, live 'apart' from the rest of the world. Every action in the world, however seemingly insignificant, has some consequence for us, as individuals, as human societies. The one blessing of the twentieth century is that we have just begun to understand this.[33]

Burnside's philosophical reflections on the large topic of responsibility to the Other become particularly strategic for his recent poetry and helps him discuss the problem of 'healing' as a kind of starting point for a non-belligerent and neo-harmonious co-existence in the world:

> My poetry works at the borderline between 'self' and 'other' – partly with a view to undermining the feelings of separateness that make us capable of damaging

the world in which we live, the meta-habitat that we must share with all other things. Of course, I have other concerns, but this is central. Naturally, this relationship between 'self' and 'other' can be explored in many ways – in the so-called 'nature poem', or in love poems, for example. At the core of these explorations, however, I believe, lies a fundamental concern with healing, in its broadest sense: not the healing of the world, or of 'the other' so much as a healing of oneself, sufficient to allow for a continuation of meaningful and non-destructive play between self and other.[34]

This is the poetics of 'tolerance' issuing forth the unsaid and unsayable details of another life. In the depth of darkness or of unconscious states, we are presented with alternative personas or untouched secrets, or with various possibilities of relating ourselves with the Other:

and someone is having the dream
I had for weeks: out walking on the beach
I lifted a pebble and split it
open, like an apricot, to find
a live child hatched in the stone . . . [35]

In his 1994 collection, *The Myth of the Twin*, Burnside engages his persona in a subtle and painful game of remembrance and invocation of his relatives, as in the poems he dedicates to his grandfather ('Grandfather' and 'A Photograph of My Grandfather'), or to his grandparents ('My Grandparents in 1963'), or to the drowned children at the pond, or to his sister, or to the dead in general. He has described invocation as 'the mode by which we reintegrate the things of the world':

One might see this mode as essentially metaphorical: for, as Hannah Arendt says, 'Metaphors are the means by which the oneness of the world is brought about'. Invocation, then, is an attempt to bring about the oneness of which Arendt speaks: a oneness which is 'out there' in the world, and is only ever fractured in our imaginations. I see the invocative aspect of poetry (of all art) as a healing power, in so far as it restores the oneness of the world, and our continuity with 'the things of the world', especially with other living things. To this extent, invocation can also be described as an ecological pursuit.[36]

Lilias Fraser has observed that

Becoming proven . . . is a process where both poet and reader can describe and recognise their adult responsibility to acknowledge where, when or how they began to grow up. Something which seems as ubiquitous as motherhood, or looking out at a street, can have all the remarkable familiarity of a 'closeness in the mind', yet it is as much a test, or proof of identity, in these poems for the poet or reader to recognise and reassess how forceful these familiar settings or words can be.[37]

While declaring his special way of shaping his own identity, Burnside professes his 'religious' attitude towards all the details of the world and questions if in his 'secular/ agnostic sacrality' there is still room for an ordinary epiphany which could reveal the very essence of a Deity:

> I would love it if more people abandoned a belief in g(G)od, but I wouldn't expect them all to start writing poetry. I think the arts generally do have a significant part to play in reminding us of the real, at transitional times (which I hope this time is), when we are shifting from one belief system to another (and I hope, rather than trust, that we are). The real is here present with us: water, air, stones, plants, animals, gravity, light. I think the best art has always worked against orthodoxies of religion and politics, to reassert the worth of the ordinary, the physical and the transient against the grandiose, puritan, metaphysical ideas of church and state. Don't the poems we love best sing of the transient beauty of hedgerow flowers, the fleeting joys and pains of love, of our occasional and tentative epiphanies in a mysterious world, as against the thousand year Reich, the tyrant's desire for immortality and the promised eternities of the official religions?[38]

In this context we might consider the following lines from The Myth of the Twin:

> In the morning you would have stood
> alone, at the edge of the world
> with your face to the light,
> and God would become the camphor in a bush,
> the whisper of something local and banal,
> a personal event, which you would grasp,
> inferred from the wind like a shiver of ash or pollen.[39]

In one of his essays Burnside talks about Paul Eluard's (1895–1952) secular programme to uncover the autremonde ('that non-factual truth of being: the missed world and, by extension, the missed self who sees and imagines and is fully alive outside the bounds of socially-engineered expectations') by means of a radical 'illumination, a re-attunement to the continuum of objects and weather and other lives that we inhabit', which becomes a way for him to define what a lyric poem really is: another point of entry to the quotidian, 'another source of that clarity of being that alchemists call pleroma':[40]

> Consider the body: changeable, incomplete,
> yet still continuous:

think how it holds the perfect likenesses
of all the former selves that it is not,
how casually it gathers and renews
the forms we have scarcely noticed

   . . .

and how, on a morning like this, with our everyday lives
suspended
        in these white parentheses

we start again from scratch: the coming night;
the ferry that runs to the island;
           the sullen ice;

the shapes we have scarcely noticed, bearing us on
to all we have yet to become
        to the blank of a future.[41]

This attempt to glimpse into the oneness of our worlds (including Eluard's otherworld, the true Kingdom of Heaven) through radical illumination invites us to use, as in many of Kenneth White's theoretical assumptions, a new strategy and a new attitude towards our environmental context, spatially, in language and in our existential selves:

> The lyric offers the same radical illumination that chance affords us when we wander off the map. For poetry works where maps are useless: like a passport, the lyric allows us to enter the otherworld, but is neither road map nor field guide. Upon arrival in Eluard's Kingdom, all we have is imagination and the difficult leap of trusting our own (many) senses; over there, we are not who we are in our public lives, but being there is how we come to be revealed.[42]

This strategy, at times seemingly unconscious or perhaps half-perceived, allows Burnside to combine a passion for sensuality with a convincingly secular empathy between humankind and our natural environment, inviting the reader to enjoy a revived sacrality relieved of institutional agendas and ceremonial convention. It becomes a compelling invitation when we consider how religious hierarchies routinely hijack the sacred from everyday lived experience and 'set it apart':

> in the tabernacle, on the altar, for [their] own purposes . . . to obtain and enjoy power: over others, over natural 'resources', over the earth itself. And poetry is a democratic art, one might say, in so far as it opposes this power with joy, with the affirmation of all that we cannot control, of everything which has no market value, of that freedom which, as Marx said, arises naturally from 'the recognition of necessity'.[43]

Whereas the prose writer is generally concerned with what Wittgenstein allows him or her to say about the world, the poet here is working in an area where the ability to speak precisely about the world needs to be informed by 'a new way of thinking' in a transforming 'song of existence', so that we are forced to press our ears to the earth and listen. If we can hear the beating of the heart, we may continue to live as humans, like the man blind from birth in Burnside's 'One Hand Clapping', still able to perceive the presence of a twin and lighter self in rainfall or the small hours:

> Remember the myth where everyone is twinned
> with something in the fog
> > a lighter self
> that knows its way by feel
> > and finds us out
> in rainfall
> > or the small hours
> > > finds us out
> and leads us home
> > where danger never goes
> to start again
> > one moment at a time
> grammar and kinship
> > wedlock
> > > collective nouns? [44]

CHAPTER NINE

Aonghas MacNeacail

Peter Mackay

Aonghas MacNeacail (1942–) is the most prolific of the generation of Gaelic poets who came to prominence in the 1970s and 1980s and who were celebrated in Christopher Whyte's 1991 anthology *An Aghaidh na Siorraidheachd/In the Face of Eternity*. MacNeacail is also an English language poet of some note; indeed it was in English that he first began writing and published his first collection, *Imaginary Wounds* (1980). Another English collection followed – *Rock and Water* (1990) – but since the early 1980s MacNeacail's output has mainly been in Gaelic with accompanying English translations: book-length poems (in collaboration with the artist Simon Fraser) *Sireadh Bradain Sicir/Seeking Wise Salmon* (1983) and *An Cathadh Mòr/The Great Snowbattle* (1984) have been followed by the collections *an seachnadh agus dàin eile/the avoiding and other poems* (1986), *Oideachadh Ceart agus Dàin Eile / A Proper Schooling and Other Poems* (1996) and *laoidh an donais òig/hymn to a young demon* (2007) as well as librettos – *An Sgathach/ Warrior Queen* and *An Turas (The Trip)* (c. 1993) – and scripts for radio, television, film and stage.

That MacNeacail writes in both Gaelic and English is no surprise. Born in the Isle of Skye in 1942, the poet was raised in Gaelic until he went to primary school, where education was entirely through the medium of English. After his schooldays (in which he learned Gaelic, in effect, as a foreign language) MacNeacail left Skye to work for British Rail, in a London housing office and also to take a degree at Glasgow University, where he was a member, along with Tom Leonard, James Kelman, Alasdair Gray and Liz Lochhead, of the Philip Hobsbaum writing group. Until 1977, when he took up the post of *sgrìobhadair*, or writer-in-residence, at Sabhal Mòr Ostaig, MacNeacail wrote poetry predominantly in English. From 1977 on he has been almost exclusively a Gaelic poet, and has used only his Gaelic name (some earlier work had appeared under the English 'Angus Nicolson'). This negotiation between Gaelic and English that MacNeacail has engaged in throughout his life, and the corresponding voyage between Gaelic and various other cultural traditions, is central to much of MacNeacail's poetry. The poetic persona that develops through these negotiations provides much of the interest, and many of the problems, in his poetry.

In English, MacNeacail's poetry is largely that of a local correspondent, a witness to the life (and especially the death) of the rural community in which he was brought up. Most of his English poetry was written in the late 1960s and early 1970s and was collected either in *Imaginary Wounds* or was incorporated alongside the poems from *Imaginary Wounds* into *Rock and Water*. *Imaginary Wounds* is largely a collection about childhood, and especially the 'fall' from innocence as the child gains knowledge of the adult world of good and evil. This is most obvious in 'epicures' where the eating of 'blaeberries' is accompanied by the fear that among the nearby cattle there might be a bull.[1] The sense of transgression, of guilty and fearful pleasure, of a burgeoning masculinity (as represented by the possible bull) and the sensuality of eating the blueberries – 'we purpled lips and tongues on / dark-blue juicefull fruit' – echo poems such as William Wordsworth's 'Nutting' or Seamus Heaney's 'Death of a Naturalist' and 'Blackberry-Picking'.[2] What marks MacNeacail out from such predecessors, however, is the sense of community that pervades these childhood narratives. The poet is rarely alone in the natural world; instead there is always a communal aspect to the adventures and the loss of innocence, whether it be the children watching kittens fighting, fighting themselves after the 'school / film-show', taking 'sides / at playtime', following a cart full of dung or the many interactions between adults and children.[3] Teachers, fishermen, parents all provide a moral lodestone for the young poet; it is not an inspirational nature that educates the young poet, but the adults around him.

Writing a community is crucial to most of MacNeacail's English poetry. This is not so much the process of 'imagining' a community – to adapt the phrase from Benedict Anderson that has gained a great deal of currency and notoriety in discussions of national and nationalist literatures – but the attempt to 'witness' the existence of a community seen to be on the verge of calamitous and disastrous change, with witnessing containing a moral imperative.[4] Rather than attempting to constitute a present and future community out of a reinterpretation of the past, MacNeacail's poetry tends towards an anthropological attempt to record a community passing out of existence (this is not, however, in any way to claim that the community he records is 'real' and not imaginatively configured). As such, *Rock and Water* is replete with vignettes about the life of community in the process of decay and dissolution. Often – as here in 'country life' – there are echoes of the Irish poet Patrick Kavanagh's anti-pastoralism, his parochialism and confidence in the 'social and artistic validity of his parish':[5]

> GOD DAMN this earth, when not alive
> with stone, it's bog, and always greedy

for dung, there aren't cows here
to shit a breakfast for spiky acres
that clamour for feast.
not since the great war
have i had peace.[6]

The narrator in 'country life' is the last member of a family – his wife dead, his sons driven away – with nothing to live for but his 'trench warfare' against the land, and he is about to lose even that; it is being repossessed by a man in a 'big black shining limousine'. The adjective 'shining' when 'shiny' is expected is wonderfully unsettling, as if the speaker is not quite in control of the language he is speaking; in the slip from shining to shiny, the limousine becomes the luminous source of the man's power rather than a symbolic reflection of it. This is a characteristic poem for the English-language MacNeacail, in as much as a rural world on the cusp of radical and irrevocable change is depicted with a precise minimalism and idiosyncratic orthography. The harshness and directness of this minimalism – especially in images such as 'to shit a breakfast' – is, however, balanced by a sense of nostalgia, and the obvious fondness and empathy with which the poet describes his characters. The air of nostalgia is made more acute – and problematised – by the fact the poems were written at two removes from the community they describe: MacNeacail wrote them while living in the city, harvesting stories from his childhood memory and from trips to the island; and they are also written in English, a language which is at least partly implicated in the cultural change the poems lament. The questions arises: who is MacNeacail witnessing this community for? The rural community itself or a distant, urban readership? Also, to what extent does the act of writing about this community in English contribute to the changes it is undergoing? These questions are all the more pressing because the poetic voice and technique that MacNeacail adopts in Gaelic is quite different.

In Gaelic, MacNeacail is an extremely diverse poet. More than any poet since Sorley MacLean (1911–96) – one of his early mentors – MacNeacail has made a concerted effort to introduce a re-invigoratingly broad range of references into Gaelic literature, while also attending deeply to the traditions of Gaelic poetry. His poetry is awash with influences, acknowledged and silent, and tends to position itself within various cultures and religions. In the Introduction to *Sireadh Bradain Sicir*, for example, MacNeacail appeals to ancient Celtic mythology, Scottish travelling tinkers, an Amerindian medicine woman, the 'African Bushman who lifts a new-born child toward the stars . . . so that the infant's heart will meet the stars and acquire immunity from fear', the poetry of Euripides, the Hindu deity Siva and 'the Nordic *Selkie of Sule Skerry*'.[7] Thematically, these accord with the Zen-inspired poems, haikus and translations of North American Indian poetry that appear in MacNeacail's early work; they also combine with – and are in part justified by – MacNeacail's association with a strain of twentieth-century American verse running from William Carlos Williams through the Black Mountain School of Poetry to the L=A=N=G=U=A=G=E poets.

MacNeacail himself has described William Carlos Williams as 'one of the most important writers and theorists on poetry this century'.[8] The poetry movements Williams inaugurated and inspired encourage an experimentation in MacNeacail's work that is not matched in the work of any other contemporary Gaelic poet (with the possible exception of Fearghus MacFhionnlaigh). The most obvious manifestation of this comes in MacNeacail's distinctive orthography. Throughout, MacNeacail's poetry uses lower case letters, and the deliberate and suggestive use of breaks and caesuras, as here in his long poem *An Cathadh Mòr/The Great Snowbattle* (1984):

a chruinne   chuir thu ort gu bhi lom

    gilead mala air bheanntan
    gilead cìch air an t-sìthean
    gilead brù air a' mhòintich
    gilead sléisde 'san achadh

gruag neòil air do sgorran
agus sgàile air d'aodann

(earth   you dressed yourself to be bare

    whiteness of brow on the mountains
    whiteness of breast on the foothills
    whiteness of belly on the moorland
    whiteness of thigh in the meadow

coif of cloud on your peaks
and a veil on your face)[9]

The visual impact of this long poem is crucial to its interpretation. The spacing of the text, interacting with Simon Fraser's illustrations, encourages the reader to treat every word or phrase as an independent entity to be savoured and spoken separately. On a thematic level, the texts (both Gaelic and English), dancing and floating around the white expanse of the page, enact the snowbattle of the English title (this effect was lost when the poem was published with a more standard typography in *an seachnadh/the avoiding*). Behind MacNeacail's orthography lies Williams's own style, which Ezra

Pound memorably described as being made up of 'volts, jerks, sulks, balks, outblurts and jump-overs'.[10] The effect of Williams's poetry was to make the reader pause, to highlight the materiality of the poem and the integrity of each phonetic and textual element, to make immediate the individual reader's experience. For Williams, this went in tandem with an emphasis on an individual's immediate relationship with the world around him or her; poetry came to be the expression of this relationship, the verbalisation of what Charles Tomlinson has described as a 'locality, seen as the jerks and outblurts of speech rendered on to the here and now of the page'.[11] The American poet Charles Olson justified his own use of a similar orthography by emphasising how the form of poetry should always be an extension of its content, and affirming the importance of 'breath' – since reading poetry is a physical act – as a form of temporal and physical spacing upon which poems should be built[12] (such a space can be seen in the line 'a chruinne   chuir thu ort gu bhi lom' in the example above).

Both Williams and Olson remind us that the textual appearance of poetry is essential to how it is read. Non-standard orthography becomes a positively disruptive force, making the reader (or the poet) pause and question how language is being used, the political or cultural significance of how language is portrayed, and the reader's own personal relationship to language. This is as much of an issue for Gaelic language poetry – despite, or indeed because of, its attenuated state – as it is for English, the lingua franca of business and politics, a language through which great power is wielded. As the number and competence of speakers of Gaelic declines there is a real risk that the possibility for radical or controversial comment be formalised out of the language in the midst of efforts to preserve the status of the language – preservation could come to stifle linguistic experimentation and renewal.

This radical orthography meets in MacNeacail's work an unprecedented willingness to dispense with the traditional patterns, rhymes and metres of Gaelic poetry. 'dol dhachaigh – 1/going home – 1', for example, is a shape poem, repeating the words 'théid mi' (I will go) and 'théid mi dhachaigh' (I will go home), interspersed with different ways of saying 'yes', in Gaelic and English: 'sin e' (that's it), 'seadh' (that's it), 'aye' and 'yes'.[13] The poem is not translated into English; instead there are six notes explaining the 'poem'; these notes are a crucial part of the poem itself, with the final note making clear its subversive thrust: '*yes*, as any teacher of english will confirm, is the "correct" word.' Despite being part of the linguistic fabric of Scotland, neither the Scots 'aye' or the Gaelic 'sin e' and 'seadh' would be considered 'correct' responses in the world of the received pronunciation of English. 'dol dhachaigh – 1/going home – 1' should not be read as one would read a sonnet; rather it highlights what it means to separate and distinguish a set of words and call them a 'poem'. It foregrounds the deconstruction and the opening out of the repeated Gaelic words, and the relationship between the Gaelic and English languages.

Other of MacNeacail's experimental poems concentrate more specifically on the renovation and restoration of the Gaelic language itself. MacNeacail is attracted to a sub-genre within contemporary Gaelic poetry, the Dwelly poem, a poem derived or inspired by Edward Dwelly's magisterial diction-ary of the Gaelic language (1901–11). The nine lines of 'éideadh/attire', for example, feature five different kinds of shirt, each one explicated in notes either glossing or directly borrowed from Dwelly; in 'ghabh mi tamall aig tobar a' chràidh/i rested a while at the well of pain' it is herbs that are listed – 'lus nan dearc . . . lus-chlòimh . . . lus a' ghràidh . . . lus na sìochaint' – and these are offered two different renderings in English, in the text as 'berry herb . . . wool herb . . . herb of love . . . herb of peace', and in notes (taken from Dwelly) as 'bilberry . . . gossamer . . . love-lies-bleeding . . . loose-strife'.[14] As with MacDiarmid's trawling of Scots dictionaries, the recovery of these words, and the cultural history contained in their layers of meaning, offers a way of renewing the language, of creating a lexical range sophisticated enough to deal with the pressures of modern life. And one side-effect of these poems (as suggested by the 'double' translation of the verbs in 'ghabh mi tamall aig tobar a' chràidh/i rested a while at the well of pain') is to high-light the textuality of everyday experience, the way in which we experience through the words we use to describe, and so the value of different linguistic perspectives – Gaelic and English – on the world.

These linguistic concerns are exacerbated by the practice of publish-ing poetry in dual-language editions, and MacNeacail is well aware of the ironies of the situation in which he finds himself, with the majority of his readers only having access to his poetry through English translation. In reply to his own question 'Why bother to translate at all?' in a 1978 interview the poet commented:

> The answer, if there was one, was simply that there was a bigger publication potential in English. Which was rather sad in the context of the truer and more original creative product. By translating it into English you felt you were doing it a disservice.[15]

MacNeacail has since been more vehement in his support for the translation of Gaelic poetry, however, especially in the 1990s, when he found himself engaged in a debate over whether it was justified or indeed desirable for Gaelic to be published in dual-language editions. He comments:

> [B]ecause I have worked creatively in English even before I did in Gaelic, I see no problem in constructing the translation as an entity that ought to work as an

independent poem in English, different in a variety of ways, but every bit as realised and, I'd hope, as effective as the original. Nor do I see this reworking as a dilution of the strength or integrity of the original.[16]

It is certainly true of MacNeacail's English 'translations' that they have a distinct life of their own (although the divergence between the two has grown smaller as his career has progressed). The exhortation in 'bratach/banner', the first poem of *an seachnadh/the avoiding*, offers a potent example: the poet introduces himself as a bard and holy fool and instructs the reader to 'amhairc is éisd rium', which is literally 'observe and listen to me'; the English text tellingly only has 'observe and listen'.[17]

The bardic pose of 'bratach/banner' is a crucial feature of MacNeacail's work. There is no doubt he sees himself as part of a long line of Gaelic bardic poets: part of the dedication of *Oideachadh Ceart/A Proper Schooling* is 'Do gach bard aithnichte is neo-aithnichte a sheinn a Ghàidhig riamh' (To every bard, known and anonymous, who ever made the Gaelic language sing).[18] However, in his Gaelic poetry MacNeacail is not 'bardic' in the traditional senses of being the chronicler and historian of a clan or society – this would be a more accurate description of his English poetry – or of writing poetry fulfilling the requirements of traditional 'bardic poetry' such as employing the strict, syllabic metres of the *dàn dìreach* and intricate end and internal assonance.[19] Instead, in Gaelic he often writes a politically engaged 'visionary' poetry – the poetry of a seer rather than a bard – elaborated in a highly rhetorical and often mesmerisingly structured verse: MacNeacail proclaims and hectors in verse that is repetitive and incantatory; he rarely narrates or argues, instead preferring to build image upon image through the related techniques of repetition and parallelism. This poetry requires a particularly willing and sympathetic audience, which will accept shamanistic poetry as a stylistic choice rather than as part of a historically grounded poetic genre, as it is for the North American Indian poets MacNeacail translated in *an seachnadh/the avoiding*. The poetry's enthusiastic reception is testament to the technical skill with which MacNeacail controls his poetic voice.

The most frequent of the rhetorical techniques in MacNeacail's work is repetition, and in particular anaphora, epiphora and epizeuxis: the repetition of words or phrases at the beginning of neighbouring clauses, at the end of successive clauses, or in immediate succession. These have several different functions in the poetry: for emphasis, to create mood, and to give a sense of continuity or connection. It is this last that is most common: repetition allows MacNeacail to juxtapose disparate concepts or contexts without any logical connection. This is the case in 'sear–siar: seunaidhean/east–west: telepathies', where the poet's observations are rather knowingly linked by the phrase 'nì nach do mhothaich thu' ('a thing you did not observe'). Though it runs the risk of condescension – with the suggestion that the poet observes more than the reader – the poem escapes this through its good humour, lightly mocking its own tendency to parallelism and accumulation in the anaphoric lines

> nì nach do mhothaich thu
>> druid
> nì nach do mhothaich thu
>> is druid
> nì nach do mhothaich thu
>> is druid is druid is druid is druid is druid

> (a thing you did not observe
> starling
> a thing you did not observe
> and starling
> a thing you did not observe
> and starling and starling
> and starling and starling and starling).[20]

Similarly, in 'gàidheal san eòrp/a gael in europe' the fourfold repetition of 'an gàidheal ag imeachd' ('the gael travelling') is a powerful tool to suggest the continuing influence of Macpherson's Ossianic poems through disparate historical contexts.[21] This poem risks, however, becoming somewhat pretentious; and there is no doubt that repetition is not always equally successful in MacNeacail's work. The balance appears to be tipped in a poem such as 'trì nithean' which ends rather flatly with 'cò leis iad/cò ghoid iad' ('whose are they/who stole them') repeated three times.[22] Like the repetition of 'an gàidheal ag imeachd' this is an example of the use of epizeuxis (immediate repetition of a phrase) for emphasis; the effect is, however, subtly different. While the repetition in 'gàidheal san eòrp/a gael in Europe' helps to stress the ongoing dispersal and movement of Gaels throughout the world, the repetition in 'trì nithean' seems instead simply to introduce greater confusion, and an undirected sense of grievance, which tends to undermine the 'obvious' suggestion that the salmon, grouse and deer in the poem belong to all of us. Similarly, in 'òran cèile/song for a spouse', the repetition of 'chan fhaca mi latha nad ghnùis / on a' chiad sealladh àlainn' ('not a day have i seen in your face / since i first glimpsed its beauty') three times in the last two stanzas undermines rather than reaffirms, and rather undesirably introduces doubt into what is otherwise a straightforward love poem.[23]

At its best MacNeacail's 'bardic' voice, through its use of repetition and parallelism, creates a swirling, hypnotic rhythm. It becomes a form of exploration – related to the quest for knowledge of *Sireadh Bradain Sicir/Seeking*

Wild Salmon – slowly expanding into a new world of meaning as it alters and develops its repetitions. In the second section of *An Cathadh Mòr / The Great Snowbattle*, for example, the crystalline images of the knives of ice develop into a standing army filling the landscape:

> sgeinean deas deighe
> sleaghan deighe
> claidheamhan deighe
> 'nan caiseanan seudach
> ris gach creig
> gach geug
> gach anainn
> freiceadain òrnaideach
>
> (honed knives of ice
> lances of ice
> claymores of ice
> in jewelled pendicles
> upon each rock
> each branch
> each gable
> ornate sentinels)[24]

Each image is partial, they flow into another and avoid final definition. In the spirit of Zen poetry they acknowledge that 'to define . . . is to limit'.[25] It is poetry of the abundance of the natural world, and of human experience of that world (as the rock and branch transforms into the gable end of a house).

And it is perhaps when MacNeacail turns his rhetorical power to political matters that this bardic stance develops its sharpest edge (and most of its critics). MacNeacail is a polemic poet of political causes, writing poems about Muslims in Bosnia, the Chernobyl disaster, the Gulf War, the closure of the Ravenscraig steel works, the return of the Stone of Destiny, the homeless in Edinburgh and – of course – the Gaelic language. 'uiseag uiseag/skylark skylark', warning of possible nuclear holocaust, exemplifies his more overt style of political poetry:

> uiseag uiseag anns na speuran
> seachain duslach dubh an dadaim
> thig e ort gun fhios gun chumadh
> thig e ort gun fhuaim gun bholadh
> uiseag uiseag anns na speuran.
>
> (skylark skylark soaring high
> beware the dark atomic dust

which comes with neither shape nor warning
which comes with neither sound nor savour
skylark skylark soaring high.)[26]

The repetition of 'uiseag' and of the whole first line; the regular, drumming tro-
chaic tetrameter; the parallel structuring of the third and fourth lines – these
combine to frame an insistent and urgent warning to the skylark (emotively
unaware 'in the skies', the literal translation of the Gaelic 'anns na speuran').
The poem brooks no dissent, allows no room for argument, admits no uncertainty – the urgency of its rhythms reflects the conviction of the poet.

This is to some extent a high-wire performance without the safety net –
which MacNeacail explicitly associates with contemporary English poetry –
of self-distancing irony (an irony which would anyway be discredited by the
urgency of MacNeacail's poem). In an essay entitled 'Poetry in Translation'
MacNeacail explained his desire to achieve a more 'committed', emotionally
engaged poetry, and how this related to the decline of the Gaelic culture:

> There was the fact that my native culture was steadily and, it seemed, inexora-
> bly, eroding. I was apart from it, and watching it die. One thing I was tiring of
> was restraint. So much contemporary English poetry is characterised by, and
> commended for, its detachment, its understatement, its gentle ironies. It is
> fashionable to be uncommitted, to see, from the seclusion of the parlour, intri-
> cate metaphors in the kitchen garden. I wanted, particularly after I had returned
> to Gaeldom, a wilder creative terrain.[27]

This position is certainly not without risk. In rejecting detachment in favour
of commitment, MacNeacail could face charges of being presumptuous,
naïve or over-simplistic. The apparent easiness of the quest for knowledge
in *Sireadh Bradain Sicir/Seeking Wild Salmon* drew mild admonishment from
Derick Thomson:

> Duine sam bith a tha a' sireadh gliocais, feumaidh e bhith greis mhòr anns an
> tòir, is a' toirt leis bloighean an-dràsda 's a-rithist mar a thig iad 'na chòir. 'S cha
> dèan math dha bhith cinnteach gun do lorg e e.

> (Anyone who is seeking knowledge has to be a long time in the hunt, and take
> with him fragments here and there when they come to him. And he shouldn't
> be certain that he has found them.)[28]

The risk Thomson highlights is that the inquisitiveness of MacNeacail's early
work will solidify into dogmatic certainty (the 'holy fool' of 'bratach/banner'
returning from the hillside with a tablet engraved with commandments).
For Thomson, the search for knowledge should not stop at answers found

too easily; the power of Zen *koans* (the unanswerable questions) is precisely that they are unanswerable. In a related criticism, Christopher Whyte questions the 'obviousness' or 'easiness' of MacNeacail's politics, quoting Joseph Brodsky: 'What's wrong with discourses about the obvious is that they corrupt consciousness with their easiness, with the speed with which they provide one with moral comfort, with the sensation of being right.'[29] MacNeacail, in this view, while rejecting the detachment of irony becomes a poet of the moral majority, a reactionary confirming and supporting the ethical attitudes of his (liberal, humanist) audience, while not encouraging them to question their belief systems and attitudes to the world radically. This is true to some extent (though debates of the relative conservatism or radicalism of a Gaelic speaking audience for poetry would require another essay) but it is also somewhat unfair. Although not offering a radical questioning of readers' attitudes to the Chernobyl disaster or the first Gulf War, the poems do serve at least to keep them as part of the public domain, while also being part of an attempt to create a public domain within the Gàidhealtachd in which such topics can be discussed (and also, more broadly, reaffirming them as topics for poetry). Were MacNeacail to stay silent about such topics and instead concentrate on delightful love lyrics (of which he has many), he would fall prey to charges of escapism, of constructing the 'intricate metaphors in the kitchen garden' he deliberately eschews.

MacNeacail's political poetry is best when it is closest to home, engaged in a rediscovery and renovation of Highland history and the Gaelic tradition (which parallels his experimental linguistic reinvigoration of the language). The title poem of *Oideachadh Ceart/A Proper Schooling* is a powerful narrative of incidents from the poet's native Skye, especially those connected with the land wars and the stories of emigration that have remained in the cultural consciousness of the people despite happening over a hundred years ago. The refrain of the poem – 'cha b' eachdraidh ach cuimhne' ('it wasn't history but memory') – suggests the personal, lived experience of history when it is passed down through oral tradition and so is retained in what could be termed 'folk memory' (this communion with the past is nowhere near as emphatic in his English poetry).[30] Access to the past is here associated with rootedness in a community, and also crucially in the culture of that community. The second motif running through the poem – 'nuair a bha mi òg' ('when I was young') – is the title of one of the most famous songs by the Skye poetess of the Clearances and the Land League, Mary MacPherson (1821–98), also known as Màiri Mhòr nan Oran.[31] MacNeacail adopts the nostalgia of MacPherson's poem – which talks blissfully of her childhood on Skye – to present an image of a community which still maintained shared memories of the past and an awareness of the great Gaelic poets of the eighteenth century named in the poem – Rob Donn Mackay, William Ross, Duncan Bàn MacIntyre and Alexander MacDonald (Mac Mhaighstir Alastair). The implication is that the association between history and memory does not continue to the present; with the attenuation of the cultural traditions of the community, the direct link to the past has been lost.

The poem suggests the ideological justification behind the exploration of cultures and religions evinced in the introduction to *Sireadh Bradain Sicir/ Seeking Wise Salmon*; cultures that could broadly – though insufficiently – be described as folk, indigenous or traditional (a fuzzily defined, new-age, 'world poetry' as counterpart to the 'world music' sections of record stores). Involved in this worldview is the valuing of local, indigenous and traditional arts, with the somewhat paradoxical notion that these different artforms are equivalent, to the extent that they are 'authentically' rooted in a particular community or culture – the more localised they are, the more easily they can be compared to similarly localised cultures elsewhere in the world, with the cumulative effect of inaugurating a broad, universal 'world culture' taken as the aggregate or shared characteristics of authentically rooted cultures. Often a deep concern for the natural world is implicated in this worldview, with cultures being rooted through a symbiotic relationship with the natural landscape; indeed it appears to depend on a mix of ecological and mystical humanism, in which individuals are tied to each other through the shared natural landscape, and tied to the natural landscape through various rituals, rites and ceremonies.

In MacNeacail's poetry, the poet then becomes not only the representative of the specific culture he composes (and from within which he composes), but also a conduit for the relationship between humanity and nature. This is, of course, not a new position. Christopher Whyte suggests as a precursor Amhairgin (or Amergin), reputedly the first Irish poet, who exclaimed in 'The Song of Amergin'

> I am the sound of the sea,
> I am a powerful ox,
> I am a hawk on a cliff,
> I am a dewdrop in the sun.[32]

(Closer to MacNeacail perhaps is Charles Olson, who offers images of humans mediating the natural landscape in such poems as 'Maximus, from Dogtown – 1': 'she is the goddess / of the earth, and night / of the earth and fish / of the little bull').[33] The role of poet as mediator of nature is inherently sensual, as the human body becomes the venue for the meeting of the natural and the cultural. Thus the traditional motif of body-as-landscape (and in particular the tendentious identification of the female body with the landscape) is the starting point for many of MacNeacail's poems: the early 'fearann mo ghaoil' ('Land of my Love: author's translation') contrasts 'do bhilean' ('your lips') and 'do bhàighean' ('your bays'), 'do chìochan' ('your breasts') and 'do chnuic' ('your hills'), and 'do shléisdean' ('your thighs') and 'do thràighean' ('your shores'),[34] while 'lili marlene san h-eileanan siar/lili marlene in the western isles' includes a description of Marlene Dietrich's hair being 'mar uillt feòir' ('like streams of hay').[35] The 'naturomorphism' of this motif – explaining human relationships in terms of the natural landscape – at times becomes a more threatening zoomorphism. Broadly speaking, naturo-morphism allows for human physical beauty to be compared to the beauty of the natural landscape while zoomorphism suggests the dark underside of this association; the extent to which humans can be understood as repeating or embodying (violent) animal instincts. This is certainly the case in a poem such as 'do chòin/your dogs':

> is mise do chù tòire
> rag
> do-cheannsachail
> nach géill nach
> fan
> gus an glas mi nam ghiall
> do thoil.

> (i am your tracking dog
> unbridled
> obstinate
> who will not yield nor
> stay
> till i clutch in my jaws
> your wish.)[36]

(This responds to a poem by Sorley MacLean, 'Coin is Madaihean-Allaidh' ('Dogs and Wolves'), sharing with MacLean's poem the hidden threat that the poet's beloved will be caught in his devouring jaws.) The naturomor-phism of these poems is counterbalanced by anthropomorphic poems such as 'A' Chlach/The Stone',[37] which erotically gives voice to a stone as it calls on the wind, sun, moon and elements to stroke it, and 'craobh na bliadhna/ the year's tree',[38] which imagines a tree as a woman. The cumulative effect of these anthropomorphic and naturomorphic poems is to emphasise the interrelationship of the human and the natural, with the human body – and especially the poet's body – as meeting point.

MacNeacail's poems linking humanity to the natural world often combine with his other great strength: love poetry. For all the power of his political poetry and the occasional bluster of his bardic stance it is in deliciously complex love lyrics that MacNeacail first found his voice in Gaelic, and for

which his poetry gains a great deal of its popularity. Alongside the conventional image of the body-as-landscape MacNeacail makes brilliant use of the
natural landscape as a feature of – or impediment to – a romantic relationship. In 'òran gaoil/love song' the poet is a boat floating in his beloved's
body, anchored.[39] In 'nuair a phòg sinn a' chiad uair/when we kissed for the
first time' the poet and his beloved are two crofters, tending quite different
crofts, who do not understand each other but can still hope to meet on the
common grazing land.[40] In 'an aimhreit/the contention' the emotional distance between a rowing couple is a kyle which will be rowed across 'le ràimh
mar sgiathan sgairbh' ('with oars like scart's [cormorant's] wings') with the
first word of reconciliation.[41] As these examples suggest, MacNeacail is not
only a love poet, but also a poet of the whole spectrum of human relationships – of first kisses, of uncomfortable silences, of disagreements, of the
happy and unhappy marriage, of break-ups, harsh words and recriminations.
In these poems the importance of love to human relationships is everything;
that the imagery used to describe these relationships is often derived from
the natural landscape offers the poetry at least a coherence and occasionally a sense of being part of ancient and powerful cycles of life. When the
symbolism of the love poetry doubles and triples to form a complex tapestry,
MacNeacail's poetry gains the depth and solemnity his bardic voice requires.
In 'an eilid bhàn/the white hind', for example, the poet's love poetry – the
hind is a traditional folk motif for love[42] – meets his concerns for his culture
(the deer also being a possible symbol of the Gaelic way of life).[43] The
meeting of the human and the natural here ends in tragedy, and the death
of the deer; the poet's repetition at the end strikes a highly evocative note
of lamentation:

ach 's ann air an t-sealg eile bhios m'inntinn
far am bi na buill-airm choma gan giùlain
air guailnean luchd-faghaid a tha
gun aithne air d'àilleachd
chan e do chniadachd a tha dhìth orra
ach an t-sealg
 an t-sealg is
 a' bhuile sgoilteach
  o m'eilid bhàn
  o m'eilid bhàn

(but my thought will be on the other hunt
where the indifferent weapons are carried
on the shoulders
of stalkers who
don't know your beauty

not your caresses they want
but the hunt
the hunt and
the gutting blow
my white hind
o my white hind)[44]

CHAPTER TEN

Kathleen Jamie

Matt McGuire

Kathleen Jamie published her first poem 'View from the Cliffs' in 1979 at the age of just seventeen. It depicts a scene from Orkney where fishermen load lobsters to be sent south to restaurants in London. In contrast to the conspicuous consumption of the metropolis the poem foregrounds the fishermen's contentment, their sense of balance and commitment to 'a walking-pace world'.[1] The poem's oscillation, from Orkney to London and back again, reveals its own preference for peripheral and more rooted forms of existence. Throughout her career this walking-pace world has offered an antidote to the increasing uncertainties of modernity and become fundamental to Jamie's poetic DNA. Equally constitutive is the notion of the chance encounter and, moreover, a willingness to submit these experiences to the rigours of poetic form. While the title alludes to a single view there are, in fact, two views in the poem: the image the poet initially stumbles upon and a second view, the aesthetic perspective offered by the poem itself. The poem becomes a form of second sight, a way of mediating and negotiating our experience of the external world. Such realisation recalls Wordsworth's manifesto in the Preface to the *Lyrical Ballads* (1798): 'to choose incidents and situations from common life' but to treat them so that 'ordinary things should be presented to the mind in an unusual aspect'.[2] The common is in fact uncommon, the prosaic deeply poetic. Jamie's poetry presents alternative ways of travelling. It is a gateway through which to access this walking-pace world. We are reminded of Frederic Jameson's definition of how good poetry functions: 'by drawing the real into its own texture, in order to submit it to the transformations of form'.[3] In the following discussion this notion of a Romantic inheritance will be used as a way of contextualising Jamie's more recent output, particularly her collections *Jizzen* (1999) and *The Tree House* (2004). The legacy of Romanticism will be used to bring into focus a number of wider issues, including Jamie's engagement with the natural world, her place in various poetic traditions, and her acute interest in the politics of the environment. This framework is echoed in a review by Andrew Marr who compares Jamie's prose writing to the work of eighteenth-century English naturalist Gilbert White. If

'View from the Cliffs' looks backwards and in doing so evokes the aesthetics of the early eighteenth century, it is also possessed of a remarkable foresight. Our own ecologically attuned senses will doubtless recognise in Jamie's poem the contemporary debate surrounding food miles and the environmental cost of global trade. From the late 1970s the poem anticipates our own age and the fraught ideological terrain of environmental politics. This chapter explores the ways in which Jamie's poetry engages with the mélange of issues that gather under this green umbrella. It suggests that her poetry reconnects us with the natural world in a way that both science and the mainstream coverage of the environmental crisis have so far failed to do.

Just as drought, hurricanes and severe weather have little respect for national boundaries, Jamie's writing disrupts the demarcation lines within recent Scottish criticism. The sensitivity of her poetry stands in contrast to the 'Caledonian brutalism' that characterises so much recent Scottish writing.[4] Her interest in green spaces situates her work in a radically different terrain, both aesthetically and ideologically, from the likes of Irvine Welsh, James Kelman and Alistair Gray. Jamie's background is markedly different from these and many of her other Scottish contemporaries. Born in Paisley, her family moved to Teeside before returning to Currie, a small town outside Edinburgh, where the poet spent the rest of her youth. A philosophy graduate from the University of Edinburgh she subsequently described herself as 'West Coast urban, Edinburgh middle class, English liberal – an outsider everywhere'.[5] This sense of the outsider pervades Jamie's earlier work. The title poem from *The Queen of Sheba* (1994) depicts a camel train from Arabia riding into the Central Belt to lay bare the cultural poverty of modern Scotland. From the same collection 'Jocky in the Wilderness' offers a full frontal assault on the kinds of warped masculinity so prevalent within contemporary Scottish literature. The poem declares:

> come hame
> when ye've learned
> to unclench your fists and heart.[6]

And when Jamie employs vernacular speech it is not to champion an underclass *a la* Kelman; instead she seeks to expose small town mentalities and peculiarly Scottish brands of philistinism. In 'Arraheids' the artistic impulse is kept in check by a voice handed down over generations: '*ye arnae here tae wonder, / whae dae ye think ye ur?*'[7]

The desire to escape the restricting force of labels has underpinned much of Jamie's travelling, both physically and aesthetically. In her twenties she travelled through Asia visiting China, Tibet and Pakistan, commenting: 'Sometimes I feel so constrained with this palaver of labelling. I just bugger off abroad where nobody knows and nobody cares.'[8] A familiar claim within recent Scottish criticism is that in the wake of the devolution debacle in 1979 a more confident Scottish literature helped fan the flames of demands for national self-government. In his Introduction to the anthology *Dream State* (1994) Donny O'Rourke argues that in the 1980s it was the poets, more so than the politicians, who set about dreaming a new state for Scotland.[9] One of only two full-length essays devoted to Jamie's work, Helen Boden's 'Semiotics of Scotland' situates the poet's work within this model of national introspection. Boden is interested in the 'interconnected matrices of national and sexual difference' within Jamie's poetry.[10] She highlights her attempts to recycle rather than reject the cultural stereotypes of Scotland, with the poet rewriting the narrative of the nation.[11] My chapter departs from this tendency within Jamie criticism. Having said this, her ability to dissect surgically contemporary Scottish politics remains highly arresting. On the much debated new Scottish Parliament she offers us 'On the Design Chosen for the New Scottish Parliament Building by Architect Enric Miralles'. The poem itself is a two line aphorism: 'an upturned boat / a watershed'.[12] The title satirises political self-importance and long-windedness. In contrast the economy of the poem is a masterclass in understated wit. The upturned boat refers to the shape of the domed roof in Miralles's design. Jamie's description of this as a watershed evinces a measured ambiguity, both celebration and warning. At long last the boat has been righted, a new voyage has begun. But as a watershed, the new parliament might be of little lasting value, a room full of hot air, or cold water, perhaps. As this and the above examples from *The Queen of Sheba* illustrate, it is not always easy to align Jamie's cold eye with an unrestrained cultural nationalism. We see again that her poetry operates in the gaps, in the places where other discourses fail to reach. As critics we must be wary of valuing a writer in terms of the ease with which they may be appropriated to any particular ideology, not least that of nationalism. Such paradigms muzzle the range of Jamie's writing. They neglect the changes in direction that her work has taken in recent years; its turn toward greener and less nation-bound issues. The extended remit of Jamie's work is also evinced in the number of UK awards her poetry has received. She has won the Forward Poetry Prize, the Somerset Maugham Award and the Geoffrey Faber Memorial Prize (twice!). Her poems have appeared on the walls of underground stations in both New York and Shanghai.

In marshalling, or at least tempering, the significance of the nation within our critical practice the Irish poet Eavan Boland is instructive. Boland reads a colonising tendency at work within certain nationalist interpretations of the literary text. The quotation below is her reaction to comments by Seamus Heaney following his inclusion in *The Penguin Book of Contemporary British Poetry* (1982). Heaney had declared: 'My passport is green / no glass of ours was ever raised to toast the Queen.'[13] Boland responds: 'Poetry is defined by its energies and its eloquence, not by the passport of the poet or the editor; or the name of the nationality. That way lie all the categories, the separations, the censorships that poetry seeks to dispel.'[14] Her statement resonates with the central premise of Christopher Whyte's study *Modern Scottish Poetry* (2004). Whyte asks: 'How realistic is it to expect that, if we were to bring together the most significant works of Scottish poetry from the last sixty years, they would dutifully reflect a growing desire for and progress towards national autonomy?'[15] Moreover, in terms of Scottish women's poetry there is little sense of an informing literary tradition. For Liz Lochhead in the 1970s the absence of a recognisable tradition was a liberation, a freedom to make things up as one went along. In terms of Scottish poetry more generally, Jamie's poetry works at a tangent to that of many of her male forebears. Whilst questions of language *are* important to her work, she wears her Scots lightly. Her poetry sidesteps the ardent linguistic politics that, in different ways, has characterised the work of writers like Hugh MacDiarmid or Tom Leonard. Jamie often employs dialect in an ironic and highly stylised manner:

> Jock's a-brawling on the Aberdeen train.
> I'll punch your heid! he says to his weans
> I'll punch *your* heid! repeat the weans.[16]

Language it would seem is not the only thing passed from one generation to the next. Arguably much of Jamie's career has been spent defying a specifically Scottish scepticism regarding the legitimacy of the female poetic voice. Again Eavan Boland provides an insight into this kind of political aesthetic:

> [M]erely by the fact of going upstairs in a winter dusk, merely by starting to write a poem at a window that looked out on the Dublin hills, I was entering a place of force. Just by trying to record the life I lived in the poem I wrote, I had become a political poet.[17]

Jamie's loyalty to her own experience demands that we attend to her poetry on its own terms before reaching for the flag and all that that entails.

Jamie's 'Meadowsweet' resonates with the kind of sentiments Boland locates within the very act of female writing. The poem begins with a preface – 'Tradition suggests that certain of the Gaelic women poets were buried face down.' The face-down burial, of course, was not solely the reserve of the female poet. It was more commonly employed as a way of interring witches; the idea being to silence them and prevent them speaking further maledictions from the grave. Jamie's poem deliberately plays on this association, interweaving images of the supernatural and otherworldly with the idea of the unreconstituted female poet. The poem begins at the funeral:

So they buried her, and turned home,
a drab psalm
hanging about them like haar[18]

Much of the mood of the first verse comes from the sonorous qualities of its language. Jamie's use of free verse suggests that it is not the line-endings but the internal rhymes of the poem we ought to attend. The lifeless, bland quality of the 'drab psalm' is emphasised through the assonance of the 'a' sounds, a tone which overspills to the 'hanging . . . haar' in the next line. The third line is itself enclosed at either end by the 'h' sounds which act like bookends. There is a feeling of entrapment, of a world imprisoned by the ubiquitous melancholy of such religiosity and its incantatory blandness. Jamie's use of the word 'haar' lends the scene specifically Scottish undertones. We are reminded of the vigour of Free Presbyterianism and its dour denial of the material world. The image of the face-down burial also suggests a communal desire to punish the female poet, to set her on her way, to hell rather than to heaven. What the community does not realise, what the haar of the drab psalm blinds it to, is the natural cycle of rebirth in which it has unknowingly placed the poet. We are told of seeds caught in her hair that will sprout and grow, nourished by her decomposing body. They will break the surface as summer flowers, meadowsweet and bastard balm. Their role: 'showing her, / when the time came, how to dig herself out'.[19] Nature possesses a force and a power that will not conform to human reckoning. Also known as Queen of the Meadow, the flowering meadowsweet carries secondary connotations to do with female empowerment. Similarly, 'bastard balm' blossoms in colourful defiance of Christian prohibitions regarding sex, marriage and childbirth. As with Arabia and small-town Scotland, Jamie looks to play differences off against one another. 'Meadowsweet' cultivates its own pairs of opposites: grey haar / colourful flowers; dour Presbyterianism / vibrant Celticism; the world above / the world below. The flowers breaking the surface defy such rigid boundaries and the community's attempts to police them. From a Christian perspective the material world is, of course, of secondary importance. It is a place of preparation, an apprenticeship for the next life. This sense of detachment, of looking elsewhere, is contrasted with the female poet who merges and becomes one with the landscape. When the time comes she will return:

to surface and greet them,
mouth young, and full again
of dirt, and spit, and poetry.[20]

Poetry refuses to remain buried. It will resurface and resume its place amid the grime and physicality of everyday life. The 'drab psalm' which opens the poem is contrasted with the soundscape of the final line, its repeated 't' sounds drumming out the guttural liveliness of the material world. Poetry is not a lifeless, foreboding mist that clouds our vision. It is textured, grainy and raw. It exists within us rather than 'hanging' over us. 'Meadowsweet' rewrites the Christian lament 'ashes to ashes, dust to dust', turning its elegiac sadness into a celebratory shout. The traditional teleology of the Christian life, earthly denial followed by heavenly fulfilment, is undone by the cyclical, regenerative processes of nature. The poet's rebirth in the form of flowers offers both literal and metaphorical riposte to the finality of death.

The fusion of the female poet and the natural environment in 'Meadowsweet' anticipates the tenor of much of Jamie's recent poetry. This heightened sense of identification can in part be traced to the poet's own recent experiences of childbirth. The word 'jizzen' which lends Jamie's 1999 collection its title is old Scots for childbed. In a sequence called 'Ultrasound' the poet describes a new found intimacy that accompanied the pregnancy and birth of her son Duncan:

arms laden with you in a blanket,
I had to walk to the top of the garden,
to touch, in a complicit
homage of equals, the spiral
trunks of our plum trees, the moss,
the robin's roost in the holly.[21]

This process of identification, of new found complicity, is a useful way of approaching Jamie's own perception of our current environmental crisis. For her the problem lies in our own growing sense of estrangement from the natural world: 'I don't recognise the idea of "the outdoors", or of "nature". We are "nature", in our anatomy and mortality. Regarding nature as the other, different, an "outdoors" an "environment" speaks volumes about our alienation from ourselves.'[22] For Jamie the problem is the language we use to speak about the natural world. Our everyday speech differentiates us, and creates an artificial barrier between ourselves and the world around us. Here we might think about the abstract rhetoric of ecology and its frequent use of intangible and apocalyptic language. Meanwhile we are paralysed amid a welter of statistics and facts, and by the sensationalist character of our twenty-four-hour media culture. Again we can turn to Wordsworth who, more than two centuries ago, diagnosed this as one of the malaises of modernity. The poet identified such experience with a loss of sensibility, one that resulted from industrialisation and the mass urbanisation of society:

[A] multitude of causes unknown to former times are now acting with a combined force to blunt the discriminating powers of the mind, and unfitting it for all voluntary exertion to reduce it to a state of almost savage torpor. The most effective of these causes are the great national events which are daily taking place, and the increasing accumulation of men in cities, where the uniformity of their occupations produces a craving for extraordinary incident which the rapid communication of intelligence hourly gratifies.[23]

Arguably we have only become more blunted, our torpor more savage, in the intervening centuries. Critic Richard Kerridge comments: 'The real, material ecological crisis, then, is also a cultural crisis, a crisis of representation. The inability of political cultures to address environmentalism is in part a failure of narrative.'[24] The ecological crisis represents a failure of the political narrative, shackled as it is to national politics and the short-termism of the four-year electoral cycle. It is a failure of the scientific narrative, where diagnosis is one thing and cure quite another. And it is a failure of the traditional narratives of the Left. In the face of such global problems, arguments over class, gender and race can seem like rearranging deck chairs on the Titanic.[25] Advances in biotechnology and agri-business mean that the relationship between nature and culture is one of the key intellectual problems of the twenty-first century. At the other end of the scale our challenge is to avoid the kind of green fascism and clichéd alternatives with which we have become familiar. Images of the dreadlocked tree-hugger spring to mind. As does Philip Larkin's ironic figure in his poem 'Poetry of Departures' which exposed the futility of 'chucking everything off' and retiring from the world 'all stubbly with goodness'.[26] Against this backdrop Kathleen Jamie offers us a poetry of reconnection and reclamation. In fact, if language has fostered our modern alienated existence, for Jamie it is poetry as a complex linguistic performance that holds the key to change:

> I used to think that language was what got in the way, that it was a screen, a dark glass. That you could not get at the world because you were stuck with language, but now I think that's wrong. Now I think language is what connects us with the world.[27]

Her recent volumes bring us closer to the natural world, to re-establish a sense of intimacy with the outdoors, to rediscover an interdependence that has been forgotten amidst the onrush of our contemporary age.

As the title of Jamie's collection *The Tree House* (2005) suggests, the poet is interested in reconfiguring our relationship with the natural world; in thinking of new ways to live a more interdependent existence. In 'The Whale-Watcher' the poet turns her back on civilisation, holing herself up in a beachside caravan in order to wait for a sign from the ocean.[28] The poem begins in declarative mood: 'And when at last the road / gives out, I'll walk –.' The end of the road has no sense of final destination, of arrival and repose. It suggests a failed or aborted journey, and that we still have some way to travel. The crumbling tarmac is highly symbolic. We are reminded again of Jamie's 'walking-pace world', only here it resonates with the specious freedoms of technology. We may think of the open road and the iconography of car advertising, in contrast to which, of course, stands the more mundane reality of the gridlocked motorway and carbon emissions. The second verse announces the poet's determination to 'hole up the cold / summer in some battered caravan'. This is a world where the seasons are out of kilter, where climate no longer functions as it should. The battered caravan reminds us of a bygone era, before the low cost airline, the package holiday, and the unseen environmental price tag. From the caravan the poet will look out at 'the brittle waves':

> till my eyes evaporate
> and I'm willing again
> to deal myself in:
> having watched them
>
> breach, breathe, and dive
> far out in the glare,
> like stitches sewn in a rent
> almost beyond repair.

The poem climaxes with the whales breaking the surface of the water. The aborted future with which it began is resolved with the poet choosing to deal herself back in. Again the soundscape of Jamie's writing is important. The rhythm of the poem is deliberately reorganised by the single syllables and open vowels of 'breach, breathe, and dive'. Both rhythmically and thematically, the poem hinges on this moment. There is a sense of a slower, deeper rhythm welling up from the bottom of the ocean. The whales' immensity adds to the weight and majesty of the image. Their deliberate, measured breath stands in contrast to the road and its sense of hurried urgency. There is a process of recalibration at work, a sense of restoring some balance. The sight of the mammals renews the poet's spirit; it reinvigorates her and enables her to rejoin the tumult of living. The organic, natural rhythm of the whales as they breach, breathe, and dive spills over into the rest of the poem, which concludes on its only full-rhyme – 'glare' and 'repair'. Again the rhythmic qualities of the poetry underpin what is happening at a thematic level. For Jamie attending to nature is its own form of catharsis and consolation. The poem echoes Samuel Johnson's pithy observation: 'The only end of writing is to enable the readers better to enjoy life, or better to endure it.'[29] The *discordia concors*, or harmonious discord, between the image of surfacing whales and the notion of stitches is doubly suggestive. It echoes both the sewing up of a

garment and the post-operative stitching of a human body. We have the everyday inextricably bound up with issues of life and death. This cross-contex-
tualisation recalls the nature of the environmental crisis, where our everyday
behaviour has potentially catastrophic consequences for life on the planet. It
calls to mind the popular environmental mantra 'Act locally, think globally'.
If the poem opens with a feeling of resignation its conclusion is slightly more
upbeat. The qualified nature of the tear, 'almost beyond repair', suggests it is
not too late, that there is a possibility to mend and fix this damage.

As 'The Whale-Watcher' reveals, Jamie's acute interest in the natural
world is informed by her own historical moment and an awareness of the
contemporary environmental crisis. Her poetry can be theorised by way
of a new school of literary studies operating under the term 'ecocriticism'.
Emerging in the 1990s, ecocriticism is interested in the relationship between
literature and the environment, particularly the representation of landscape,
the treatment of wildlife and the economy of the natural world. It represents
a change in emphasis, a digression from the more familiar literary analysis
premised on gender, race, class and so on. The emergence of ecocriticism also
reflects the changing political landscape of the 1990s and the emergence of
environmentalism as part of our everyday vocabulary. This essay has already
invoked Wordsworth twice. His importance to this new critical movement
can be traced back to Jonathan Bate's *Romantic Ecology* (1991). Bate sought
to revisit Romanticism, and particularly the work of Wordsworth, to interrogate the aesthetic politics of this period and in particular its depictions of
landscape and environment. According to Bate, rather than representing
merely another modish trend in the academic study of literature, ecocriticism
is part of an ongoing attempt to understand our relationship to the natural
world: '[I]f one historicises the idea of an ecological viewpoint – a respect
for the earth and a scepticism as to the orthodoxy that economic growth
and material production are the be-all and end-all of human society – one
finds oneself squarely in the Romantic tradition.'[30] The current ecological
crisis is a consequence of the ideological assumptions that underpinned the
Enlightenment in the late eighteenth century. Bate continues: '[T]he human
claim to understand nature has led to Western humankind's understanding
of itself as apart from nature and therefore able to use and reshape nature at
will.'[31] This sense of distance and estrangement accords with Jamie's own
diagnosis above. We might also recall 'Meadowsweet' and its depiction of a
recalcitrant natural environment; one which acted in defiance of the human
community's desires to bury the female poet. Humanity's domination and
exploitation of the natural world are fundamental to the contemporary
environmental crisis. Such readings of modern ecology situate it within a
wider debate about the core values of the Enlightenment and the belief in
scientific rationalism as the engine of human progress. As a result we may

locate ecocriticism within a wider tradition; one that includes thinkers like
Theodore Adorno and Jurgen Habermas, and is highly sceptical regarding the
ideological foundations of modernity.[32]

Jamie's poetry is interested in the tension between the economy of nature
and the economy of human society. In contrast to human domination, her
poetry enters into what Richard Mabey describes as 'a conversation with the
natural world'.[33] Like 'The Whale-Watcher' there is a sense of recalibration
at work, an attempt to reset the balance of power. The natural is not a passive
object, but is instead replete with signification. Jamie's more recent poetry
features the personification of trees, birds and animals. They speak through the
poems as the poet asks them: 'how to live / on this damp ambiguous earth?'[34]
Jamie's openness to the environment, her willingness to seek out its 'edgy
intelligence' resonates with the work of the nineteenth-century American
writer Henry David Thoreau.[35] For Thoreau the outdoors was not merely an
economic resource to be harvested, it existed as a source of instruction: '[I]
n wilderness is the preservation of the world.'[36] Jamie can be seen to adopt a
similar position in her poem 'Alder'. Looking upon an old tree in bad weather
she asks: 'Are you weary, alder tree / in this, the age of rain?'[37] The rain conjures images of tearfulness, sadness and sorrow. We are also reminded of acid
rain and the threat posed by the devastation of the tropical rainforest. The 'age
of rain' might also imply a second diluvian flood, with an angry God punish-
ing mankind's greedy exploitation of the world. In contrast to Enlightenment
aspirations to understand and master nature, Jamie's poems adopt an uncertain and questioning tone. In her most recent prose work *Findings* (2005) she
speaks of trying to recapture the original meaning of the word 'essay' which
comes from French verb *essayer* meaning to try or endeavour.[38]

We might also align Jamie's poetry with the Russian writer Anton
Chekhov's definition of how art works: 'It is the business of art to pose questions in interesting ways, not to provide answers.'[39] Her poetry inverts the
arrogance of humanism and mankind's wish to regard himself as the measure
of all things. Jamie comments: 'Poets use language as a form of "seeing". More
and more, however, I think the job is to listen, to pay attention . . . '[40] Such
comments echo the work of another Romantic poet, William Blake, who
was profoundly influenced by the power of vision: 'To the Eyes of a Miser a
Guinea is far more beautiful than the Sun . . . The tree which moves some
to tears of joy is in the Eyes of others only a Green thing which stands in the
way.'[41] In 'Alder' Jamie acknowledges the tree's historic pedigree. It unfolded
'before the glaciers' and as such partakes in a deep sense of time, one which
predates human memory. The tree's vintage is offered as a foil to humanity's
youthful arrogance. Like 'The Whale-Watcher' the poem shuns the advances
of modernity, again foregrounding a slower wisdom and a walking-pace
world. Rather than a passive object the alder tree is something to be spoken

to and learned from. It offers us access to a deeper form of cultural memory. Modern history is overshadowed; given a new perspective by a passage of time far greater than human reckoning.

If the official discourses of environmentalism alienate us through the sheer scale of their terms, poetry attempts to operate at a much more personal and subjective level. As Samuel Taylor Coleridge commented: 'He prayeth best, who loveth best / All things both great and small.'[42] Shunning the grandiose and the abstract, Jamie's poetry delights in the minutiae of the natural world. It is pipistrelles, sparrows and frogs rather than epic and emotive scenery that capture her imagination. Her work stands in contrast to some of the more affected poses of traditional Romantic poetry. Her experience of the natural world is fleeting, stolen amidst the hustle and bustle of everyday life: 'Between the laundry and the fetching kids from school, that's how birds enter my life. I listen. During a lull in the traffic: oyster-catchers; in the school-playground, sparrows.'[43] 'The Buddleia' addresses the idea of such snatched moments in contrast to the more contrived and orchestrated epiphanies which poetry often offers us.[44] The poem opens with Jamie in high aesthetic pose, ironically contemplating the metaphysics of existence.

> When I pause to consider
> a god, or creation unfolding
> in front of my eyes –
> is this my lot?

The self-conscious tone of this verse has Jamie raise an eyebrow at the dramatic postures often associated with her craft. The use of the indefinite article 'a god' distances the poem from any affiliation with Christianity and its more dogmatic metaphysics. The mood of abstract musing, generated by the rhythm of the longer line, is cut short with the four short syllables 'is this my lot?' The poet is woken from her reverie by the most mundane objects, her parents with their broken Hoover and her quarrelling kids. The stylised musings of poetry are suddenly unhinged by the more mundane concerns of daily life. The second verse sets about reconciling this tension. Beginning 'Come evening, it's almost too late / to walk in the garden' it continues the sense that daily life is intrinsically inimical to the more meditative and enriched aspects of poetic experience. She attempts to 'retire the masculine / God of my youth', evoking the plants around her, the lupins, foxloves and buddleia, from which the poem takes its title. It is this last plant that the poet pauses over and describes. The 'heavy horns' of the buddleia:

> open to flower, and draw
> these bumbling, well-meaning bees

which remind me again,
of my father . . . whom, Christ,
I've forgotten to call.

Here it is nature's own organic process rather than the deliberate imagining of the poet that creates the association and subsequent moment of revelation. In contrast to the opening verse with the poet deliberately mining for metaphysical truth, it is the natural processes of the garden that enable her realisation. The poem stumbles upon these resemblances in an almost unconscious manner. It is not an abstract, heavenly quality but 'the bumbling, well-meaning' aspect of Jamie's father that is evoked. This leads to the understated disclosure of their deep bond and the remembrance of a forgotten phone call. We are cast back to the description in the first verse and 'my suddenly elderly parents'. The single word 'suddenly' reminds us of our tendency to take things for granted, to be blinded by our search for what we imagine to be a more meaningful encounter with the world. The shock of 'Christ, / I've forgotten to call' is a moment of reawakening. The poet realises something she always knew. The title 'The Buddleia' also invites us to consider the origin or seed of such thoughts, their own moment of budding. It is through being mindfully present, allowing nature to reveal itself, that the poetic insight is achieved. This sense of listening and the spiritual value in paying attention pervades *The Tree House*. In 'Pipistrelles' the poet watches a group of bats which 'vanished, suddenly, before we'd understood'.[45] In 'Daisies' it is the flowers themselves that are imbued with a sense of composure and self-awareness:

We are flowers of the common
sward, that much we understand.
of everything else
we're innocent.[46]

This mindfulness revisits the heightened state of consciousness to which her early travels through Buddhist Tibet exposed Jamie. In a poem from *The Autonomous Region* (1993) she imagines a fourth-century Chinese Buddhist monk setting out on a journey of discovery:

And our horse mayn't be divine,
we must ride it and be astonished and glad
to arrive at a clutter of gold roofs
cupped in a valley:
with a scented tree
whose every leaf
shimmers with the face of the divine.[47]

In Jamie's poetry it is the realisation of the physical world that offers a gateway to philosophical revelation. Where *The Tree House* marks something of a departure is not only in its acute interest in the natural world, but in its paring down and Jamie's preference for the shorter lyric. Does such economy speak to our contemporary urge to recycle and live less wasteful lives? Perhaps. Where there is definite resonance is with Jamie's desire to attend to the world around her and elevate its importance. In this her poetry resembles the work of the Scottish poet Norman MacCaig. At the foot of one of the poet's favourite hills in the Scottish Highlands, Stac Polly, is a bench with a carving quoting MacCaig: 'I took my mind a walk.' It is this combination of earthy and Eastern, mountain and metaphysical, that Jamie's work also develops. The MacCaig line comes from his poem 'An Ordinary Day' which is a highly appropriate note on which to end:

> and my mind observed to me,
> or I to it, how ordinary
> extraordinary things are or
>
> how extraordinary ordinary
> things are, like the nature of the mind
> and the process of observing.[48]

CHAPTER ELEVEN

Kenneth White

Cairns Craig

Kenneth White does not appear in Robert Crawford and Mick Imlah's *Penguin Book of Scottish Poetry*, and gets five pages in the much shorter time-frame of Douglas Dunn's *Faber Book of Twentieth-Century Scottish Poetry* (less than Robin Fulton or Alan Bold). Despite a special issue of the magazine *Chapman* devoted to his work in the 1980s, the critical literature on his work largely comes from France, where he has lived since the 1960s, and where he became Professor of Poetics at the Sorbonne in 1983. In France his work has won major awards, and the Centre for Geopoetics that he established in Paris in 1989 represented a groundbreaking introduction of environmental issues into contemporary literature, one which confirmed him as a culture-hero of the post-communist, and yet anti-capitalist, French intelligentsia. White has stood as the representative of an alternative to modern industrial society, as a pathbreaker for a new ecological awareness, as a writer whose work is *engaged* – in the tradition of Jean Paul Sartre's *littérature engagée* – but engaged with the world we inhabit rather than the history we had hoped to create. Such a career might make him, also, a culture-hero of Scotland, a Scotland turned towards its European destiny in the aftermath of Empire. And yet White, it seems, remains marginal to modern Scottish poetry – let alone to Scottish culture in general. Enormous admiration among a small group of followers committed to the ideology of 'geopoetics' seems to ensure a profound scepticism on the part of the general public for poetry (if such a thing can be said to exist). Neither a poet in the line of writing in Scots established by Hugh MacDiarmid's early work in the 1920s, nor one of those sophisticated experimenters with the traditional forms of English literature in the line of MacCaig and Dunn; neither an assertive promoter of working-class language, like Tom Leonard, nor an inquisitive ear upon contemporary Scottish *mores* like Liz Lochhead, White has generally been regarded as an outsider to Scottish writing.[1] In so far as he forms part of a tradition of Scottish writing, it is the tradition that Hugh MacDiarmid proposed in 'The Kind of Poetry I Want' –

A poetry the quality of which
Is a stand made against intellectual apathy,
Its material founded, like Gray's, on difficult knowledge.[2]

– a tradition which has been more honoured in the description than in the reading. So although Mainstream published both a collected shorter poems, *Handbook for the Diamond Country* (1990), and a collected longer poems, *Bird Path* (1990), followed by Polygon's *Open World: Collected Poems 1960– 2000* (2003), much of White's work, written in English but published in French, remains unavailable to the anglophone reader. White is, therefore, quite literally, *eccentric* to modern Scottish poetry, existing on its margins, as though his choice of a life in France (he became a French citizen in the 1980s) had disenfranchised him as a Scottish poet and as a contributor to Scottish culture.

Given this isolation from the mainstream of modern Scottish culture (how ironic the name of his Edinburgh publisher in the 1990s!), the fact remains that no modern Scottish poet has been more concerned than Kenneth White to situate his work in very specific Scottish traditions and to use Scottish predecessors as models for his own life choices and poetic commitments. The very decision to root himself in France is one he relates to the tradition of the 'wandering Scot', seeing himself treading in the footsteps of the many distinguished Scots, from John Mair (professor at the Sorbonne) and George Buchanan (Mair's student at St Andrews, who followed him to Paris and then became professor at Bordeaux, where he wrote his major works), to David Hume (who wrote his *Treatise of Human Nature* in France) and Patrick Geddes (who built a new *Collège des Écossais* at Montpellier in the 1920s, in emulation of the original Scots College, established in Paris in 1325). He might equally have cited Andrew Michael Ramsay, author of *The Travels of Cyrus*, published in Paris and in French in the 1720s, and which probably counts as the first Scottish novel, or J. D. Fergusson, whose Modernist technique was developed in Paris in the years before World War One, and who believed that 'to go to Paris was the natural thing for the Scot . . . it doesn't seem to have occurred to the modern Scot that the Scottish Celt, when in France, was among his own people, the French Celts.'[3] For White, those Scottish intellectuals who have sought to make Scottish ideas flourish in French soil represent one of the major traditions of Scotland's intellectual history, one which justifies his own choice of French domicile as the territory for the development of his Scottish agenda. Those Scottish migrants in France were themselves, however, in White's view, travelling in the footsteps of the Celtic missionaries who came from Ireland and Scotland to bring Christianity, or a certain form of Christianity, to a barbarised Europe:

Brandan, born in Kerry, founds a monastery at Clonfert, and then when a certain Barintus tells of a trip he made to visit a disciple of his on a distant island, embarks for the Hebrides, Iceland, Brittany, and maybe farther. St Malo, St Pol, St Renan settle in Brittany. Others come to Reims, Cambrai, Soissons. There were so many of them at Péronne the place was called Perrona Scottorum.[4]

These 'scotic' wanderers were disrupters of convention – 'Their existence was extravagant, their encyclopaedic knowledge was overwhelming, their intellectual acuity was disquieting and unorthodox, and their ideas were incomprehensible, but definitely heretical';[5] they were rebels in favour of freedom – 'When Belgian abbeys on the Scarpe and the Escaut began to draw up "charts of liberty", the inspiration can be traced back to Scotic influence';[6] they were examples of the 'nomadic intellect' which refuses incorporation into the fixed structures of an existing society and seeks 'always how, against the mechanics of history, to maintain some dynamic that transcends history'.[7]

It is through such predecessors that White justifies the pattern of his own career: he is a nomad whose territory is European in scope rather than confined by the boundaries of the nation; his connections are with 'a much older tradition'[8] of Scottish intellectuals than those shaped by the Unions of Crown and Parliaments since the seventeenth century; and if MacDiarmid needed to go 'Back to Dunbar' to find the resources for a modern Scottish poetry, White is determined to go even further back – to Pelagius, who challenged the Augustinian emphasis on original sin;[9] to the ninth-century theologian John Scot Erigena, 'one of the prime examples of the Celtic intellectual';[10] or Michael Scot,

In the early 13th century
        an 'internationalgebildeter Mann'
    with a mass of knowledge
        crystallising in his brain.[11]

That these Celtic and Scottish precursors all precede the formation of the nation of Scotland is significant: like many Scottish poets of the twentieth century, White regards historical Scotland, the Scotland 'marked by Calvinism, Victorianism, and an industrial revolution',[12] as a country not only 'bruised and numb',[13] but riven by 'Anglo-Scotic schizophrenia'.[14] It is a place which, *as a historical nation*, is incapable of providing support for creativity: that support has to come not from the nation's history but from the place's geography, from the 'attempt to get back into the living forest, the archaic ground':[15]

A country is that which offers resistance. The word itself says it, stemming as it does from *contra* (same thing in the German *Gegend*, region, district, which contains *gegen*, against). But in the course of time, the resistance wears down, the country gets covered with cliché and becomes couthy, or even cruddy. Alba is Scotland un-couthied, un-crudded, re-discovered. Scotland after all is a colonial term, and Scotland has been over-colonied. Post-colonial Scotland means getting back down to Alba, to original landscape-mindscape, and connecting them, wordscape.[16]

The business of the Scottish poet, then, is to get beyond existing Scotland – if necessary by leaving it altogether – and to discover another that will be 'devoid of romantic sentimentality, Gaelic piety and Lowland reductiveness – a ground we lost long ago, which went subterranean'.[17] Getting back to the ground demands, for White, both a cultural archaeology designed to find the fundamental forces of creativity that link apparently discrete environments – 'Over the years, I have come to see a connexion between Celtic naturalism, Eskimo vision, Siberian shamanism, Amerindian religion and Japanese Shinto continued into Zen'[18] – and an exploration of actual territories that have resisted the 'autobahn of Western civilization',[19] as, for instance, in these first three sections of 'On Rannoch Moor':[20]

> 1.
> Here, where the glacier started
> snow hardening into ice and
> slowly moving –
> sculpting the tertiary terrain.

> 2.
> This morning
> (a few millennia later)
> a chill wind blowing
> on original ground.

> 3.
> An erratic boulder
> let it be the centre
> from it, the eye travels
> tracing the circle . . .

The 'accidental' centre – from the viewpoint of history – is the real centre for poetry because it provides a place of vision – 'the eye travels' – from which can be discovered an 'original ground':

> 9.
> On this plateau
> has taken place

the ultimate union
of matter and space.

The merely historical 'unions' in which the state of Scotland has existed are
irrelevant in comparison to this 'ultimate union' of which its landscape is a
symbol. At this level the local and universal are one, since 'poetry signifies
the transcendence of individual conscience and the introduction to a world
(a cosmos, a beautiful whole in movement)'.[21] The search for this transcendence is best conducted at the margins of the defined territory of the nation:
the Ayrshire coast of his boyhood explorations; Pau, in the Pyrenees, on the
borders of France and Spain and the Basque country, where he lived in the
1970s; Brittany and the Atlantic coast, where he has been settled since 1983.
These are places where national culture peters out and where the messages
come not from an economically-driven state but from beyond the limits of
the human world:

The sounding of the silence here
is a *kerrak-rrok-rrok*
pronounced by dark birds

the endless emptiness of the sky
is filled with slowmoving cloud
from the open ocean

meditation is and is not the name for what goes on

a single, sun-bright concentration
while a thousand blue waves break on the horizon.[22]

The 'open ocean' is an opening through which it is possible to glimpse the
world as it is in itself, in its 'silence', before it submits to the imposition of
human meanings: to rediscover that ground it is necessary to escape the
ground as defined by the nation.

Because of his French literary success, and his French domicile, White's
presentation of his relationship to Scotland and its culture may have its own
particular emphases but its structure is, in fact, very familiar: like Edwin
Muir, he rejects the Calvinist–Industrial complex of modern Scotland in
favour of an alternative, more archetypal Scotland; like Neil Gunn, he
gathers inspiration from Celtic sources that are seen as closely linked to
Eastern religions; like MacDiarmid, he seeks a poetry of erudition – 'A
poetry concerned with all that is needed / Of the sum of human knowledge
and expression'[23] – that engages with the languages of Scotland in order to
come to terms with the fact that

What happens to us
Is irrelevant to the world's geology
But what happens to the world's geology
Is not irrelevant to us.[24]

So poem III of *Walking the Coast* hails the gulls – 'ah, the gulls:' – in their many Scots forms:

baagies bluemaws aulins badochs
goos scutiallans
cobbies and scarts

This list concludes with a name – *weathergaw* – which recalls MacDiarmid's first poem in Scots – 'The Watergaw' – and invokes the new science of chaos with the same sense of revelation with which MacDiarmid, in 'On a Raised Beach', declared that 'All is lithogenesis':[25]

swabies
tarrocks and weathergaws –
all haphazardly manoeuvring
a hymn to chaoticism
out in the wind
and the lifting waters
and myself there maybe no more
staring from my mind's wide-open door[26]

White's invocation of the 'mind's wide-open door' echoes MacDiarmid's vision of the stones on his raised beach – 'I know their gates are open too, / Always open, far longer open, than any bird's can be'[27] – and invokes, too, the bird imagery which MacDiarmid uses as a symbol of mind's flight into otherness: 'For an instant I seemed to see into the bird's mind / And to thrill with its own exhilaration of assured safety.'[28] White's self-conscious location of his own work as a continuation of MacDiarmid's later poetry ('It is a *difficult* area. MacDiarmid talked about it and certainly knew it'),[29] and of Gunn's work (in whose writings 'there is not only the motivation of my own early work, but its leitmotivs. It was full of cold images, in particular that of the gull, and was based on the triple notion of primordial contact, ecstatic experience and the search for a logic, a language to make it last'),[30] effectively situate him as the true descendant of the Scottish Renaissance. Or, rather, as a descendant of the *true* Scottish Renaissance – one defined not by MacDiarmid's adoption of an assertive nationalism projected through 'synthetic Scots' but White's insistence on a 'movement back to the ancient Gaelic classics and then North to Iceland and then East to Persia and India' as 'the course the refluence of

Gaelic genius must take'.[31] For White, the Scottish Renaissance of synthetic
Scots promotes 'work that is obviously enough Scottish, but shows no sign of
what he is recommending' in terms of work of 'a certain scope and height'.[32]
This contradiction between MacDiarmid's agenda for poetry and his agenda
for Scotland, between his universalism and his nationalism, is one that White
exploits to situate himself as the successor of MacDiarmid's truly ambitious
poetic project, formulated in *In Memoriam James Joyce*, a book White read as
a student in Glasgow in the 1950s:

> the poetry I seek
> Must be the work of one who has always known
> That the Tarim Valley is of more importance
> Than Jordan or the Rhine in world history.[33]

If the *real* Scottish Renaissance is defined by MacDiarmid's work rather
than his assertions, then it is to be found in the poetry of his later period,
a poetry of

> the artful tessellation of commonplaces
> Expressed with so exact a magnificence
> That they seem – and sometimes are – profound.[34]

Such poetry is not something new and disconnected from its Scottish
context, however, because it is already predicted by, or founded upon, an
earlier Scottish Renascence, the one inspired by the work of Patrick Geddes
in the 1890s. Geddes represents for White the generalising, totalising intellect that refuses to limit itself to the empirical and atomising tendencies of
institutional forms of knowledge in the modern age. Geddes, who challenged
Darwinian conceptions of evolution because they failed to acknowledge the
evolutionary advantage provided by a species committed to community and
to love, offers White an intellectual ground not only committed to rethinking humanity's relationship with its environment but also with one already
constructed from a Franco-Scottish interaction, since Geddes's theories
developed from the work of the French sociologist and anarchist, Frederic
le Play. In Geddes, White finds conceptions of an alternative trajectory
for Western civilisation which foreshadows – in a way that MacDiarmid's
Marxism could not – his own conception of 'geopoetics':

> Paleotechnics [industrial society] meant waste of natural resources, blighted
> landscapes, pandemoniac cities full of factories, offices, slums and stunted
> human lives. Neotechnics meant the use of non-polluting energy and the
> attempt to reunite utility with beauty, city with landscape. Biotechnics would
> promote new life thinking, leading to more developed human lives, more

expanded psyches. As to geotechnics, it was the means for human beings to learn how to really and fully inhabit the earth.[35]

Geddes had defined the ground on which MacDiarmid's Marxism and Gunn's Celticism, with their rejection of urban, industrial civilisation as the end and aim of human progress, had been built: but for White the task is to get back to that ground and to define it outwith the assumption of the national historical trajectory that still haunts MacDiarmid's and Gunn's rejection of modernity. In Geddes's work, it is the region and its cultural inheritance that is crucial, rather than the nation, and a region is defined by the geological structure of the land and the work that that imposes and makes possible for human beings, by the relation of country to city, and of city to river and sea. It is the regionalism of Geddes's 'Scottish Renascence' rather than the nationalism of MacDiarmid's to which White is inheritor, a renascence more concerned with Celtic traditions of identification with the land than with the construction of a proletarian society or the adoption of 'synthetic Scots'. 'If Geddes was and is mainly known as a town-planner, a city-surveyor,' White comments, 'he was also looking to a new exodus into "the outside world", that of the other animals, of plants and rocks':

> ... perhaps one who knows
> even one rock thoroughly
> in all its idiosyncrasy
> and relatedness
> to sea and sky
> is better fit to speak
> to another human being
> than one who lives and rots perpetually
> in a crowded society
> that teaches him
> nothing essential.[36]

What Geddes sought, White was also determined to find, 'a great "single discipline", which is "complex indeed, but no more a mere maze than a mere chaos" and which leads to "a single presentment of the world", "a growing Cosmos, a literal Uni-verse".'[37]

Placing Geddes's 'Renascence' at the core of the project of MacDiarmid's 'Renaissance', allows us to see, perhaps, a pattern in the development of twentieth-century Scottish art that the traditional focus on MacDiarmid's linguistic experiments in the 1920s conceals. For Geddes, modern art should not derive – as it did for much of English-language Modernism – from the aestheticism of 'art for art's sake', with its assumption of the autotelic autonomy of the art work. This could lead only to the 'decadence' which Geddes's 'Renascence'

aimed at transforming by reintegrating art back into the active life of community – as in his resuscitation of the 'masque' as a celebration of communal
life.[38] Such art allowed its human actors to be, quite literally, reinformed by
their cultural traditions and through those traditions reconnected with their
environment. It was such a reconnection that J. D. Fergusson, Scotland's
leading visual artist in the first half of the twentieth century who worked in
Paris before World War One, believed Cubism to have made possible, because
its abstract forms were not simply the expression of Parisian modernity but a
return to the abstract art forms of the Celts. For Fergusson, modern art was not
founded on urban cosmopolitanism but rather in 'the atavistic unconscious',
which 'provides a formidable extension to the individual's experience, and it
is not surprising that most of the world's best artistic work proves on examina-
tion to be, not cosmopolitan, however international its appeal, but racial and
national'.[39] Such a return to a Celtic 'atavistic unconscious' has two related
consequences which might be seen as shaping a tradition of Scottish writing
influenced by Geddes's conception of 'Renascence': first, it directs attention to
the environment and to an alternative conception of our relationship with it,
one for which Celtic culture stands as an emblem; second, it produces a crisis
of language, since the English language can never be 'at home' in that recu-
perated environment. That crisis of language can be seen in the work of poets
like Norman MacCaig and W. S. Graham, as well as in White's work, and its
consequence can perhaps be seen most clearly in the work of Ian Hamilton
Finlay, who describes his move into concrete poetry and then into garden art
as resulting from 'the extraordinary (since wholly unexpected) sense that the
syntax I had been using, *the movement* of language in me, at a physical level,
was no longer there – so it had to be replaced with something else'.[40] To turn
to – or return to – the garden as the environment of poetry is a rooted equivalent of White's travels at the margins of modernity: it makes art, as Geddes
would have believed, consequential upon action, dependent on interaction
with an environment recreated or rediscovered as a tradition. In Finlay's art,
language is always environmental, dependent for its significance on its place,
whether on the page or in the garden. The garden poet is engaged in 'a revolution of the word'[41] not by its deconstruction, but by its relocation. In 'Autumn
Poem' of 1966, for instance, Finlay not only fractures words, but sets them in a
picture of a faded square of earthclods and leaves:

Turn
-ing
o-
ver

the
earth

This kind of turning over, which the gardener does in preparing ground for planting, is then juxtaposed with another phrase which is set in a circle that looks like cloud and land on an earth seen from space:

the
earth

turn
-ing
o-
ver [42]

The word 'earth' changes its meaning depending on context but the two contexts reveal the interdependence of the earth turning over, and earth being turned over. Language has be put back *in place* to become properly meaningful, and when it is put back in place it forces us to engage not just with the poem as a linguistic structure but the poem as a relationship to an environment, a demand for engagement with the environment. (The garden in which Finlay's poem-sculptures are set has to be maintained by effort if the works are to remain meaningful.) The crisis of language that afflicts this tradition of Scottish poets demands a going beyond language into action, and, like Hamilton Finlay's transformation of a once bleak hillside in the southern uplands into a recuperation of the whole history of European gardens, a refusal to accept the environment that history has imposed on us.

It is a similar refusal that defines White's 'open world', a world released from the directionality of history, a world open to the possibility of a higher integration that escapes the categories of our historically-constituted intellectual disciplines. Poetry is the medium of this engagement because poetry has always remained outside the assumptions that have driven all the other disciplines that we have inherited from the Enlightenment. Those disciplines take history as the 'ground' upon which knowledge is constructed, whereas, for White, it is precisely the movement beyond, to the side of, out of the way of that ground that will allow us to discover the real ground of knowledge. White 'peregrinates' casually, randomly, apparently without direction, in order to encounter a world, a ground, that has been bypassed by the determined purposiveness of history. The apparently casual title of *Walking the Coast*, the best of his long poems, points to precisely this rejection of the way of history for the path of geology, for submitting himself to the shapes produced by the collision between the elemental territories of our natural world:

Like this rock now before me
    Facing the tide

An outcrop
      Of dark grey sandstone
      (so the ones on which
            as children
we chiselled our signs)
with a blaze
      of white granite
running right through it –

understand this, poet.[43]

To understand this poet we have to grasp his relationship to rocks, to sea; and we have to see his work as an attempt to discover the 'blaze / of white granite' that runs through modernity, that will not be eroded and that is impervious to merely human signs.

This is the paradox on which 'White poetics' is based: that 'poetry' in its real sense is the medium of our connection with that which is necessarily beyond all language. As he puts it in 'Tractatus Cosmo-Poeticus',

it is difficult
to avoid drawing distinctions and conclusions
so pleasant
to enter an area
beyond the climate of opinion
and over-particularized existence
where the less you say
the more is said

I think of a room in Otterthal
And snow drifting
Across a silent window frame.[44]

Otterhal is the town in which Ludwig Wittgenstein, having given up philosophy, was fulfilling the injunction of his own *Tractatus* that 'whereof you cannot speak, thereof you must remain silent'. White's poetics reverses Wittgenstein's scrupulous limitation of language by daring to speak in order to bring us into contact with silence:

A bird yell
emptied my skull

ricks of hay
lined the fields

a fishing smack
lay at quiet anchor

it was Kyle of Tongue
on a blue morning.[45]

On the Kyle of Tongue, the tongue is silent and yet the landscape speaks, and speaks the language beyond language that its epigraph – 'Fuzeshin, fuzebutsu, fuzemotsu' – invokes from the text *The Gateless Gate*: 'Neither mind, neither Buddha, nor a thing'.[46] The very title of White's collected poems – *Open World* – enacts the paradox, the 'O' being the blank, the zero before the 'pen' inscribes meanings on it. This is why – to the vast annoyance of some commentators – he finds everywhere the 'white' of his own name as the ground upon which the world is inscribed:

> Always the metaphysical landscape
>   but more and more abstract
>   yet more abrupt
>   where the farthest of unrealities
>   are the reality
> and life
>   that dancing flurry
> that line of white
>   that incandescent edge
>   advancing
>   beyond meaning and problem.[47]

The 'line of white' that is 'beyond meaning' is what the poetic line – the black line on the white background – is forever seeking, but what it finds, necessarily, is a 'mindscape' as well as a 'landscape', the ground of the transcendental self as well as the ground of an external reality. White's sculptural use of typography in the distribution of the lines, with their continual displacement from a fixed point of beginning, make the reading eye aware both of the 'white' on which they are defined, and the intervention of the White who has defined them. Poet and poem move through self-development towards a self-erasure that will also be a revelation of meaning beyond language:

> Now I have burnt all my knowledge
> and am learning to live with the whiteness naked
>
> what I call art now is nothing made
> but the pure pathology of my body and mind
>
> at the heart of a terrible and joyous world.[48]

To some this is a poetics that can never become a poetry, since the poetry can only gesture towards meanings which it cannot communicate,[49] but for White such conceptions of poetry reduce it to 'an ego-limited conscience, with more or less skill, taste, sensitivity, etc.'.[50] Poetry, real poetry, has, for White, a broader and a deeper significance, for it is the response to a world in which 'the mind cries out for unity, for a unitive experience', it is the 'desire of a whole world',[51] and, as such, it is an act which is more than linguistic – a 'sheer experience of the nakedness and loveliness of everything, an ecstatic existence, expanding to the sense of cosmic unity'.[52] The achievement of this experience depends on being able to come close to the thingness of the world, its *thisness* – what Duns Scotus called its *haecceitas* – but that individuality is precisely what language, in its ordinary operation, refuses, since language brings the uniqueness of individual things into general categories – not this specific, unique tree but *a* tree, one of a type. To enter the 'white world' is, as in 'Letter to an Old Calligrapher', to circumvent this abstracting function of language itself:

A hundred days
along shore and mountain

with eye open
for heron and cormorant

now writing this
at the world's edge

in a silence become
a second nature

coming to know
in brain and in bone

the path of emptiness.[53]

As a linguistic structure the poem is a 'second nature', a duplication of the real, but behind the linguistic structure is another 'second nature', the second nature of 'silence', of the end of language and division and the beginning of unity.

In the 1970s and 1980s, these 'white poetics' aligned Kenneth White with the reconceptualisation of the relationship of modern thought to the past of Western culture that characterised the work of Foucault, Deleuze and Derrida, and which can be traced to the influence of Edmund Husserl and Martin Heidegger, and through Heidegger to the Nietzsche by whom White was obsessed in his early years as a student in Glasgow. Nietzsche's demand for a transcendence of the Christian tradition and a recovery of the tragic world that was last experienced in ancient Greece, re-emerged in Husserl and Heidegger as the dismissal of the history of Western philosophy as a mistake, a mistake which could only be corrected by getting back to pre-Socratic insights in order to begin again:

> hare pads
> lightning flash
> written rocks
> begin again.[54]

Husserl, according to White, identified the rise of philosophy in ancient Greece as the beginning of a destructive dislocation of humanity from its engagement with a whole world:

> What happened in the modern age was that rationality turned into rationalism, which means, among other things, a loss of the sense of world, a culture that rings more and more hollow (hardly helped by periodical attempts to give it more substance via naturalism, social realism or oneiric fantasy), and a proliferation of narrow specialities. How that move from 'full world' and knowledge of whole being to 'objective world', unilateral conceptions and endless series of sterile research came about is the history of Western philosophy, to which Husserl devoted a great deal of his thinking and teaching.[55]

White's poetry can be read as a dramatisation of that philosophical effort to undo the destructiveness of Western tradition, not only by an engagement with Eastern religious philosophies but by a return to European origins before the baleful effects of philosophy took hold:

> I'm idiomatic
> I'm idiosyncratic
>
> I'm pre-socratic.[56]

The means of that return to origins White attributes to his discovery of shamanism, a discovery both biographical – his childhood creation of a hut which formed a kind of shrine full of magic objects – and intellectual, in his reading of Mircea Eliade's Shamanism – The Archaic Techniques of Ecstasy (1970):

> As I read through that book, I came across more and more correspondences between what he was laying out and my own early experience. In other words, I had stumbled on to shamanism, had practised a kind of home-made shamanism, that is, an immemorial tradition going back to neolithic, paleolithic and

prelithic times, elements of which can be found all over the world . . . This isn't really so surprising as it may sound. It's almost certain that, given enough scope, enough freedom, a child will go though all the past phases of humanity, from fishes to philosophers.[57]

Shamanism is, for White, one of the elements of Celtic tradition, so that both in his person and in his cultural inheritance he is able to re-enact the search for a new totality that Heidegger illustrates though a saying of Heraclitus: 'The familiar abode is for man the open region for the presencing of god (the unfamiliar one).'[58] The shaman is he who makes the gods, the unfamiliar ones, present themselves; he gives voice to that which lives beyond the boundaries of the community, thereby 'giving it breathing space'.[59] The shamanism through which White discovered the 'open world' connects directly, as his meditation on 'Heidegger at Home' reveals, to Husserl and Heidegger's effort to get back beyond Socratic philosophy:

> On the steep slope
> of a mountain valley
> a little chalet
> eighteen feet by twenty
>
> all around
> meadow and pinewood
>
> when snow surrounded the house
> *that* was the time for philosophy:
> following all those
> secret, silent paths
> till cogitation turned into sight
>
> like this high summer morning
> and two hawks gliding
> round and round
> in the absolute light.[60]

The poem, ironically entitled 'Black Forest', travels from the ordinary world – in which poetry is characterised by mere rhyme: 'valley', 'chalet' – towards that transcendence in which 'being' steps forth 'into the open region that lights the "between" within which a "relation" of subject to object can "be"'.[61] Such moments of revelation, however, are precisely the ones that allow us to know ourselves to be 'at home' in the world, despite the alienation that modern civilisation imposes on us: the 'white world', he tells us, is 'where poetry and metaphysics meet'.[62] Without that meeting 'culture, as Nietzsche foresaw, would go to the dogs, that is, to what he called the "last men", hideously productive, but creatively nil'.[63]

This challenge to Western metaphysics and the challenge of 'geopoetics' to the economism of modern civilisation – whether of the failed Marxism of 1968 or the neo-liberal 'free enterprise' of the 1980s – made White one of the leading spokespersons in French radical culture in the 1980s and 1990s. The work he produced in this period he divided into three different forms: 'way books', describing his travels on the margins of the modern world, essays, in which he sought to 'draw up a new mental cartography';[64] and poems, some short insights which he calls 'diamond-type' and longer 'peregrine' poems: 'I've likened this triple writing activity to the parts of an arrow: the essays are the feathers, giving direction; the way-books are the shaft, ongoing movement; and the poems are the arrow-head.'[65] For White, then, the poems do not stand alone, and the prose works are not simply occasional supplements: they form a single body of work (even though it is a body of work which is not – as yet – all available to the anglophone reader). White's very success in locating himself within the theoretical concerns of post-Heideggerian philosophy in France, however, may have alienated some of his anglophone critics, since, despite intense debates about Derrida's deconstruction or Deleuze's theory of difference, so-called 'continental philosophy' remains an alien realm to many British academics, let alone to a general readership. That this should be so is deeply ironic from a Scottish perspective, since German philosophy was largely introduced into British philosophy in the nineteenth century by Scots, from Thomas Carlyle in the 1830s to the dominance of Edward Caird's Kantianism at Oxford in the 1880s; and since the major translations of Kant, Hegel and, indeed, of Heidegger himself were all carried out by Scots (Norman Kemp Smith, William Wallace and John MacQuarrie respectively). In fact, Heidegger's earliest work was on Duns Scotus and Deleuze's was on David Hume, so that in engaging with this intellectual tradition White is actually re-engaging with an earlier phase of Scottish intellectual history, one that has been largely, and unjustly, disowned by contemporary commentators despite its considerable influence on the continent.[66] As a 'metaphysical' poet White can be seen as fulfilling what MacDiarmid himself regarded as one of the distinctive characteristics of Scottish poetry, and, as White points out in 'The High Field', MacDiarmid makes clear reference to Heideggerian philosophy in *In Memoriam James Joyce*:

Even so, Conscience calls the self of *Dasein*
Out of the state in which it is lost

. . .

To call the self back into the silence
Of the 'existent' potentiality of being.[67]

The direction of continental metaphysics cannot, therefore, be regarded as a direction *away* from Scotland: if anything, it is a challenge to White's readers to recover important but undervalued Scottish traditions.

What has taken White away from the mainstream of Scottish poetry, arguably, is not the content of his work but its style. Like many poets of the 1950s and 1960s in Britain, White found his voice not by imitating his British predecessors but by learning from transatlantic traditions. Unlike most of his contemporaries, however, it was not through Robert Lowell's or Sylvia Plath's confessional poetry that he found his own way, but through the radical poetics of an earlier American generation, through the work of Ezra Pound and William Carlos Williams, in which the traditional metrical or rhythmic 'line' of poetry is replaced with a typographic line which marks units of significant meaning, or by the line defined by the 'breath', by shapes of sound. It is in this radical poetics of visual structure shaped by the contours of the breath that White's work has developed:

> yet the mind moves here with ease
> advances into the emptiness
>
> *breathes*
>
> and line after line
> something like a universe
> lays itself out[68]

'Line after line' such poetry isolates each line as a breath which makes us pause over its reference and its connection, producing a poetry that is more mosaic than narrative even when it is apparently telling a story:

> *To the Bone*
>
> Hearing a bird cry
>
> back up there
> in the field behind Fairlie
>
> an autumn afternoon
> the air chill
> the gold sun turning red
>
> reality right to the bone.[69]

The title hesitates between an address – a poem invoking a bone – and the phrase which it will become at the poem's conclusion; the first line reads like a title, in its isolation from what follows; 'back up there' oscillates between time and place as 'right' hovers between 'justified' and 'essential'. Like William Carlos Williams, White turns the ordinary into the profound by unlocking the linear order of the sentence and replacing it with a visual order of breaths that produces, at its best, a mosaic of 'idea-energies'.[70] A poetry at once of the present and of presence:

> This is today
>   raised out of history [71]

CHAPTER TWELVE

Don Paterson

Alan Gillis

Don Paterson was born in Dundee in 1963. To date he has published five collections of verse: *Nil Nil* (1993), *God's Gift to Women* (1997), *The Eyes* (1999), *Landing Light* (2003) and *Orpheus* (2007).[1] He has also written several dramatic works (including four for radio), published two books of aphorisms, essays on poetic craft, and is a prolific editor and anthologist. He is one of the most lauded poets of his generation in Britain. Robert Crawford has written: '[Paterson's] sudden rise to pre-eminence . . . is as astounding as it is justly merited. Not since the work of Hugh MacDiarmid in the 1920s has Scottish poetry felt such a remarkable surge of marvellously controlled poetic language.'[2]

The first poem in *Nil Nil* is 'The Ferryman's Arms'.[3] It begins:

> About to sit down with my half-pint of Guinness
> I was magnetized by a remote phosphorescence
> and drawn, like a moth, to the darkened back room
> where a pool-table hummed to itself in the corner.
> With ten minutes to kill and the whole place deserted
> I took myself on for the hell of it.

As an introduction to Paterson's work, these lines are incisive. His pages are plagued by pulls towards recesses, the subconscious and negation, often figured through a play between darkness and light. The seemingly throwaway phrase of the sixth line could stand as Paterson's motto: 'I took myself on for the hell of it.'

The poem's speaker beats himself:

> I went on to make an immaculate clearance.
> A low punch with a wee dab of side, and the black
> did the vanishing trick while the white stopped
> before gently rolling back as if nothing had happened,
> shouldering its way through the unpotted colours.

The poem then casts its eyes beyond the bar, turning to the symbolic freight of its title:

> The boat chugged up to the little stone jetty
> without breaking the skin of the water, stretching,
> as black as my stout, from somewhere unspeakable
> to here, where the foaming lip mussitates endlessly,
> trying, with a mutter's persistence, to read
> and re-read the shoreline. I got aboard early,
> remembering the ferry would leave on the hour
> even for only my losing opponent;
> but I left him there, stuck in his tent of light, sullenly
> knocking the balls in, for practice, for next time.

Patrick Crotty has rightly hailed this display of what he calls Paterson's 'extraordinary facility for embedding mythical materials in familiar locales', praising the poem's 'beautifully precise conjuring' in bringing 'the waters of Leith and Lethe to effortless confluence'.[4] Indeed, it becomes impossible to separate the quotidian from the symbolic. The black and white of the half-pint of Guinness (which would be colloquially termed, at least in parts of Ireland, a half-pint of 'double') finds its echo in the play of black and white balls on the pool table (the speaker sinks the black on two levels). The manner in which the colours are left untouched hints at how the realm of the chromatic – what Paterson calls the realm of 'mundane and quotidian diffraction, where all the stories, the details and the differences are' – will frequently be pierced through, in the existential x-ray of his verse, to explore underlying black-and-white binaries.[5] Meanwhile, the Guinness finds its fullest double in the black waters outside. As the speaker drinks his half-pint (implying 'foaming lips'), the 'foaming lips' of the briny shore take on a kind of symbolic sensibility, stretching from 'somewhere unspeakable / to here', bent towards the seemingly intractable task of making sense of the shoreline, of the palpable here-and-now.

The speaker seems happy to board the ferry, victoriously leaving his doppelganger behind. Yet he ends up in the arms of the ferryman, on his way from 'here' to 'somewhere unspeakable' on black waters, leaving behind his double 'stuck in his tent of light'. The irony seems open-ended. The game has turned into a tussle for the soul, of white and light against darkness. Clearly, the speaker feels he has won. But who has ended up better off? The poem has split into two realms: the familiar, solid world of pub, half-pint and pool game; and a more mysterious symbolic realm. But which realm is the 'real' one, and which the mythic?

In the popular imagination, Charon the ferryman stands as a grim reaper, transporting us from the realm of life to the realm of death. More particularly, in *The Aeneid*, Charon distinguishes between the restful dead and the tormented dead. Because the Underworld is the natural place for the dead, and not a realm of punishment, it is much better to be on board Charon's ferry than not (once you are dead, that is).[6] Meanwhile, in Dante's *Inferno*, Charon transports the dead to Hell, rather than the Underworld. Perhaps less believably, this is also a good thing, because the sinful dead, we are told, naturally choose and desire Hell. Here, the banks of the river (now the Acheron, rather than the Styx) are again thronged with sufferers in a terrible state of limbo.[7] Those left behind by Charon, in Dante's poem, are 'so-so' fence-sitters: the indifferent, those who never did good or bad; and they are joined by the angels who were neither for God nor for Satan, when it mattered, but who stayed neutral to look after themselves. Dante writes of them: 'These grey people have no hope of death; / so low and wretched is their blind existence.'[8] Again, then, it's actually better to be in the arms of the ferryman than not, even if this is a rather twisted scenario. But most crucially, Aeneas and Dante, in these respective poems, are granted an unusual concession. Normally the living are barred from the ferryman's arms. To be permitted aboard Charon's boat is to receive a privileged poetic passport into realms customarily kept from mortal knowledge. The pilgrimages of Aeneas and Dante endow their respective poems with a totality of vision beyond everyday perception and experience.

As such, the first poem of Paterson's first book announces a serious ambition. If we follow the allusive trail of Charon, we can say the poem's persona has indeed won a victory. He has left behind another version of himself in an artificially-lit limbo of perpetual torment, a realm of 'so-so' shiftless banality. The persona may be heading towards 'somewhere unspeakable', but this is better than being imprisoned in a one-dimensional here and now. From this perspective, the poem suggests our everyday world already constitutes a kind of death-realm. Writing on Rilke's *Die Sonette An Orpheus*, Paterson writes: 'Man is probably unique amongst the mammals in that he has conscious foreknowledge of his own death. Knowing he will die means he acts, in part, as if he were already dead.'[9] He continues: 'The Sonnets imply that how well a man or woman deals with their twin citizenship determines the degree of their authenticity.' Ultimately, 'the answer is to live in the heart of the paradox itself, to form a stereoscopic view of the world with one eye in the land of the living and one eye in the land of the dead, in the breathing present and in atemporal eternity.'[10]

In 'The Ferryman's Arms' the persona leaves the light for the darkness (one of Paterson's aphorisms reads: 'We turn from the light to see').[11] Symbolically, his poems will traverse the continuum between our habitual reality and its 'unspeakable' shadows, in order to voice themselves authentically. Negation is a necessity. Paterson argues that we spend most of our time lost in a dream in which 'everywhere we look, we see the world purely in the highly restricted synecdoche of its human *use*.'[12] He claims: 'We live in a human dream; being one in which everything appears purely in the guise of its human utility.'[13] In this potentially catastrophic hallucination, our dream 'becomes so heavily constructed and all-pervasive that we begin to mistake it for our element'.[14] As such, one of the poet's primary functions is the age-old task of making the normal and habitual appear newly strange. Paterson writes: 'Every evening, part of me still wants to rush into the Street screaming "Jesus, can't you people see? It's getting *dark* . . . "'[15]

However, a crucial aspect of 'The Ferryman's Arms' remains its verisimilitude. Paterson is one of the most precise and effective engineers of grounded context, detail and atmosphere in British verse since Philip Larkin. He has stated: '[A]stonishment, in the mind of the reader, always works from the familiar to the unfamiliar, as gravity works from the ground up. There must always be a little of the quotidian to contextualise the omen, shock or surprise.'[16] The familiarity of the beginning of 'The Ferryman's Arms' endows the poem with its matter of fact, 'it could happen to you' credibility. It enables the poem to suggest that the here and now is *always* infected; that the continuum between here and 'somewhere unspeakable' is an ever-present shadow.

Another key to the success of the poem is the ambivalent tilt and angle with which it lifts the veil. The poem's open-ended ambiguity ensures there can be no clear-cut moral distinction between realms (the light seems bad, the dark seems better, but it is difficult to be certain). Indeed, the full impact of the poem relies on the contradictory sense that the 'opponent' left behind in the 'tent of light' is a kind of ideal self inhabiting a kernel of inviolate truth. [17]

A further pivotal aspect of the poem is its revelation of a bifurcation, a split between realms, *within* a seamless and measured continuum. At a basic level, the persona has merely taken himself on; the split is an internalised one. But splits or sutures within apparent wholes are explored throughout Paterson's work more broadly. The title *Nil Nil* itself suggests a bifurcated and dualistic nullity. The book's original cover featured an illustration of a goalpost with its crossbar snapped, serving up an impression of structure and symmetry that is fractured. This crack in the crossbar calls to mind the missing dash one would find in a football score: 'Nil–Nil'. In turn, this title speaks, not just of stalemate and banality, but of a stasis which has resulted from play, energy, competition and, in a sense, conflict.[18] In any case, in his poems, the structure is as important as the fracture; one cannot exist without the other.

In such a manner, Paterson's poems tend to be dramatically poised, their meanings refracted through contradictions, tonal reverberations, inflections and connotations. The quotidian and the symbolic, truth and delusion, black and white, positive and negative: these are not structured oppositions, but are more ambivalently and intimately intertwined. His great success as a poet is bound up with the manner in which this antinomical aesthetic surges from the foundations upwards; it is never imposed or didactic. Matter and anti-matter seethe into one another at a virtually physical level. As such, the revelation of a poem such as 'The Ferryman's Arms' is not experienced as enlightenment, but rather as a removal of the ground from under our feet.

With typical cheer, Joseph Conrad wrote in *Lord Jim*: '[O]nly a meticulous precision of statement would bring out the true horror behind the appalling face of things.'[19] In such a spirit, through the concision of Paterson's verisimilitude, something more than the mere establishment of a solid bedrock to the lyric ground occurs. In 'The Ferryman's Arms', the pool table humming to itself introduces an abiding concern, throughout Paterson's oeuvre, with the quiddity and haecceity of things, which frequently surfaces in such a way that the object world is rendered with some unnerving and inscrutable form of agency, or spectral menace. In lines not quoted above from 'The Ferryman's Arms', while the speaker's back is turned, the pool table seemingly operates itself. This nods, of course, towards a phantasmagorical trope of the common ghost story, creating an uncanny ambience. But it also introduces a central motif in Paterson's poetic regarding the world's essential lack of solidity. As the poem puts it: 'physics itself becomes something negotiable.'[20]

Throughout Paterson's poems, the otherness of things feeds into a broadly malevolent sense of alienation sprung, not only from the disorientation of everyday experience, but also from the estrangement of mundane things in themselves – from physical objects, rooms, houses, towns – in a chain of dissolution that ultimately registers an enduring sense of how all objects and subjects are constantly breaking down to the vibrating mass of particles and entropic energy that constitutes their innermost and unknowable reality. Paterson writes: 'Almost everything in the room will survive you. To the room, you are already a ghost, a pathetic soft thing, coming and going.'[21] In 'The White Lie', the crowning poem of *Landing Light*, we read:

> But consider this: that when we leave the room,
> The chair, the bookend or the picture-frame
> We had frozen by desire or spent desire
> Is reconsumed in its estranging fire.[22]

In a poem, of course, the physical world and the world of the mind are both manifested through the selfsame medium. To focus, for a short moment, merely on diction: listen again to 'mussitates' from 'The Ferryman's Arms'. Such a word could not fail to have an aesthetic effect, helping to occasion this poem's preternatural shift from the everyday to the symbolic. The word's basic strangeness in itself augurs an indefinite but uncanny significance of tone and mood. To mussitate is to mutter, so the word is supremely apt: its denotation chimes with the 'nutter's persistence, to read / and re-read the shoreline'. But the word also *sounds* like it should mean 'suffocates'; it *seems* redolent of the effects of a disease or infection. Compellingly, Paterson has written of the synaesthetic aspect of a lyric poem's connotative power, describing it as a bodily, sensual, morphing, indeterminate field of force.[23] In such a way, the word 'mussitates' pivotally affects the tenor of the dark water stretching 'from somewhere unspeakable / to here'. The word indicates how the object world and the world of speculative thought almost melt into one another, when Paterson is at his best, through the 'estranging fire' of his language. When mediated through the virtuosity of his lyric craft, the physical becomes mental, and the mental becomes physical.

Paterson's poetry is notable for the intensity with which its poems are clamped to their particulars. The manner in which they play indefinite and disturbing suggestion off detailed but askew imagery is striking, and their absorption in peculiar detail creates an ambivalence through which they evoke deeper significance. Or, rather, their weird specificity seems confidently pitched to suggest such deeper significance, but this often remains unfixed, lurking below, or beyond, or within, their alternately supple and gnarled textures. When successful, this has the effect of infusing the slanted detail of the verse with an unspecified but teeming charge of imminent revelation, the quality and substance of which is affected by every minute detail, every nuance of tone. At their best, his poems create an affecting sense of a multiplicitous, contradictory, disturbed and contoured backdrop against which, it is implied, the ludic surface of existence plays itself out.

To be sure, some early poems are too compressed and coiled to uncork in the reader's consciousness. *Nil Nil* is striking, at times, for abstruse and rebarbative qualities which, in places, seem overcooked, but which infiltrate to the core of the book's overall tenor, as casual menace is expressed through nihilistic fantasias in aggressively hermetic fusions of audacity and opacity. And so, if we are sometimes left in the dark, this is, at least, a violently charged, pungently eroticised, hallucinogenic darkness, and the opaque poems do create an atmosphere of violation and foreboding which vitally seeps into the book's invigorating successes.

Discomposing sexuality, class inequality, urban deprivation, metaphysical angst and existential violence: these are all sources of alienation, aggression, estrangement, or the 'unspeakable' in Paterson's early poems. Most often, the speakers of the poems are dramatic personae, precluding the reader from assuming a straight relationship with the poetic voice. The most forthright example of this occurs at the end of 'An Elliptical Stylus'.[24] The poem tells of how the speaker joined his father in visiting a shop to buy a better needle for their 'beat-up Phillips turntable' to enhance its sound quality ('music billowed into three dimensions / as if we could have walked between the players'). On reaching the shop:

> We had the guy in stitches: 'You can't . . .
> er . . . you'll have to *upgrade your equipment.*'
> Still smirking, he sent us from the shop
> with a box of needles, thick as carpet-tacks,
> the only sort they made to fit our model.

The final stanza ends with father and son driving home 'slowly, as if we had a puncture', with 'that man's laugh / stuck in my head'. However, the poem then self-reflexively breaks off; pointedly refusing to go where the reader might have expected. The poem insists it will not

> cauterize this fable
> with something axiomatic on the nature
> of articulacy and inheritance.

It ends:

> But if you still insist on resonance –
> I'd swing for him, and every other cunt
> happy to let my father know his station,
> which probably includes yourself. To be blunt.

By so turning against the reader, Paterson turns the poem on its head. What else is such a poem for, if not 'something axiomatic on the nature / of articu-lacy and inheritance'?

The poem makes clear that classic working-class *inarticulacy* is not what has been inherited, because this poem is manifestly another consummate display of lyric craft. Strikingly, a parenthetical stanza gives us the poem the speaker might have written if he had been the smirking salesman's son. In other words, with a sophisticated formal spin, the speaker shows a deft ability to empathise with different perspectives and imagine different roles, which is precisely what is being refused the reader. The poem has its cake and eats it. In many ways, the poem's aesthetic poise is itself a retrospective 'swing' for the salesman. Yet this is not enough, and the poem reverts to a stereotypical response of aggression. The poem wants to out-articulate you, the reader, and then perhaps swing for you anyway.

The overriding effect is to give us a voice which arrestingly declaims its otherness, not through overt formal disjunctiveness or hermetic stylistic dis-order, but through lyric skill and poise. The poem's apparently confessional style would seem to *depend* upon readerly identification, which makes the snub of its ending more jarring. Because 'something axiomatic on the nature / of articulacy and inheritance' is being refused, the private realm is kept private and uncorrupted. Inheritance and familial bonds are laid bare, but, precisely because they are not open for discussion, they are kept pure, in their own 'tent of light', as it were. And yet, in a double movement, the poem's rhetorical turn also wields a sucker-punch of hurt and anger about implied shame. The split or bifurcation opening out to the 'unspeakable' has again happened *within* the seams of the 'normal'. When the reader is instructed to think again, at the end of the poem, the disturbance to his or her habitual presumptions, the jolt to 'the dream', is all the more troublesome, even as the poem invigorates with its primal, contradictory cussedness. The crucial effect is that the emotional and psychological scars of alienation, the schisms and ruptures of class inequality, are not related passively. Instead, through the poem's turn against the reader, they become a dynamic and active experience.

Another poem, 'Amnesia', also shows fissures opened by class, memory and change.[25] It opens with a startling scene of glossolalia:

> my eyes rolled back to show the whites, my arms
> outstretched in catatonic supplication
> while I gibbered impeccably in the gorgeous tongues
> of the aerial orders.

This strangely savage evangelism melds with scenes of impoverishment and degraded sexuality: 'The room was ripe with gurry and old sweat' (gurry is either diarrhoea or fish-offal). We hear of a blind evangelist who dies in squalor 'above the fishmonger's', whose

> eyes had been put out before the war,
> just in time to never see the daughter
> with the hare-lip and the kilt of dirty dishtowels
> who ran the brothel from the upstairs flat.

This, in turn, is juxtaposed with a scene from 'four years later', where the same building has been transformed through (knowingly arch) student-like affectations:

> Smouldering frangipani;
> Dali's *The Persistence of Memory*
> . . .
> a sheaf of Penguin Classics,
> their spines all carefully broken in the middle.

The 'Amnesia' of the title would seem to refer to the gap between the two scenarios. Although it would be heavy-handed, we might take this as a kind of allegory for how a bourgeois and recognisably 'normalised' contemporary Scottish culture emerges from, and overlaps awkwardly with, more retrograde and impoverished sectors. The poem ends with a character, Sue, complaining: '*It was a nightmare, Don. We had to gut the place.*' However, the nightmare of the past and of the unpalatable persists: it cannot quite be gutted. In the second section, the speaker describes his actions:

> One hand was jacked up her skirt, the other trailing
> over the cool wall behind the headboard
> where I found the hole in the plaster again.

Having been gouged in the first section, this hole in the plaster forms a kind of portal between the two realities of past and present. But, crucially, so does the speaker. His nonchalant hand 'jacked up her skirt' nods back to his earlier patronage of the hare-lipped and dirty dishtowel-kilted daughter's brothel (he 'earnestly' paid with his bus-fare). First and foremost, then, the poem presents an odd disjunction between realms (this time socio-economic and historical). But at the same time, these realms overlap in a peculiarly uncanny manner. Specifically, they overlap through the speaker's predacious sexuality. This, in turn, renders both realms somehow fraudulent; or, at least, it gives each a kind of indefinite, unsettled edge.

A central trope in Paterson's work is the disconcerting mask of the Lothario. The casual braggadocio and venereal intent voiced by a string of his sexually charged personae introduce a distinctive element rare in contemporary verse. His most immediate precursor in this respect is surely Paul Muldoon, whose *Quoof*, in particular, was so marked by misogynistic sexual violence.[26] *Quoof* explored masculine menace and volatility in a context in which Northern Irish political violence and the pathologies of fundamentalism overlapped with the sexual mores of contemporary culture. Innocent of such a particular context, Paterson's work bracingly explores the pathology of male sexuality more generally. The sexual edge and anxiety of his verse springs from supposed normality.

In this sense, the obsessive and phobic sexuality of his verse returns to the fundamental roots of the love lyric, re-introducing the predatory sensibility of much Renaissance and Restoration verse. Driven by 'the imperatives of sex and Calvinism', at times, his poems are racked and riddled with angst, disgust and cruelty.[27] Indeed, you probably need to return to early T. S. Eliot to see carnality handled with such loathing. At other times, however, his poetry gobsmacks with erotic intimations of assuagement, grace and beauty. At all times, sexuality is an unsettlement.

Like the more abstracted negation figured by the dark waters of 'The Ferryman's Arms', and like the class inequality of 'An Elliptical Stylus', the split between body and mind becomes a weapon, in Paterson's verse, used to violate habitual normality. No moment, no thought, no act of love, no social engagement, no representation of self – indeed, nothing touched by human-ity – is ever neutral. And, as 'Amnesia' suggests, this perpetual undermining of the habitual ultimately infects the poetry's sense of time and historical reality. As these poems show, any turn to the self, in Paterson's work, is a turn to something that is compellingly appetitive and insistent, but which is also combative, inconstant, shadowed, disturbing and ungraspable. Strikingly, his poems treat the social fabric of culture and history in a similar manner.

'The Alexandrian Library' – the long poem at the heart of *Nil Nil* – explicitly introduces two other tropes central to Paterson's verse: the idea of entropy, and the idea of the Borgesian labyrinth.[28] In Jorge Luis Borges's 'The Garden of Forking Paths', we are told: 'In all fictions, each time a man meets diverse alternatives, he chooses one and eliminates the others . . . *He creates*, thereby, "several futures", several *times*, which themselves prolifer-ate and fork.'[29] As such, our world consists of 'an infinite series of times, a growing, dizzying web of divergent, convergent, and parallel times'; and this 'fabric of times that approach one another, fork, are snipped off, or are simply unknown for centuries, contains *all* possibilities'.[30] In a manner that will ramify throughout the rest of Paterson's oeuvre, a pursuit to grasp the moment, grasp the self, grasp historical reality, in 'The Alexandrian Library', leads to a slip into such labyrinthine complexity. Moreover, the pursuit ultimately leads to an intuition of ever-diminishing end-points, in a kind of teleological trajectory marked by the absence of a telos.

The poem begins with a train journey to Cowdenbeath, and its opening shares a sense of the past with 'Amnesia':

> peeling the gaffa-tape back from the map
> you uncover the names of decanonized saints
> and football clubs, now long-extinct.[31]

Underneath the present, the past, cut off by extinction, exists in a kind of parallel universe. These 'decanonized saints' suggest history's changes through time, rewritten at the whim of the proclivities of the present; but they also suggest a past or shadowy realm of botches, mistakes, error, and futility. The journey proceeds across a Lowlands landscape:

> These were the battlegrounds
> abandoned in slaughter, the borders no more
> than feebly disputed; a land with no history,
> there being no victors to write it. You lean

from the window to use the last shot in the spool:
the print slinks out like a diseased tongue.[32]

This wholesale refusal of a nationalist history disenfranchises Scottish culture
of any purposeful narrative, condemning it to the botched parallel realm,
associated with the individual and collective unconscious, soon to be item-
ised in the 'library'. Meanwhile, the Polaroid photograph's 'diseased tongue'
renders realist representation (and, by extension, normative ideas of reality
and history) as an infection.

Accordingly, on alighting at Cowdenbeath, the poem's dream logic takes
over. It turns out there is, and has been, 'no train' and 'no tracks'.[33] From this
ghost-train, we move towards a council estate peopled by 'girls with disastrous
make-up and ringworm', towards a house, passing through and out its back-
door, to be faced with 'twelve . . . blue doors' surrounded by 'thirteen allot-
ments'.[34] In other words, we get a sense of a movement back in time towards
a putative point of origin or key memory, confused by a Borgesian sense of
multiple portals and narrative strands.

An epigraph to 'The Alexandrian Library' introduces François Aussemain,
a fictive philosopher, to Paterson's oeuvre. In a subsequent epigraph to 'Nil
Nil', Aussemain writes of 'all our abandoned histories': 'those ignoble lines
of succession that end in neither triumph nor disaster, but merely plunge
on into deeper and deeper obscurity'.[35] Meanwhile, the epigraph to 'The
Alexandrian Library' argues: 'Nothing is ever lost; things only become irretrievable.' Aussemain continues: 'What is lost, then, is the method of their
retrieval, and what we rediscover is not the thing itself, but the overgrown
path, the secret staircase, the ancient sewer.'[36] But what is the difference
between being lost and being irretrievable? Being lost suggests total absence,
while the irretrievable, by contrast, is *there* yet out of reach. Once again, we
have the idea of a parallel realm.

The two Aussemain epigraphs together gesture towards a poetics of
haunting and failure. Any attempt to grasp at truth, or reality, or the past,
is doomed to fail as these perpetually recede in reaction to their pursuit.
But at the same time, nothing is ever lost. Thus we intuit a dizzying web of
divergent, convergent and parallel dimensions. As such, the world's fractures,
banalities and maladies seem to be symptoms that suggest both the absence
and the retrievability of The Real. Paterson argues:

There's this idea, explicit in Buddhist teaching but which you can infer in
Borges, Calvino, Jung, Derrida and a thousand other writers, that God dispersed
after the Big Bang, or the Fall, and shattered into a million pieces, like a great
glass hologram. The pieces are us. A poem is the literary analogue . . . and the
whole is subtly implied in the fragmentary narratives that we write.[37]

The great synecdoche of truth is shattered by the irony of time and difference. This, in turn, leads to the seemingly-denying-what-it-asserts vision of
Paterson's verse. He writes:

> Most people are convinced that the path of the departing spirit is distinguished
> by its scatter of holy detritus . . . but the one thing of which God is incapable is
> fragmentation. The path He has taken is distinguished only by its godlessness.
> When we stumble upon anything — a bottle of wine, a poem, a poor suburb, a
> railway platform – that is incontestably the worst of its kind, we know for
> certain that we have picked up the trail again.[38]

As this suggests, the *via negativa* is not a straightforward path.

Returning to 'The Alexandrian Library': it may be the case that nothing
is ever lost, but the method of retrieval is not, apparently, to be consciously
controlled. Rather, consciousness is beset by amnesia, as this intensely self-
reflexive poem muses on the brain's 'aeons / of failure to recollect something
important', and ponders

> the synaptic lacuna
> where the spark of your most-treasured memory
> finally fails in the crossing
> and sinks in the gap
> like Leander.[39]

So the attempt to sensibly locate 'something important' in the memory (and by
extension in history) is doomed to failure. At which point, we enter the 'library'
(in the shape of Harry Sturgis's remaindered and second-hand bookstore).

What follows is a dextrous and hugely enjoyable riff through a motley of
unlikely and undesirable reads:

> *Diabetic Desserts All the Family Will Love;*
> *Origamian* specials – *The Scissor Debate;*
> *Urine – The Water of Life; The King's Gambit –*
> *Play it to Win.*[40]

The library is a chaotic storehouse of flotsam, error, absurdity and misdi-
rected energy.[41] In turn, the discombobulations of the library, or bookshop
(reflecting the chaos of the mind), begin to suggest the disorder of entropy.
Entropy might be defined as the absence of form, pattern or differentiation;
but also the process of decay that leads to this. Thus entropy describes both
the whirl of bamboozlement, as we are spun from one scenario to the next
through the dream logic of the poem; and also the poem's trajectory of perpetual recession.

As it happens, the poem ultimately conjures some form of nightmarish 'horror'. This lacks total conviction, but is perhaps symbolic of a primal fault or wrong in the depths of the unconscious. And thus while the portals of retrieval (of the truth, or reality, or the past) might remain, implicitly approachable through the dream of art, the poem concludes that what we might retrieve is potentially dangerous, or, at least, destabilising:

> the archives are always somewhere intact –
> in the world, or that part of the mind that the mind
> cannot contemplate.[42]

'Nil Nil', the final poem of Nil Nil, also explores the idea of entropy, but this time in a less overtly nightmarish atmosphere. Then again, while 'The Alexandrian Library' allows for an awakening from its perturbed dream of perpetual regression, in 'Nil Nil', we can't escape. Instead, 'Nil Nil' concludes with a gorgeous vista of supermundane diminishment:

> following the trail as it steadily fades
> into road-repairs, birdsong, the weather, nirvana,
> the plot thinning down to a point so refined
> not even the angels could dance on it.[43]

To get to this point, or absence of point, the poem catapults the reader along a fantastical, speeded-up reversal through space and time. With football as the theme, we are led from the first division to the second division, and then downwards on a swift

> descent into pitch-sharing,
> pay-cuts, pawned silver, the Highland Division,
> the absolute sitters ballooned over open goals,
> the dismal nutmegs, the scores so obscene
> no respectable journal will print them

and on to

> unrefereed thirty-a-sides,
> terrified fat boys with callipers minding
> four jackets on infinite, notational fields

until we end with two boys, and then just one, kicking a stone into a gutter.[44]

Although logically regressive, the poem's intuitive effect is expansive; its swoop propelled through a broadly dactylic rhythm. A reversal of the full-on 'da-da-dum / da-da-dum' throttle of anapests, the more rare pulse of these dactyls ('*dum-da-da* / *dum-da-da*') creates a paradoxical momentum. This is a poem of what might best be called backward velocity, of inverted enlargement. It seems to hit upon a nerve-centre, an archetype of vanishing youth and innocence, as its 'out the rear window' momentum and nostalgic vistas sum up a history of embattled community fortitude, endeavour and stoicism in the face of change and the vicissitudes of modernity. All headed down the gutter.

In a striking turn (it should by now be clear that Paterson is adept at the 'twist' or the 'turn of the screw'), the poem suddenly switches to the pathos of a 'lone fighter-pilot', killed when trying to parachute from his crashing plane, because his parachute was replaced by a 'flurry of socks' in an April Fools Day joke. (As always, in Paterson, the pathos is spiked with venom.) Again, the juxtaposition of this military-industrial scene with the preceding vision of football seems archetypal: it harks back to our cultural store-house of contrasts between innocence and war (even, somewhere in the background, of football in the trenches), while it is also mordantly acute about how this sepia-tinged juxtaposition is complicated by the impinging inhumanity of technology – the true vanishing point of communal fortitude. In such a way, the poem, with its stunning combination of a calculated and cuttingly intelligent conceit, with a compassionate and dramatically resonant form, creates an extraordinary impression.

In conclusion, it must be said that, since *Nil Nil*, Paterson's writing has evolved and improved. It seems clear that poems such as '11:00 Baldovan' and 'A Private Bottling' from *God's Gift to Women*, and 'Letter to the Twins' and 'The White Lie' from *Landing Light*, among others, are major works of their time. As such, they demand close and scrupulous consideration, the space for which is unavailable here. Yet the poems discussed here are themselves major British poems of the 1990s. Besides, criticism of Paterson is in its infancy, and it seems essential that discussion of his oeuvre is grounded upon the foundations of these first published poems. Moreover, while his work has moved on from the poetics of *Nil Nil*, it would be false to say its stylistic and thematic concerns have been superceded. His oeuvre, while dynamic and varied, has been highly consistent.

Entropy; labyrinths; the almost unpalatable splendours and tremors of experience; parallel worlds; futility; antagonism; the violations and captivations of sexuality; class inequality; social disparity and hardship; fluid shiftings between apprehensions of oblivion and apprehensions of mythic significance; fluid shiftings between acts of memory and acts of invention; the unquantifiable enigmas of the internal, subjective world; of the external, objective world; of their crossing: these themes continue to pervade his work. Moreover, many of the stylistic and tonal features of *Nil Nil* become core facets of his whole oeuvre. His work remains marked by its dramatic open-endedness within rhetorically rounded and conclusive forms. It remains distinguished by his ability to forge ambiguous nuance with compelling force to create emphatic ambivalence. The fusion, in his poems, of agility with compression is often remarkable; but 'The Alexandrian Library' and 'Nil Nil' also indicate his sweep and widescreen innovation. Any account of his poetic will be incomplete if it does not allow for his vim and unpredictable energy, his fresh-air inventiveness and wit.

To contextualise Paterson further, he needs to be discussed in terms of predecessors and influence. There is no doubt that scrutiny of his work in relation to immediate contemporaries such as Simon Armitage (1963–), Michael Donaghy (1954–2004), Kathleen Jamie, Glyn Maxwell (1962–), Robin Robertson (1955–) and Jo Shapcott (1953–) is now seriously overdue; likewise, his work's relationship with poets such as Douglas Dunn (1942–) Derek Mahon (1941–), Paul Muldoon (1951–); as well as W. S. Graham (1918–86), W. H. Auden (1907–73) and Louis MacNeice (1907–63), among others. Beyond that, his work has striking affinities with Hugh MacDiarmid and with W. B. Yeats (1865–1939), as much as with Rainer Maria Rilke (1875–1926) or Antonio Machado (1875–1939). And then, there is his engaged relationship with the 'canon' (not just anglophone) in all its unending, coiled sprawl. In the best possible sense, the deeply literate nature of his poetry is innate.

Meanwhile, for cultural and historical contextualisation, critics will need to attend to his Scottishness, or his Britishness, with care. His verse doubts the stability and knowability of the self, and then some. Therefore its relationship with concepts such as nations tends to be tentative, while nevertheless searching, and often searing. Rooted in tradition and grounded in local specificity, the work also vituperates with sceptical and voracious individualism, and it will react badly to artificially superimposed circumscriptions.[45] And yet his poetic does seem an intricate model of the permeable and labyrinthine complex of contexts in which they are written – local, regional, national, international – each interacting with distinctive, changing nuance.

Architectonically impressive, his lines and stanzas are deftly crafted to create a lasting tonal vibrance, replete with dramatic animation, embedded sensuality, crisp intelligence and haunted numinosity. In terms of diction, phrasing and intonation, his voice is distinctive but broad-ranged: distilled from the copious hybridity of sources and currents that constitute the English language in Scotland. With its provocative blend of dark beauty and ferocity, its rage for originality, its dynamic grasp of tradition, this is verse of unsettling audacity and unsettled grace.

Endnotes

Introduction – McGuire and Nicholson

1. D. O'Rourke (ed.), *Dream State: The New Scottish Poets* (Edinburgh: Polygon, [1994] 2002), pp. 280–1.
2. Berthold Schoene, 'Going Cosmopolitan: Reconstituting "Scottishness" in Post-Devolution Criticism', in B. Schoene (ed.), *The Edinburgh Companion to Contemporary Scottish Literature* (Edinburgh: Edinburgh University Press, 2007), pp. 7–16.
3. Kathleen Jamie, *Jizzen* (London: Picador, 1999), p. 5.
4. Donnie O'Rourke (ed.), *Dream State*, p. 281.
5. Edward Soja, *Postmodern Geographies* (London: Verso, 1989), p. 6.
6. Fredric Jameson, *Postmodernism, or the Cultural Logic of Late Capitalism* (London: Verso, 1991), pp. 364–5.
7. The phrase is from Iain Crichton Smith, *Towards the Human: Selected Essays* (Edinburgh: Macdonald, 1986), pp. 13–70.
8. Michael Keith and Steve Pile (eds), *Place and the Politics of Identity* (London: Routledge, 1993), p. 38.
9. Neil Smith and Cindi Katz, 'Grounding Metaphor: Towards a Spatialised Politics', in Michael Keitt and Steve Pile (eds), *Place and the Politics of Identity*, p. 69.
10. Tom Leonard, *Radical Renfrew: Poetry from the French Revolution to the First World War* (Edinburgh: Polygon, 1990), p. xxi.
11. Jacques Rancière, 'The Thinking of Dissensus: Politics and Aesthetics', paper presented at the conference 'Fidelity to the Disagreement: Jacques Rancière and the Political', Goldsmith College, London, 16–17 September, 2003.
12. Cairns Craig, 'Scotland and Hybridity', in G. Carruthers, D. Goldie, A. Renfrew (eds), *Beyond Scotland: New Contexts for Twentieth-Century Scottish Literature* (Amsterdam: Rodopi, 2004), p. 240.
13. John Macmurray, *Persons in Relation* (London: Faber, 1983 [1961]), p. 158.
14. Edwin Muir, *An Autobiography* (Edinburgh: Canongate, 2000 [1954]), p. 47.

15. Julia Kristeva, *Desire in Language: A Semiotic Approach to Literature and Art*, ed. L. S. Roudiez, trans. T. Gora, A. Jardine and L. Roudiez (London: Blackwell, 1984), p. 74.

16. John Macmurray, *Persons*, p. 24.

17. Gaston Bachelard, *The Poetics of Space*, trans. Maria Jolas (Boston: Beacon Press, 1994 [1958]), pp. xxvi–xxvii.

Chapter 1 – Riach

1. Roderick Watson, *The Literature of Scotland* (London: Macmillan, [1984] (2007)); Cairns Craig (ed.), *The History of Scottish Literature*, 4 vols (Aberdeen: Aberdeen University Press, 1986–7); Marshall Walker, *Scottish Literature Since 1707* (London and New York: Longman, 1996); Douglas Gifford and Dorothy McMillan (eds), *A History of Scottish Women's Writing* (Edinburgh: Edinburgh University Press, 1997); Alasdair Gray, *Lanark: A Life in Four Books* (Edinburgh: Canongate, 1981); Edwin Morgan, *Sonnets from Scotland* (Glasgow: Mariscat Press, 1984); Liz Lochhead, *Mary Queen of Scots Got Her Head Chopped Off: and Dracula* (Harmondsworth: Penguin Books, 1989).

2. Iain Crichton Smith, 'The Beginning of a New Song' and Anne Frater, 'Divorce', in Douglas Gifford and Alan Riach (eds), *Scotlands: Poets and the Nation* (Manchester: Carcanet; and Edinburgh: Scottish Poetry Library, 2004), pp. 243–5.

3. Walter Benjamin, 'The Work of Art in the Age of Mechanical Reproduction' [1936], in Hannah Arendt (ed.), *Illuminations* (London: Pimlico, 1999), pp. 211–44.

4. Anne Frater, 'Divorce' in *Scotlands*, p. 243.

5. Edwin Morgan, 'For the Opening of the Scottish Parliament, 9 October 2004', in *A Book of Lives* (Manchester: Carcanet, 2007), p. 9.

6. Alastair Reid, 'Scotland', in *Scotlands*, p.175.

7. Donald Allen (ed.), *The New American Poetry* [1960], reprinted in an expanded edition as Donald Allen and George F. Butterick (eds), *The Postmoderns: The New American Poetry Revised* (New York: Grove Press, 1982).

8. Duncan Glen, 'The Hert o Scotland', in *Collected Poems 1965–2005* (Kirkcaldy: Akros, 2006), pp. 76–7.

9. Douglas Dunn (ed.), *Twentieth-Century Scottish Poetry* (London: Faber, [1992] 2006); Robert Crawford, *A Scottish Assembly* (London: Chatto and Windus, 1990), p. 41; Robert Crawford, *Masculinity* (London: Jonathan Cape, 1996), p. 31.

10. Janice Galloway, *boy book see* (Glasgow: Mariscat Press, 2002); A. L. Kennedy, *Absolutely Nothing* (Glasgow: Mariscat Press, 1998).

11. Adrienne Rich, 'Diving into the Wreck', in Nina Baym (ed.), *The Norton Anthology of American Literature*, Volume 2 (New York and London: W.W. Norton, 1998), vol. 2, pp. 2719–21.

12. Jackie Kay, 'In my Country', in *Scotlands*, p. 230.

13. Edwin Morgan, 'A Demon', from the sequence 'Demon' [1999], in *Cathures: New Poems 1997–2001* (Manchester: Carcanet Press; and Glasgow: Mariscat Press, 2002), p. 93.

14. Edwin Morgan, 'Flood-Tide', in *A Book of Lives*, p. 80.

15. Alec Finlay and Kevin MacNeil (eds), *Wish I Was Here: A Scottish Multicultural Anthology* (Edinburgh: Pocketbooks, 2005); Alec Finlay, *Without Day. Proposals for a New Parliament* (Edinburgh: Pocketbooks, 1998).

16. Peter McCarey, 'Referendum Day 3', in *Scotlands*, p. 220.

17. www.thesyllabary.com/

18. Daniel O'Rourke (ed.), *Dream State: The New Scottish Poets* (Edinburgh: Polygon, 1994); Donny O'Rourke (ed.), *Dream State: The New Scottish Poets*, 2nd edn (Edinburgh: Polygon, 2002).

19. Andrew McNeillie, 'Cynefin *Glossed*', in *Slower* (Manchester: Carcanet Press, 2006), p. 28.

20. See *Archipelago* 2 (spring, 2008).

21. Stephen Rodefer, 'Codex', in *Four Lectures* (Berkeley: The Figures, 1982), p. 69.

22. Edwin Morgan, 'Lines for Wallace', in Lesley Duncan and Elspeth King (eds), *The Wallace Muse: Poems and Artworks Inspired by the Life and Legend of William Wallace* (Edinburgh: Luath Press, 2005), p. 15.

Chapter 2 – Wilson

1. Janet Paisley, 'Poets or What? An Off the Cuff "Dear Jon"', *Chapman* 91 (1998), p. 22.

2. Tessa Ransford, Review of *Coming Out With It*, by Angela McSeveney, *Harpies and Quines* 7 (June/July 1993), p. 43; Christopher Whyte, *Modern Scottish Poetry* (Edinburgh: Edinburgh University, 2004), p. 111.

3. Denise Riley, '*Am I That Name?*': Feminism and the Category of 'Women' in History* (Minneapolis: University of Minnesota Press, 1988), p. 2; Douglas Gifford and Dorothy MacMillan (eds), *A History of Scottish Women's Writing* (Edinburgh: Edinburgh University Press, 1997), p. xiv.

4. Alice Entwhistle, 'Scotland's New House: Domesticity and Domicile in Contemporary Scottish Women's Poetry', in Berthold Schoene (ed.), *The Edinburgh Companion to Contemporary Scottish Literature* (Edinburgh: Edinburgh University Press, 2007), p. 115.

5. Colin Nicholson, *Poem, Purpose and Place: Shaping Identities in Contemporary Scottish Verse* (Edinburgh: Polygon, 1992), p. 223.

6. Liz Lochhead, 'The Grim Sisters', in *Dreaming Frankenstein and Collected Poems* (Edinburgh: Polygon, 1984), pp. 82–3.

7. Ibid., 'What the Pool Said on Midsummer's Day', p. 3.

8. Christopher Whyte, *Modern Scottish Poetry*, p. 189.

9. Liz Lochhead, 'Mirror's Song', in *Dreaming Frankenstein*, p. 75.
10. Liz Lochhead, 'Kidspoem/Bairnsang', in *The Colour of Black and White: Poems 1984–2003* (Edinburgh: Polygon, 2003), pp. 19–20.
11. Donny O'Rourke (ed.), *Dream State: The New Scottish Poets* (Edinburgh: Polygon, 2002), p. xxii.
12. Carol Ann Duffy, 'Standing Female Nude', in *Selected Poems* (London: Picador Books, 1994), p. 20.
13. Carol Ann Duffy, 'Recognition', in *Selling Manhattan* (London: Anvil, 1987), p. 24.
14. Ibid., 'Foreign', p. 47.
15. Ibid., 'Homesick', p. 19; 'Strange Place', p. 55.
16. Carol Ann Duffy, 'Originally', in *The Other Country* (London: Anvil, 1990), p. 7.
17. Ibid., 'The Way My Mother Speaks,' p. 54; 'In Your Mind,' p. 55.
18. Ibid., 'Originally', p. 7.
19. Jackie Kay, 'The Waiting Lists', in *Darling: New and Selected Poems* (Tarset: Bloodaxe Books, 2007), p. 20.
20. Ibid., 'Black Bottom', p. 29.
21. Ibid., 'Race, Racist, Racism', p. 128.
22. Ibid., 'The Broons' Bairn's Black', p. 159.
23. Ibid., 'Pride', pp. 161–2.
24. Jackie Kay, 'Life Mask', in *Life Mask* (Tarset: Bloodaxe Books, 2005), p. 198.
25. Janet Paisley, 'Poet's or What? An Off the Cuff "Dear Jon"', *Chapman* 91 (1998), p. 22.
26. Ibid.
27. Janet Paisley, 'Conjugate', in *Alien Crop* (Edinburgh: Chapman, 1996), p. 9.
28. Ibid., 'Sinking the Ship', p. 9.
29. Ibid., 'Storm Warning', p. 35.
30. Janet Paisley, 'Morag: Witchcraft', in *Ye Cannae Win* (Edinburgh: Chapman, 2000), p. 70.
31. Angela McSeveney, *Coming Out With It* (Edinburgh: Polygon, 1992), p. 12.
32. Ibid., 'Ponytail', p. 92.
33. Ibid., 'The Fat Nymphomaniac's Poem', p. 22.
34. Ibid., 'Exposure', p. 12.
35. Ibid., 'Vivisection', p. 76.
36. Ibid., 'Stretch Marks', p. 21; 'Breast Exam', p. 60.
37. Ibid., 'Ultrasonic Scan', p. 34.
38. Dilys Rose, interview in Gillian Somerville and Rebecca Wilson (eds), *Sleeping with Monsters: Conversations with Scottish and Irish Women Poets* (Edinburgh: Polygon, 1990), p. 209.
39. Dilys Rose, 'No Name Woman', in *Madame Doubtfire's Dilemma* (Blackford: Chapman, 1989), p. 7.
40. Ibid., 'Sister Sirens', p. 15.

41. Ibid., 'Caryatid', p. 17.
42. Ibid., 'Figurehead', p. 14.
43. Dilys Rose, 'Siguiriya in Scotland', in *Bodywork* (Edinburgh: Luath Press, 2007), p. 3.
44. Kate Clanchy, 'Men', in *Slattern* (London: Chatto and Windus, 1995), p. 1.
45. Ibid., 'Men from the Boys', p. 10.
46. Ibid., 'Men', p. 1.
47. Ibid., 'Tip', p. 2.
48. Kate Clanchy, 'Spell', in *Samarkand* (London: Picador, 1999), p. 35.
49. Ibid., 'Travel', p. 2.
50. Ibid., 'The Bridge Over the Border', p. 1.

Chapter 3 – Hubbard

1. Pearse Hutchinson, 'The Frost is All Over', in *Collected Poems* (Oldcastle: Gallery Books, 2002), p. 172.
2. Philip Hobsbaum, 'Speech Rather Than Lallans: West of Scotland Poetry', *Lines Review* 113 (January, 1990), pp. 5–10.
3. W. N. Herbert, 'The Hermitage', in *Sharawaggi* (Edinburgh: Polygon, 1990), p. 137.
4. W. N. Herbert, 'First Fit', in *The Laurelude* (Newcastle upon Tyne: Bloodaxe, 1998), p. 92.
5. George Gunn, 'Wake Up!', *Spectrum* 6 (1994), p. 67.
6. Richard Price and Donny O'Rourke, *Eftirs/Afters* (Glasgow: Au Quai, 1996), p. 8.
7. Tom Hubbard (ed.), *The New Makars: Contemporary Poetry in Scots* (Edinburgh: Mercat, 1991), pp. 54–9.
8. John Manson, *Frae Glesca til Manila* (Kirkcudbright: Markings, 2000), p. 6.
9. John Law, *The Heichts o Macchu Picchu* (Edinburgh: Chapman, 2006), pp. 15, 16.
10. Tom Hubbard, 'Skulls and Stoaters', *Poetry Ireland Review* 93 (2008), p. 92.
11. John Corbett, 'Now You See 'Em: The Visibility of Scots Translators', *Cadernos de Tradução* 4, quoted in John Manson, *Frae Glesca*, back cover.
12. Michael Cronin, *Translation and Globalization* (London: Routledge, 2003), p. 164.
13. J. Derrick McClure, 'Villon in Scots: The Translations of Tom Scott', in Armand Michaux (ed.), *English Studies 2: Essays in Honour of Marie-Thérèse Schroder-Hartmann* (Luxembourg: Publications du Centre Universitaire de Luxembourg, 1990), p. 109.
14. J. Derrick McClure, 'Scots – A Language for Poetic Translation?' [followed by the texts of his Kollerisch translations], *Metamorphoses* (spring 2008), pp. 144–53.

15. J. Derrick McClure, 'Fower Poems bi Schoschana Rabinovici', *Lallans* 69 (wunter, 2006), pp. 57–9.
16. George Bruce, 'Minding David Murison', in *Pursuit: Poems 1986–1998* (Edinburgh: Scottish Cultural Press, 1999), p. 30.
17. Ibid., 'Weys o Self-Preservin Natur', p. 43.
18. Ibid., p. x.
19. See Duncan Glen and Tom Hubbard (eds), *Fringe of Gold: The Fife Anthology* (Edinburgh: Birlinn, 2008), p. 52–3.
20. William Hershaw, *Fifty Fife Sonnets Coarse and Fine* (Kirkcaldy: Akros, 2006), p. 21.
21. Maureen Macnaughtan, 'The Duncan Glen Interview', *Fife Lines* 1 (September, 1998), p. 57.
22. Duncan Glen, *Collected Poems 1965–2005* (Kirkcaldy: Akros, 2006), p. 178.
23. William Neill, 'C. F. Meyer Owerset bi William Neill', *Lallans* 59 (hairst, 2001), pp. 10–17.
24. William Neill, *Seventeen Sonnets by G. G. Belli, Translated from the Romanesco* (Kirkcaldy: Akros, 1998), p. 5.
25. Rab Wilson, 'Cormilligan', in *Accent o the Mind* (Edinburgh: Luath, 2006), p. 21.
26. Liz Niven, 'Merrick tae Criffel', in *Burning Whins* (Edinburgh: Luath, 2004), p. 59.
27. Matthew Fitt, *Kate o Shanter's Tale* (Edinburgh: Luath, 2003), pp. 49–50.
28. Ellie McDonald, 'Smeddum', in *The Gangan Fuit* (Edinburgh: Chapman, 1991), p. 12.
29. Janet Paisley, *Pegasus in Flight* (Edinburgh: Rookbook Publications, 1989).
30. Raymond Vettese, 'A Keen New Air', in *A Keen New Air* (Edinburgh: Saltire Society, 1995), p. 35.
31. Ibid., 'Edna', p. 57.
32. Sheena Blackhall, *Pandora's Box* (Aberdeen: the author, 2004), p. 23.
33. Sheena Blackhall, 'The Auldest Profession', in *On Brigid's Day* (Aberdeen: Malfranteaux Concepts, 2007), p. 8.
34. Sheena Blackhall, 'Scotch n' Watter', in *Indian Peter* (Aberdeen: the author, 2004), p. 25.
35. *A Small Book of Translations*, http://www.scottishcorpus.ac.uk/corpus/
36. James Robertson, *Fae the Flouers o Evil: Baudelaire in Scots* (Kingskettle: Kettillonia, 2001); James Robertson, 'Three Poems bi Louis Duchosal', *Lallans* 59 (hairst, 2001), pp. 22–30.
37. Arthur Rimbaud, *Alchemie o the Word* (Leven: Scots Glasnost, 1990).
38. Robert Calder, 'The Old West', *Lallans* 61 (hairst, 2002), p. 28.
39. Robert Calder, 'Greenfield the Name o the Pit', *Lallans* 56 (voar, 2000), p. 110.
40. Robert Calder, 'Fae "Griencide"', *Lallans* 71 (wunter, 2008), pp. 8–21.

Chapter 4 – O'Gallagher

1. See Sorley MacLean, *Poems to Eimhir*, trans. Iain Crichton Smith (Newcastle-upon-Tyne: Northern House, 1971). *Nua-Bhàrdachd Gàidhlig* was followed by MacLean's selected poems, *Reothairt is Contraigh*, featuring his own, much less successful English versions of the 'Dàin do Eimhir' in 1977.

2. Aonghas MacNeacail, *an seachnadh agus dàin eile/the avoiding and other poems*, (Edinburgh: Macdonald, 1986), pp. 10–11.

3. Aonghas MacNeacail, 'oideachadh ceart', in *Oideachadh Ceart agus Dàin Eile* (Edinburgh: Polygon, 1996), pp. 12–13.

4. Aonghas MacNeacail, 'dèanamh ime', in *Laoidh an Daonais Òig* (Edinburgh: Polygon, 2007), pp. 56–7.

5. Myles Campbell, 'An Referendum . . . ', in *Breac-a'-Mhuiltein*, trans. NO'G (Dublin: Coisceim, 2007), pp. 33–4.

6. Ibid., trans. 'Rud a Thachair', pp. 248–50.

7. Christopher Whyte, 'Dàin Eadar-Theangaichte bho Ritsos agus Cavafy', *Gairm* 123 (samhradh, 1983), pp. 259–61.

8. Christopher Whyte, *Uirsgeul/Myth: Gaelic Poems with English Translations* (Glaschu: Gairm, 1991), pp. 62–3.

9. See Niall O'Gallagher, 'Cainnt agus Balbhachd ann am Bàrdachd Chrìsdein Whyte', in Gillian Munro (ed.), *Cànan agus Cultar: Rannsachadh na Gàidhlig 4* (Edinburgh: Dunedin Academic Press, 2009).

10. The poem is due to be republished, with an English translation by Sally Evans, in *Bho Leabhar-Latha Maria Malibran* (Steòrnabhagh: Acair, 2009).

11. Christopher Whyte, Maria Malibran, trans. NO'G, *Gairm* 175 (samhradh, 1996), p. 272.

12. Christopher Whyte, Maria Malibran, trans. NO'G, *Gairm* 176 (foghair, 1996), p. 372.

13. Meg Bateman, 'Because I was So Fond of Him', in *Aotromachd agus Dàin Eile/Lightness and Other Poems* (Edinburgh: Polygon, 1997), p. 5. The Gaelic text is slightly revised in this later version from the original, which appeared in Meg Bateman, *Òrain Ghaoil* (Baile Àtha Cliath: Coiscéim, 1991), p. 10.

14. Meg Bateman, 'Aotromachd', in *Aotromachd agus Dàin Eile/Lightness and Other Poems*, pp. 48–9. Again this version is slightly revised from the original which appeared in *Òrain Ghaoil*.

15. Meg Bateman, 'Ceòl san Eaglais', in *Soirbheas/Fair Wind* (Edinburgh: Polygon, 2007), pp. 36–7.

16. Rody Gorman, 'Fax', in *Fax and Other Poems* (Edinburgh: Polygon, 1996), pp. 10–11.

17. McClure's Scots versions of MacLean's 'Dàin do Eimhir' remain unpublished.

18. Angus Peter Campbell, *An Oidhche Mus do Sheòl Sinn* (Inbhir Nis: Clàr, 2003); *Là a' Dèanamh Sgèil do Là* (Inbhir Nis: Clàr, 2004) and *An Taigh-Samhraidh* (Inbhir Nis: Clàr, 2007).

19. Angus Peter Campbell, 'Ceàrd na Bàrdachd Gàidhlig', in *Meas air Chrannaibh*, p. 28.
20. Martin MacIntyre, 'Glaschu-an', in *Dannsam led Fhaileas* (Edinburgh: Luath 2006), p. 64.
21. Derick Thomson, 'Air Sràidean Ghlaschu', in *Smeur an Dòchais* (Edinburgh: Canongate, 1991), pp. 22–3.
22. Derick Thomson, 'Glaschu-an', in *Sùil air Fàire* (Steòrnabhagh: Acair, 2007), pp. 68–9.

Chapter 5 – Matthews

1. Christopher Whyte, *Modern Scottish Poetry* (Edinburgh: Edinburgh University Press, 2004), p. 9.
2. Donny [Daniel] O'Rourke (ed.), *Dream State: The New Scottish Poets*, 2nd edn (Edinburgh: Polygon, 2002), p. 70.
3. Elizabeth Burns, 'Valdas Poem', in *Ophelia and Other Poems* (Edinburgh: Polygon, 1991), p. 19.
4. Ibid., p. 19.
5. Ibid., 'Work and Art', p. 45.
6. Ibid., *Ophelia*, p. 45.
7. Ron Butlin, 'Inheritance', in *Ragtime in Unfamiliar Bars* (London: Secker and Warburg, 1985), p. 43.
8. Ibid., 'Claiminig my Inheritance', p. 45.
9. Ron Butlin, 'Poem for my Father', in *Creatures Tamed by Cruelty* (Edinburgh: EUSPB, 1979), p. 12.
10. Ibid., 'Two handscapes', p. 19.
11. Ibid., 'Strangers', p. 17.
12. Ron Butlin, 'My Inheritance', in *Ragtime in Unfamiliar Bars*, pp. 50–1.
13. Ron Butlin, 'This Embroidery', in *The Exquisite Instrument* (Edinburgh: Salamander Press, 1982), p. 14.
14. Ron Butlin, 'Three Biographies', in *Histories of Desire* (Newcastle upon Tyne: Bloodaxe, 1995), p. 46.
15. Ibid., p. 47.
16. Jon Corelis, 'From Scotland to Suburbia: A Landscape of Current British Poetry', *Chapman* 87 (1997), pp. 15–16.
17. Roddy Lumsden, 'Marmalade', in *The Book of Love* (Newcastle upon Tyne: Bloodaxe, 2000), p. 20.
18. William Shakespeare, *Hamlet*, ed. Harold Jenkins (London: Thomson Learning, 2000), I, iii, pp. 78–81.
19. Maud Sulter, 'Womanist Conception', in *Zabat: Poetics of a Family Tree* (Hebden Bridge: Urban Fox Press, 1989), p. 24.
20. Maud Sulter, 'As a Blackwoman', in *As a Blackwoman: Poems 1982–1985* (Hebden Bridge: Urban Fox Press, 1985), p. 11.

21. Robert Garioch, 'Review of *Each Bright Eye*', in *Lines Review* 65 (1978), p. 33.
22. Valerie Gillies, 'Sangam, Mysore State', in *Each Bright Eye* (Edinburgh: Canongate, 1977), p. 3
23. Tom Pow, 'The River', in *Rough Seas* (Edinburgh: Canongate, 1987), p. 7.
24. Ibid., 'The Ship', p. 8.
25. Ibid.
26. Brian McCabe, 'Object', in *Body Parts* (Edinburgh: Canongate, 1999), p. 7.
27. Brian McCabe, 'The Cartographer', in *Spring's Witch* (Glasgow: Mariscat Press, 1984), p. 14.
28. Brian McCabe, 'Sangam, Mysore State', in *Body Parts*, p. 17.
29. Ibid., 'Coal', p. 26.
30. Brian McCabe, 'To Make', in *One Atom to Another* (Edinburgh: Polygon, 1987), pp. 12–13.
31. Brian McCabe, 'The Rat Catcher', in *Body Parts*, pp. 51–5.
32. Ibid., 'The Kite', p. 17.
33. Ibid.
34. Donny O'Rourke, *Dream State*, p. 286.
35. Carol Gow, Review of *First and Last Songs*, in *Lines Review* 137 (1996), p. 59.
36. Robert Lowell, *Imitations* (London: Faber, 1961), p. xiii.
37. Alan Riach, *First and Last Songs* (Edinburgh: Chapman, 1995), pp. 63–4.
38. César Vallejo, *Obra poética completa* (Lima: F. Moncloa, 1968), p. 236. Author's translation.
39. Alan Riach, 'Going Under the Bridge', in *First and Last Songs*, p. 39.
40. Donny O'Rourke, 'Musick Eftir a Readin', in *The Waistband and Other Poems* (Edinburgh: Polygon, 1997), p. 49.
41. Valéry Larbaud, 'Musique aprés une lecture', in *Les Poésies de A. O. Barnabooth* (Paris: Gallimard, 1966), p. 50; 'Music Eftir a Readin', p. 139 Author's translation.
42. Donny O'Rourke, 'Musik Eftir a Readin', in *The Waistband*, p. 50.
43. Frank Kuppner, 'West Åland', in *A God's Breakfast* (Manchester: Carcanet, 2004), p. 125.
44. Donny O'Rourke, 'Musik Eftir a Readin', in *The Waistband*, p. 49.
45. David Kinloch, 'Lorca on Morar', in *Un Tour d'Ecosse* (Manchester: Carcanet, 2001), p. 64.

Chapter 6 – Nicholson

1. 'Love and Loss': an interview with Nicholas Wroe, www.guardian.co.uk/books/2008/mar29/featuresreviews.guardianreview 16
2. Robin Robertson, 'At Roane Head', *London Review of Books*, 14 Aug. 2008, p. 19.
3. Edwin Muir, *Scottish Journey* (London: Heinemann, 1935), p. 94.
4. Nicholas Wroe, 'Love and Loss', p. 16.
5. Ibid.

6. Robin Robertson, *Medea* (London: Vintage, 2008), p. xix.

7. Nicholas Wroe, 'Love and Loss', p. 16.

8. Robin Robertson, 'Holding Proteus', in *Swithering* (London: Picador, 2006), p. 80.

9. Nicholas Wroe, 'Love and Loss', p. 16.

10. Billy Collins, http://www.blueflowerarts.com/index.html

11. Robin Robertson, 'Three Ways of Looking at God', in *A Painted Field* (London: Picador, 1997), p. 4.

12. Robin Robertson, 'These Days', in *Slow Air* (London: Picador, 2002), p. 44.

13. Ibid., p. 25 'Between the Harvest and the Hunter's Moon, in *Swithering*, p. 22 and 'The Flamingos', in *Slow Air*, p. 34.

14. Robin Robertson, 'Entropy', in *Swithering*, p. 34.

15. Nicholas Wroe, 'Love and Loss', p. 16.

16. Robin Robertson, 'Apart', in *Slow Air*, p. 3.

17. Nicholas Wroe, 'Love and Loss', p. 16.

18. Robin Robertson, 'The Thermal Image', in *Slow Air*, p. 37.

19. Ibid., 'Wedding the Locksmith's Daughter', p. 5.

20. Robin Robertson, 'In Memoriam David Jones', in *A Painted Field*, p. 27.

21. Ibid., 'First Winter', p. 29.

22. Ibid., 'The Gift of Tantalus', p. 67.

23. Ibid., 'Fugue for Phantoms', p. 34.

24. Robin Robertson, 'Camera Obscura', in *A Painted Field*, pp. 61–87.

25. Robin Robertson, 'Actaeon: The Early Years' in *Swithering*, p. 53.

26. Stewart Conn, *Distances: A Personal Evocation of People and Places* (Dalkeith: Scottish Cultural Press, 2001), p. 23.

27. Stewart Conn, 'Heirloom', in *Ghosts at Cockcrow* (Tarset: Bloodaxe Books, 2005), p. 35.

28. Ibid., 'Roull of Corstorphine' pp. 52–72.

29. Tessa Ransford, 'With Gratitude to India', and 'Winter Sunrise in Edinburgh', in *Not Just Moonshine: New and Selected Poems* (Edinburgh: Luath Press, 2008), pp. 21, 22.

30. Ibid., 'My Indian Self', p. 80.

31. Tessa Ransford, 'February 14th' in *Shadows from the Greater Hill* (Edinburgh: Ramsay Head, 1987), pp. 20, 46.

32. Tessa Ransford, *Medusa Dozen and Other Poems* (Edinburgh: Ramsay Head, 1994), p. 5.

33. Ibid., 'Medusa Eight', p. 12.

34. Tessa Ransford, 'August 11th', in *Shadows*, p. 27.

35. Tessa Ransford, 'Medusa Nine', in *Medusa*, p. 13.

36. Pete Barry, *Contemporary British Poetry and the City* (Manchester: Manchester University Press, 2000), p. 235.

37. Tom Leonard, 'Unrelated Incidents I' in *Intimate Voices: Selected Poems 1965–1983* (Newcastle: Galloping Dog Press, 1984), p. 86.

38. Tom Leonard, *Radical Renfrew: Poetry from the French Revolution to the First World War* (Edinburgh: Polygon, 1990), p. xxxi.

39. Tom Leonard, 'The Locust Tree in Flower', in *Intimate Voices*, pp. 95–6.

40. Ibid., 'Unrelated Incidents II', p. 87.

41. Tom Leonard, *Situations Theoretical and Contemporary* (Newcastle: Galloping Dog Press), n. p.

42. Leonard, 'Unrelated Incidents III', in *Intimate Voices*, p. 88.

43. Alison Flett, 'ikariss', in *Whit Lassyz Ur Inty* (Edinburgh: Thirsty Books, 2004), p. 48.

44. A. L. Kennedy, *Night Geometry and the Garscadden Trains* (London: Phoenix, 1990), p. 64.

45. Tom Leonard, 'Fathers and Sons', in *Intimate Voices*, p. 140.

46. Mick Imlah, 'The Lost Leader', in *The Lost Leader* (London: Faber, 2008) pp. 41–3.

47. Ibid., 'Muck', pp. 3–5.

48. Ibid., 'The Prophecies', p. 8.

49. Ibid., 'Steven Boyd', p. 98.

50. Ibid., 'Namely', p. 61.

51. Douglas Dunn, 'Memory and Imagination', in *Northlight* (London: Faber, 1988), p. 70.

52. Edwin Morgan, 'The Race' in *Virtual and Other Realities* (Manchester: Carcanet, 1997), p. 67.

53. Edwin Morgan, 'John Hunter' in *Cathures* (Manchester: Carcanet, 2002), p. 19.

54. Lucretius, *De Rerum Natura*, trans. W. H. D. Rouse (London: Heinemann, 1947), p. 71.

55. Edwin Morgan, http://www.edwinmorgan.com/news_index.html

56. Robert Alan Jamieson, *Shoormal* (Edinburgh: Polygon, 1986), p. 12.

57. Ibid., pp. 12, 18.

58. Christine De Luca, *Plain Song: Poems in English and Shetland Dialect* (Lerwick: Shetland Library, 2002), p. 49.

59. Christine de Luca, 'Wast wi da Valkyries', in *Wast wi da Valkyries: Poems in English and Shetland Dialect* (Lerwick: Shetland Library, 1997), pp. 6–7.

60. Robert Alan Jamieson, *Nort Atlantik Drift: Poyims ati'Shaetlin* (Edinburgh: Luath, 2007), p. 11.

61. Morag MacInnes, 'Mapping a Continent', in *Alias Isobel: an Orkney Narrative* (Stromness: Hansel Cooperative, 2008), p. 25.

62. Ibid., 'Language', p. 7.

63. Morag MacInnes, www.scottisharts.org.uk/1/artsinscotland/scots/poemofthe-month.aspx

Chapter 7 – McGuire and Nicholson

1. Umberto Eco, 'Postscript' in *The Name of the Rose*, trans. W. Weaver (London: Secker and Warburg, 1983), p. 65.

198 ENDNOTES

2. T. J. Clark, 'Origins of the Present Crisis', *New Left Review* 2 (second series) (March–April 2000), pp. 85–96; Perry Anderson, *The Origins of Postmodernity* (London: Verso, 1998); Fredric Jameson, *The Cultural Turn: Selected Writings on the Postmodern, 1983–1998* (London: Verso, 1998). Anderson's 'Origins of the Present Crisis' first appeared in *New Left Review* 23 (January–February 1964), was reprinted in *Towards Socialism* (London: New Left Books, 1965), and revised for inclusion in Perry Anderson, *English Questions* (London: Verso, 1992), pp. 15–47.

3. T. J. Clark, 'Origins of the Present Crisis', p. 91.

4. Hugh MacDiarmid, *The Golden Treasury of Scottish Poetry* (London, 1940), p. xvii.

5. Edwin Morgan, 'A Mirrear Dance Mycht Na Man See', *Times Literary Supplement*, 20 March 1998, p. 26.

6. Fredric Jameson, *The Political Unconscious: Narrative as a Socially Symbolic Act* (London: Routledge, 1989), p. 280.

7. Edwin Morgan, *Scottish Satirical Verse: An Anthology* (Manchester: Carcanet, 1980), p. xix.

8. Edwin Morgan, 'The Beatnik in the Kailyard', in *Essays* (Cheshire: Carcanet, 1974), pp. 174–5.

9. Salman Rushdie, *In Good Faith* (London: Granta, 1990), p. 14.

10. Paul Virilio, *The Lost Dimension* (New York: Semiotext, 1991), p. 110, cited in Andrew Gibson, *Towards a Postmodern Theory of Narrative* (Edinburgh: Edinburgh University Press, 1996), pp. 8–9.

11. Glasgow University Library, MS Morgan 650 ff.

12. Daniel O'Rourke (ed.), *Dream State: The New Scottish Poets* (Edinburgh: Polygon, 1994), pp. 280–1.

13. Quoted in ibid., p. 281.

14. Raymond Williams, *On Television: Selected Writings*, ed. Alan O'Connor (London: Routledge, 1989), p. 9. Robert Hughes, *Nothing If Not Critical* (New York: Penguin, 1990), p. 14.

15. Guy Debord, *The Society of the Spectacle* (London: Rebel Press, 1983 [1967]), n. p.

16. Jean Baudrillard, *For a Critique of the Political Economy of the Sign*, trans. C. Levin (New York: Telos, 1981), p. 172.

17. Fredric Jameson, *Postmodernism or the Cultural Logic of Late Capitalism* (London: Verso, 1991), p. 74.

18. Fredric Jameson, 'Imaginary and Symbolic in Lacan: Marxism, Psychoanalytic Criticism and the Problem of the Subject', *Yale French Studies* 55–6 (1977), p. 352.

19. Louis Althusser, 'Ideology and Ideological State Apparatuses', in *Lenin and Philosophy and Other Essays*, trans. Ben Brewster (London: New Left Books, 1971), p. 15; Fredric Jameson, *The Cultural Turn*, p. 68.

20. Jean-François Lyotard, *The Post Modern Condition* (Manchester: Manchester

University Press, 1984), p. 60; Fredric Jameson, *The Political Unconscious*, p. 123.

21. Edwin Morgan, *Tales from Baron Munchausen* (Glasgow: Mariscat, 2005), p. 7.
22. Alasdair Gray, *Lanark* (London: Picador, 1994 [1981]), p. 243.
23. Edwin Morgan, 'The Second Life', in *New Selected Poems* (Manchester: Carcanet, 2000), p. 35.
24. Ibid., pp. 34–5.
25. Lucretius, *De Rerum Natura*, trans. W. H. D. Rouse (London: Heinemann, 1947), p. 71.
26. Edwin Morgan, 'Pelagius', in *Cathures* (Manchester: Carcanet, 2002), p. 10.
27. Colin Nicholson, 'Edwin Morgan: Rampant with Memory', *Cencrastus* 82 (2005), p. 31.
28. Edwin Morgan, 'Louis Kossuth', in *Cathures*, p. 26.
29. Edwin Morgan, letter to the *London Review of Books*, 25 May 2002.
30. Edwin Morgan, 'Merlin', in *Cathures*, p. 13.
31. Ibid., 'A Professorial Trinity', p. 42.
32. Ibid., 'A Hearse Reborn', p. 43.
33. Ibid., 'A Gull', p. 45.
34. Ibid., 'Gasometer', p. 46.
35. Edwin Morgan, 'Freeze-Frame', in *Love and a Life* (Glasgow: Mariscat, 2003), p. 7.
36. Ibid., 'The Top', p. 8
37. Ibid., 'Tracks and Crops', p. 9.
38. Ibid., 'Jurassic', p. 10.
39. Ibid., 'Crocodiles', p. 11.
40. Ibid., 'Touch', p. 12.
41. Ibid., 'When in Thrace', p. 42.
42. Ibid., 'November Night', p. 49.
43. Ibid., 'Spanish Night', p. 50.
44. Ibid., 'Cape Found', p. 18.
45. Ibid., 'Scan Day', p. 34.
46. Ibid., 'Skeleton Day', p. 35.
47. Ibid., 'The Last Dragon', p. 32.

Chapter 8 – Fazzini

1. Edward Said, *Representations of the Intellectual: The 1993 Reith Lectures* (London: Vintage, 1994), pp. 35, 40–4, 42.
2. From an unpublished interview with Marco Fazzini, 2005.
3. Kenneth White, *The Wanderer and His Charts* (Edinburgh: Polygon, 2004), p. vi.
4. Kenneth White, 'Walking the Coast', in *The Bird Path: Collected Longer Poems 1964–1988* (Edinburgh: Mainstream, 1989), p. 68.

5. Kenneth White, *L'Esprit nomade* (Paris: Grasset, 1987), p. 68.
6. Michel Butor, 'Le Voyage et l'écriture', *Romantisme* 4 (1972), p. 7.
7. Kenneth White, *Pilgrim of the Void: Travels in South-East Asia and the North Pacific* (Edinburgh: Mainstream, 1992), p. 163.
8. Kenneth White, 'In the Nashvak Night', in *The Bird Path*, p. 187.
9. Kenneth White, *Coast to Coast: Interviews and Conversations 1985–1995* (Glasgow: Mythic Horse Press, 1996), p. 37.
10. Kenneth White, 'The Residence of Solitude and Light', in *The Bird Path*, p. 170.
11. Letter to the present writer, 2 September 1996.
12. Christopher Whyte, *Modern Scottish Poetry* (Edinburgh: Edinburgh University Press, 2004), p. 27.
13. Kenneth White, 'Into the Whiteness', in *Handbook for the Diamond Country: Collected Shorter Poems 1960–1990* (Edinburgh: Mainstream, 1990), p. 52.
14. Letter to the present writer, 2 September 1996.
15. Gary Snyder, *Good Wild Sacred* (Hereford: Five Seasons Press, 1984), p. 24.
16. Kenneth White, 'A Shaman Dancing on the Glacier', in *On Scottish Ground: Selected Essays* (Edinburgh: Polygon, 1998), p. 48.
17. Kenneth White, *Coast to Coast*, p. 34.
18. Kenneth White, *Le Plateau de l'albatros: Introduction à la géopoétique* (Paris: Grasset, 1994), pp. 21–42.
19. Anne McClintock, *Imperial Leather: Race, Gender and Sexuality in the Colonial Context* (London: Routledge, 1995), p. 392.
20. Kenneth White, 'Walking the Coast, 31', in *The Bird Path*, p. 59.
21. Ibid., 'Scotia Deserta', p. 127.
22. 'John Burnside in Conversation with Marco Fazzini', *Il Tolomeo* 1 (8) (2008), p. 95.
23. Ibid., p. 96.
24. John Burnside, 'Travelling into the Quotidian: Some Notes on Allison Funk's "Heartland" Poems', *Poetry Review* 95 (2) (2005), p. 60.
25. Ibid., p. 61.
26. John Burnside, 'Out of Exile', in *The Hoop* (Manchester: Carcanet, 1988), p. 49.
27. Ibid., 'Exile's Return', p. 50.
28. 'John Burnside in Conversation', p. 97.
29. John Burnside, 'Aphasia in Childhood', in *Feast Days* (London: Secker and Warburg, 1992), pp. 3, 8.
30. Ibid., 'Urphänomen', p. 27.
31. André Gorz, *Critique of Economic Reason* (London: Verso, 1989), pp. 91–103.
32. Jean Baudrillard, 'Toward a Principle of Evil', in T. Docherty (ed.), *Postmodernism: A Reader* (London: Harvester Wheatsheaf, 1993), pp. 255–61.
33. 'John Burnside in Conversation', p. 98.
34. Ibid., p. 98.

35. John Burnside, 'The Myth of the Twin', in *The Myth of the Twin* (London: Cape, 1994), p. 3.
36. 'John Burnside in Conversation', p. 97.
37. Lilias Fraser, 'New Scottish Poetry', in Marco Fazzini (ed.), *Alba Literaria: A History of Scottish Literature* (Venezia Mestre: Amos Edizioni, 2005), p. 754.
38. 'John Burnside in Conversation', p. 96.
39. John Burnside, 'Faith', in *The Myth of the Twin*, p. 20.
40. John Burnside, 'Travelling into the Quotidian', pp. 60, 61.
41. John Burnside, 'Ama et fac quod Vis', in *Gift Songs* (London: Cape, 2007), p. 9.
42. Burnside, 'Travelling into the Quotidian', p. 61.
43. 'John Burnside in Conversation', p. 96.
44. John Burnside, 'One Hand Clapping', in *The Good Neighbour* (London: Cape, 2005), p. 13.

Chapter 9 – Mackay

1. Aonghas MacNeacail, *Rock and Water* (Edinburgh: Polygon, 1990), p. 25.
2. William Wordsworth, *Complete Poetical Works* (Oxford: Oxford University Press, 1936), p. 147; Seamus Heaney, *Death of a Naturalist* (London: Faber, 1966), pp. 5–6, 11.
3. Aonghas MacNeacail, *Rock and Water*, pp. 22, 20.
4. C.f. Benedict Anderson, *Imagined Communities* (London and New York: Verso, [1983] 1991) and Cairns Craig, *The Modern Scottish Novel: Narrative and the National Imagination* (Edinburgh: Edinburgh University Press, 1999), pp. 11 ff. for a discussion of the contested notion of the 'imagined community' within nationalist and anti-nationalist approaches to Scottish literature.
5. Patrick Kavanagh, *Kavanagh's Weekly*, 24 May 1952; reprinted in Patrick Kavanagh *Collected Prose* (London: MacGibbon and Kee, 1967), p. 282.
6. Aonghas MacNeacail, 'Country Life', in *Rock and Water*, p. 63.
7. Aonghas MacNeacail and Simon Fraser, *Sireadh Bradain Sicir/Seeking Wise Salmon* (Nairn: Balnain Books, 1983), p. 5.
8. Aonghas MacNeacail, 'The Prospects for a Gaelic Writer', *Books in Scotland* 4 (1979), p. 11.
9. Aonghas MacNeacail and Simon Fraser, *An Cathadh Mòr/The Great Snowbattle* (Nairn: Balnain Books, 1984), p. 17.
10. Ezra Pound, 'Review of *Al Que Quiere!* by William Carlos Williams'. Quoted in Charles Tomlinson, 'Introduction', in William Carlos Williams, *Selected Poems* (London: Penguin, 1976), p. 11.
11. Ibid., p. 11.
12. Charles Olson, 'Projective Verse' in *Collected Prose* (Berkeley, London: University of California Press, [1950] 1997), pp. 239–49.

13. Aonghas MacNeacail, 'dol dhachaigh – 1 / going home – 1', in *Oideachadh Ceart agus Dáin Eile / A Proper Schooling and Other Poems* (Edinburgh: Polygon, 1986), pp. 52–3.

14. MacNeacail, 'éideadh/altire', in *an seachnadh agus dain eile/the avoiding and other poems* (Edinburgh: Macdonald, 1986), pp. 102–3, 46–7.

15. Aonghas MacNeacail, 'English as a Function for Gaelic', *Books in Scotland* 3 (1978–9), p. 6.

16. Aonghas MacNeacail, 'Being Gaelic, and otherwise', *Chapman* 89–90 (1998), p. 155.

17. Aonghas MacNeacail, 'bratach/banner', in *an seachnadh*, pp. 10–11.

18. Aonghas MacNeacail, *Oideachadh Ceart*, p. 5.

19. C.f. Eleanor Knott, *Irish Classical Poetry, commonly called Bardic Poetry*, (Dublin: Sign of the Three Candles, 1960), pp. 11–14.

20. Aonghas MacNeacail, 'sear-siar: seunaidhean/east-west: telepathies', in *Oideachadh Ceart*, pp. 88–91. When this poem was first published, in *Chapman* 41 (1985), pp. 50–1, the layout was subtly different:

> nì nach do mhothaich thu
>> druid
> nì nach do mhothaich thu
>> is druid
> nì nach do mhothaich thu
>> is druid is druid is druid is druid is druid.

21. Ibid., 'gàidheal san eorp/agael in europe', pp. 18–19.

22. Aonghas MacNeacail, 'trì nithean', in *laoidh an donais òig/hymn to a young demon* (Edinburgh: Polygon, 2007), pp. 6–7.

23. Aonghas MacNeacail, 'òran cèile/song for a spouse', in *laoidh an donais òig*, pp. 44–5.

24. Aonghas MacNeacail, 'An Cathadh Mòr/The Great Snowbattle,' in *Oideachadh Ceart agus Dàin Eile*, pp. 72–3.

25. Lucien Stryk, 'Introduction', in *The Penguin Book of Zen Poetry* (London: Penguin, 1991), p. 12.

26. Aonghas MacNeacail, 'uiseag uiseag/skylark skylark', in *Oideachadh Ceart*, pp. 38–9.

27. Aonghas MacNeacail, 'Poetry in Translation', *Edinburgh Review* 70 (1985), p. 112.

28. Derick Thomson, review of *Sireadh Bradain Sicir/Seeking Wise Salmon*, *Gairm* 126 (1984), p. 191. Author's translation.

29. Joseph Brodsky, 'Uncommon Visage', Nobel lecture, 8 Dec. 1987, quoted Christopher Whyte, 'Review of *Oideachadh Ceart, Aotromachd* and *Fax*', *Lines in Review* 141 (1997), p. 46.

30. Aonghas MacNeacail, 'oideachadh ceart', in *Oideachadh Ceart*, pp. 12–15.

31. C.f. Donald Meek (ed.) *Caran an t-Saoghal/The Wiles of the World* (Edinburgh: Birlinn, 2003), pp. 20–3.
32. Christopher Whyte, 'Review' quoting Patrick K. Ford and J. E. Caerwyn Williams, *The Irish Literary Tradition* (Cardiff: University of Wales Press, 1992), p. 32.
33. Charles Olson, 'Maximus, from Dogtown', in *Selected Poems* (Berkeley, Los Angeles and Oxford: University of California Press, 1993), p. 143.
34. Aonghas MacNeacail, 'fearann mo ghaoil', *Gairm* 80 (1972), p. 359.
35. Aonghas MacNeacail, 'lili marlene san h-eileanan siar/lili marlene in the western isles', in *laoidh an donais òig*, pp. 48–9.
36. Aonghas MacNeacail, 'do chòin/your dogs', in *Oideachadh Ceart*, pp. 66–7.
37. Aonghas MacNeacail, 'A' Chlach/The Stone', in *laoidh an donais òig*, pp. 80–1.
38. Ibid., 'craobh na bliadhna/the year's tree', pp. 46–7.
39. Aonghas MacNeacail, 'òran gaoil/love song', in *an seachnadh*, pp. 16–17.
40. Ibid., 'nuair a phòg sinn a' chiad uair/when we kissed for the first time', pp. 18–21.
41. Ibid., 'an aimhreit/the contention', pp. 30–1.
42. Cf. Aonghas MacNeacail, 'Poetry in Translation', p. 107.
43. The symbol of the deer has a complicated history in Gaelic poetry, as both a representation of clan chiefs and also a signifier of the Clearances of the Highlands; in recent poetry it most famously appears in Sorley MacLean's 'Hallaig' as 'time, the deer' which the poet shoots to ensure the temporary survival of his culture. C.f. Sorley MacLean, *O Coille gu Bearradh* (Manchester and Edinburgh: Carcanet), pp. 226–31.
44. Aonghas MacNeacail, 'an eilid bhàn/the white hind', in *an seachnadh*, pp. 92–3.

Chapter 10 – McGuire

1. Kathleen Jamie, 'View from the Cliffs', in *Mr and Mrs Scotland are Dead: Poems 1980–1994* (Newcastle-upon-Tyne: Bloodaxe, 2002), p. 1.
2. Quoted in M. H. Abrams (ed.), *The Norton Anthology of English Literature* (London: Norton, 1993), pp. 142–3.
3. Frederic Jameson, *The Political Unconscious: Narrative as a Socially Symbolic Act* (London: Metheun, 1981), p. 81.
4. Ian Jack, quoted in Kirsty Scott, 'In the Nature of Things', *The Guardian*, 18 June 2005, p. 20.
5. Kathleen Jamie interviewed by Richard Price, *Verse* 8 (3)/9 (1) (winter/spring 1992), pp. 103–6, 103.
6. Kathleen Jamie, 'Jocky in the Wildirness', in *Mr and Mrs Scotland are Dead*, p. 139.
7. Ibid., 'Arraheids', p. 137.

8. Kathleen Jamie interviewed by Richard Price, *Verse* 8 (3)/9 (1) (winter/spring 1992), p. 103, p. 104.

9. Daniel O'Rourke, *Dream State: The New Scottish Poets* (Edinburgh: Polygon, 1994), p. 281.

10. Helen Boden, 'Kathleen Jamie: Semiotics of Scotland', in Aileen Christianson and Alison Lumsden (eds), *Contemporary Scottish Women's Writing* (Edinburgh: Edinburgh University Press, 2000), p. 29.

11. Ibid., p. 30.

12. Kathleen Jamie, 'On the Design . . . ', in *Jizzen* (London: Picador, 1999) p. 48.

13. Seamus Heaney, *An Open Letter* (Derry: Field Day, 1983), p. 9.

14. Quoted in Edna Longley, *Poetry in the Wars* (Newcastle-upon-Tyne: Bloodaxe, 1986), p. 199.

15. Christopher Whyte, *Modern Scottish Poetry* (Edinburgh: Edinburgh University Press, 2004), p. 8.

16. Kathleen Jamie, 'Jocky in the Wildirness', in *Mr and Mrs Scotland are Dead*, p. 139.

17. Eavan Boland, *Object Lessons: The Life of the Woman and the Poet in Our Times* (London: Vintage, 1995), p. 183.

18. Kathleen Jamie, 'Meadowsweet', in *Jizzen*, p. 35.

19. Ibid.

20. Ibid.

21. Ibid., 'Vetrasound', p. 13.

22. Interview with Kathleen Jamie in *Books from Scotland*, www.booksfromscotland.com/Authors/Kathleen-Jamie/Interview (25 July 2008).

23. William Wordsworth, 'Preface' to *Lyrical Ballads*, in M. H. Abrams (ed.), *The Norton Anthology of English Literature* (New York: Norton, 1993), vol. 2, p. 145.

24. Richard Kerridge, 'Introduction', in Richard Kerridge and Neil Samuels (eds), *Writing the Environment: Ecocriticism and Literature* (London: Zed Books, 1998), p. 4.

25. Feminists, Marxists and race campaigners would probably argue that it is rich, white men who are most acutely responsible for exacerbating the current environmental crisis. Moreover, as the twenty-first century unfurls these political inequalities will only become more significant in the competition for scarce resources.

26. Philip Larkin, 'Poetry of Departures', in *Collected Poems* (London: Faber and Faber, 2003), p. 64.

27. Quoted in Kirsty Scott, 'In the Nature of Things', p. 20.

28. Kathleen Jamie, 'The Whale-Watcher', in *The Tree House* (London: Picador, 2005), p. 25.

29. Samuel Johnson, 'Review of a Free Inquiry into the Nature and Origin of Evil', in *The Works of Samuel Johnson*, 12 vols (London: 1801), vol. 8, p. 48.

30. Jonathan Bate, *Romantic Ecology: William Wordsworth and the Environmental Tradition* (London: Routledge, 1991), p. 9.
31. Jonathan Bate, 'Poetry and Biodiversity', in Richard Kerridge and Neil Samuels (eds), *Writing the Environment: Ecocriticism and Literature* (London: Zed Books, 1998), p. 53.
32. See the Introduction to Thomas Docherty (ed.), *Postmodernism: A Reader* (London: Longman, 1992).
33. Quoted in Kirsty Scott, 'In the Nature of Things', p. 20.
34. Kathleen Jamie, 'Alder', in *The Tree House*, p. 7.
35. Ibid., 'Pipistrelles', p. 30.
36. Henry David Thoreau, 'Walking', in Will H. Dicks (ed.), *Essays and Other Writings* (London: Walter Scott, 1895), p. 14.
37. Kathleen Jamie, 'Alder', in *The Tree House*, p. 7.
38. Quoted in Kirsty Scott, 'In the Nature of Things', p. 20.
39. Avrahm Yarmolinsky (ed.), *The Letters of Anton Chekov* (London: Cape, 1974), p. 88.
40. Interview with Kathleen Jamie in *Books from Scotland*, www.booksfromscotland.com/Authors/Kathleen-Jamie/Interview (25 July 2008).
41. William Blake, 'Letter to the Revd Dr Trisler (23 August 1799)', in Geoffrey Keynes (ed.), *Complete Writings* (London: Oxford University Press, 1925), p. 793.
42. Quoted in Cleanth Brooks, *The Well Wrought Urn: Studies in the Structure of Poetry* (London: Dobson, 1968), p. 4.
43. Kathleen Jamie, *Findings* (London: Sort of Books, 2005), back cover.
44. Kathleen Jamie, 'The Buddleia', in *The Tree House*, p. 27.
45. Ibid., 'Pipistrelles', p. 30.
46. Ibid., 'Daisies', p. 32.
47. Kathleen Jamie and Sean Mayne Smith, 'The Panchen Lama Rides from Lhasa to Kumbum', in *The Autonomous Region: Poems and Photographs from Tibet* (Newcastle-upon-Tyne: Bloodaxe, 1993), p. 67.
48. Norman MacCaig, 'An Ordinary Day', in *The Poems of Norman MacCaig* (Edinburgh: Polygon, 2005), p. 164.

Chapter 11 – Craig

1. See Gavin Bowd, *The Outsiders: Alexander Trocchi and Kenneth White: An Essay* (Kirkcaldy: self-published, 1998).
2. Hugh MacDiarmid, 'The Kind of Poetry I Want', in Michael Grieve and W. R. Aitken (eds), *Complete Poems 1920–1976* (London: Martin Brian & O'Keefe, 1978), vol. 2, p. 1013.
3. J. D. Fergusson, *Modern Scottish Painting* (Glasgow: Wm MacLellan, 1943), p. 69.
4. Kenneth White, 'The Scot Abroad', in *On Scottish Ground: Selected Essays* (Edinburgh: Polygon, 1998), p. 105.

5. Ibid., p. 106.
6. Ibid., p. 107.
7. Ibid.
8. 'Scotland, History and the Writer', in *On Scottish Ground*, p. 162.
9. Kenneth White, 'Pelagius', in *Open World: The Collected Poems 1960–2000* (Edinburgh: Polygon, 2003, p. 9):

   'but was there ever, I ask you
   a brighter mind
   a more diamond being

   in all the murky history of knowledge?'.

10. Ibid., Note to 'Report to Erigena', p. 606.
11. Ibid., 'Walking the Coast', p. 170.
12. Kenneth White, 'Kentigern on Atlantic Quay', in *On Scottish Ground*, p. 195.
13. Ibid.
14. Ibid., 'Scotland, History and the Writer', p. 153.
15. Ibid., 'The Archaic Context', p. 31.
16. Ibid., 'The Alban Project', p. 3.
17. Ibid., 'A Shaman Dancing on the Glacier', p. 41.
18. Ibid., 'The Archaic Context', p. 33.
19. Ibid., 'Scotland, Intelligence, Culture', p. 91.
20. Kenneth White, 'On Rannoch Moor', in *Open World*, pp. 100–1.
21. Kenneth White, 'Into the White World', in *On Scottish Ground*, p. 58.
22. Kenneth White, 'The Island without a Name', in *Open World*, p. 337.
23. Hugh MacDiarmid, *Complete Poems 1920–1976* (Manchester: Carcanet 1978), vol. 2, p. 1004.
24. Ibid., 'On a Raised Beach', vol. 1, p. 428.
25. Ibid., p. 422.
26. Kenneth White, 'Walking the Coast', in *Open World*, p. 129.
27. Hugh MacDiarmid, 'On a Raised Beach', in *Collected Poems*, vol. 1, p. 422.
28. Ibid., 'Direadh III', vol. 2, p. 1189.
29. Kenneth White, 'The High Field', in *On Scottish Ground*, p. 173.
30. Ibid., 'The Archaic Context', p. 15.
31. Ibid., 'The High Field', p. 175; quotation from the 'Introduction' to Hugh MacDiarmid, *The Golden Treasury of Scottish Poetry* (London: Macmillan, 1948).
32. Ibid., 'The High Field', p. 176.
33. Ibid. The Tarim Basin is a desert region of China crossed by the silk roads and therefore a series of crossing points of East and West.
34. Hugh MacDiarmid, 'The Kind of Poetry I Want', in *Complete Poems*, vol. 2, p. 1013.

35. Kenneth White, 'Looking Out: From Neotechnics to Geopoetics', in *On Scottish Ground*, p. 147.
36. Kenneth White, 'Walking the Coast, LII', in *Open World*, p. 178.
37. Kenneth White, 'Looking Out: From Neotechnics to Geopoetics', in *On Scottish Ground*, p. 142.
38. Geddes's *Masque of Learning*, produced in 1912, presented 'the procession of European cultural ideals from pre-classical times to the present': Philip Mairet, *Pioneer of Sociology: The Life and Letters of Patrick Geddes* (London: Lund Humphries, 1957), p. 144.
39. *Arts and Letters*, 1, 4 (1944).
40. Letter to Pierre Garnier, September 1963, in *Image* (December, 1964); quoted Yves Abrioux, *Ian Hamilton Finlay: A Visual Primer* (Chicago: University of Chicago Press, 1992), p. 220.
41. 'Revolution of the word' was the subtitle of Colin MacCabe's work on James Joyce, which was one of the early contributions by a British critic to the deconstructive reading of literature: *James Joyce and the Revolution of the Word* (London: Palgrave Macmillan, 1979).
42. Yves Abrioux, *Ian Hamilton Finlay*, p. 280.
43. Kenneth White, 'Walking the Coast, LIII', in *Open World*, p. 179.
44. Ibid., 'Tractatus Cosmo-Poeticus', p. 195.
45. Ibid., 'Last Page of a Notebook', p. 123.
46. White's note, *Open World*, p. 609.
47. Ibid., 'The Region of Identity', p. 202.
48. Ibid., 'Into the Whiteness', p. 109.
49. See, for instance, Robin Fulton's comments in *Contemporary Scottish Poetry: Individuals and Contexts* (Loanhead: Macdonald, 1974), to which White responded in 'The High Field', *On Scottish Ground*, p. 171.
50. Kenneth White, 'Into the White World', in *On Scottish Ground*, p. 58.
51. Ibid., pp. 60, 61.
52. Ibid., p. 64.
53. Kenneth White, 'Letter to an Old Calligrapher', in *Open World*, p. 106.
54. Ibid., 'Chant', p. 57.
55. Kenneth White, 'Talking Transformation', in *On Scottish Ground*, p. 184.
56. Kenneth White, 'Interpretations of a Twisted Pine', in *Open World*, p. 213.
57. Kenneth White, 'A Shaman Dancing on a Glacier', in *On Scottish Ground*, p. 37.
58. Martin Heidegger, 'Letter on Humanism', in Lawrence E. Cahoone (ed.), *From Modernism to Postmodernism* (Oxford: Blackwell, 1996), p. 303.
59. Kenneth White, 'A Shaman Dancing on a Glacier', in *On Scottish Ground*, p. 38.
60. Kenneth White, 'Black Forest', in *Open World*, p. 92.
61. Martin Heidegger, 'Letter on Humanism', p. 299.
62. Kenneth White, 'The High Field', in *On Scottish Ground*, p. 179.

63. Ibid.
64. Ibid., 'Scotland, History and the Writer', p. 163.
65. Ibid.
66. Here the work of George Davie has had a particularly destructive effect, since he sees the Kantians and Hegelians of nineteenth-century Scottish philosophy as betrayers of the tradition of 'Scotch metaphysics'.
67. Kenneth White, 'The High Field', in *On Scottish Ground*, p. 174; original in Hugh MacDiarmid, *In Memoriam James Joyce* (Glasgow: William Maclellan, 1956), p. 48.
68. Kenneth White, 'White Valley', in *Open World*, p. 52.
69. Ibid., 'To the Bone', p. 53.
70. Ibid., 'The Chaoticist Manifesto', p. 550.
71. Ibid.

Chapter 12 – Gillis

1. All five collections published by Faber. *The Eyes* is a version of Antonio Machado's; *Orpheus* a version of Rilke's *Die Sonette An Orpheus*.
2. Robert Crawford, *Scotland's Books: The Penguin History of Scottish Literature* (Harmondsworth: Penguin, 2007), p. 724.
3. Don Paterson, 'The Ferryman's Arms', in *Nil Nil* (London: Faber, 1993), p. 1.
4. Patrick Crotty, 'Between Home and Rome', review of Don Paterson's *Landing Light*, *Times Literary Supplement*, 12 December 2003, p. 5.
5. Don Paterson, *The Eyes* (London: Faber, 1999), p. 59.
6. Virgil describes a 'huge throng' of dead souls, 'helpless, still not buried', gathered on the banks of the Styx. Charon will transport only those who 'rest in peace', leaving behind the others in an awful limbo:

   > A hundred years they wander, hovering round these shores
   > till at last they may return and see once more the pools
   > they long to cross.

   Charon chooses who is in, and who is not: 'the grim ferryman ushers aboard now these, now those, / others he thrusts away, back from the water's edge' (Virgil, *The Aeneid* (Bk 6, ll. 338–76), trans. Robert Fagles (London: Penguin, 2006), pp. 192–3).
7. Dante describes this limbo:

   > such a commotion of groans and wails of woe
   >   . . .
   > howls, shrieks, grunts, gasps, bawls,
   > a never-ending, terrible crescendo. (*The Inferno of Dante Alighieri* (Bk 3, ll 22–30), trans. Ciaran Carson (London: Granta 2002), p. 16).
8. Ibid., p. 17.

9. Don Paterson, *Orpheus* (London: Faber, 2006), p. 68. One of Paterson's aphorisms reads: 'Time + consciousness = foreknowledge of our passing. Our only *unique* gift; we can act knowing, in some sense, that we are already dead' (*The Book of Shadows* (London: Picador, 2004), p. 81).
10. Don Paterson, *Orpheus*, p. 69.
11. Don Paterson, *The Book of Shadows*, p. 39.
12. Don Paterson, *Orpheus*, p. 71.
13. Don Paterson, *The Book of Shadows*, p. 13.
14. Paterson continues: 'We are then in danger of blithely or accidentally destroying our real element and habitat, with which we no longer feel any physical continuity' (*Orpheus*, p. 71).
15. Don Paterson, *The Book of Shadows*, p. 64.
16. Don Paterson, 'Introduction', Don Paterson and Charles Simic (eds), *New British Poetry* (Saint Paul: Graywolf Press, 2004), p. xxxi.
17. Another aphorism reads: 'Art is the prism by which the white light – that synaesthetic radiance that we usually indicate with the word truth – is diffracted into its constituent frequencies' (*The Book of Shadows*, p. 164).
18. The illustration is by Toby Morrison.
19. Joseph Conrad, *Lord Jim* (London: Penguin, [1900] 1989), p. 65.
20. Don Paterson, 'Ferryman's Arms', in *Nil Nil*, p. 1.
21. Don Paterson, *The Book of Shadows*, p. 22.
22. Don Paterson, 'The White Lie', in *Landing Light* (London: Faber, 2004), p. 82.
23. Don Paterson, 'The Lyric Principle, Part 1: The Sense of Sound', *Poetry Review* 97 (2) (summer, 2007), pp. 56–72.
24. Don Paterson, 'An Elliptical Stylus', in *Nil Nil*, pp. 20–1.
25. Ibid., 'Amnesia', pp. 22–3.
26. Paul Muldoon, *Quoof* (London: Faber, 1983).
27. Don Paterson, *Nil Nil*, p. 46.
28. 'Part II' and 'Part III' of 'The Alexandrian Library' appear in *God's Gift to Women* and *Landing Light* respectively.
29. Jorge Louis Borges, 'The Garden of Forking Paths' in, *Collected Fictions*, trans. Andrew Hurley (New York: Penguin, 1998), p. 125.
30. Ibid., p. 127.
31. Don Paterson, 'The Alexandrian Library', in *Nil Nil*, p. 25.
32. Ibid., p. 26.
33. Ibid.
34. Ibid., pp. 26–7.
35. Don Paterson, *Nil Nil*, p. 51.
36. Ibid., p. 25.
37. Don Paterson, 'The Dilemma of the Peot [sic]', in Tony Curtis (ed.), *How Poets Work* (Bridgend: Seren, 1996), p. 157.
38. Don Paterson, *The Book of Shadows*, p. 148.
39. Don Paterson, 'The Alexandrian Library', in *Nil Nil*, p. 27.

40. Ibid., p. 29.
41. François Aussemain's epigraph to 'Nil Nil' – talking about 'all our abandoned histories' which 'plunge on into deeper and deeper obscurity', concludes: 'only in the infinite ghost-libraries of the imagination . . . can their ends be pursued, the dull and terrible facts finally authenticated' (*Nil Nil*, p. 51).
42. Don Paterson, 'The Alexandrian Library', in *Nil Nil*, p. 33.
43. Ibid., 'Nil Nil', p. 53.
44. Ibid., pp. 51–2.
45. Of course, it might be argued this is a recognisably Scottish literary trait.

Further Reading

Abad-Garcia, Pilar, 'Generic Description and the Postmodern Lyric Discourse/ Mode: Carol Ann Duffy's "Anne Hathaway"', in Eva Müller-Zettelmann and Margarete Rubik (eds), *Theory into Poetry: New Approaches to the Lyric* (Amsterdam: Rodopi, 2005), pp. 265–76.

Abrioux, Yves, *Ian Hamilton Finlay: A Visual Primer* (Cambridge: Cambridge University Press; and Chicago: University of Chicago Press, 1992).

Allen, Donald and George F. Butterick (eds), *The Postmoderns: The New American Poetry Revised* (New York: Grove Press, 1982).

Anderson, Linda, 'Autobiographical Travesties: The Nostalgic Self in Queer Writing', in David Alderson and Linda Anderson (eds), *Territories of Desire in Queer Culture: Refiguring Contemporary Boundaries* (Manchester: Manchester University Press, 2000), pp. 68–81.

Anderson, Perry, *The Origins of Postmodernity* (London: Verso, 1998).

Bachelard, Gaston, *The Poetics of Space*, trans. Maria Jolas (Boston: Beacon Press, [1958] 1994).

Barry, Pete, *Contemporary British Poetry and the City* (Manchester: Manchester University Press, 2000).

Baxter, Judith (ed.), *Four Women Poets* (Cambridge: Cambridge University Press, 1995).

Bell, Eleanor, *Questioning Scotland: Literature, Nationalism, Postmodernism* (Basingstoke: Palgrave, 2004).

Bell, Eleanor and Gavin Miller (eds), *Scotland in Theory* (Amsterdam: Rodopi, 2004).

Bertram, Vicki (ed.), *Kicking Daffodils: Twentieth Century Women Poets* (Edinburgh: Edinburgh University Press, 2005).

Beveridge, Craig and Ronald Turnbull, *The Eclipse of Scottish Culture: Inferiorism and the Intellectuals* (Edinburgh: Polygon, 1989).

Bibliography of Scottish Literature in Translation, www.nls.uk/catalogues/ resources/boslit/index.html

Birrell, Ross and Alec Finlay (eds), *Justified Sinners – An Archaeology of Scottish Counter-Culture (1960–2000)* (Edinburgh: Pocketbooks, 2002).

Black, Ronald (ed.), *An Tuil: Anthology of 20th Century Scottish Gaelic Verse* (Edinburgh: Polygon, 1999).

Blyth, Caroline, 'Autonomies and Regions: An Interview with Kathleen Jamie', *Oxford Poetry* 7 (2) (1993), pp. 7–12.

Boddy, Kasia, 'Edwin Morgan's Adventures in Calamerica', *Yale Journal of Criticism* 13 (1) (2000), pp. 177–91.

Boland, Eavan, 'Making the Difference: Eroticism and Ageing in the Work of the Woman Poet', *PN Review* 20 (4) (1994), pp. 13–21.

—, *Object Lessons: The Life of the Woman and the Poet in Our Times* (London: Vintage, 1995).

Bowd, Gavin, 'Poetry after God: The Reinvention of the Sacred in the Work of Eugène Guillevic and Kenneth White', *Dalhousie French Studies* 39–40 (1997), pp. 159–80.

Bowd, Gavin, Charles Forsdick and Norman Bissell (eds), *Grounding a World: Essays on the Work of Kenneth White* (Glasgow: Alba, 2005).

Broom, Sarah: *Contemporary British and Irish Poetry: An Introduction* (London: Macmillan, 2006).

Brown, Clare and Don Paterson (eds), *Don't Ask Me What I Mean: Poets in Their Own Words* (London: Picador, 2003).

Brown, Ian (ed.), *The Edinburgh History of Scottish Literature, Volume Three: Modern Transformations: New Identities (from 1918)* (Edinburgh: Edinburgh University Press, 2007).

Brown, Matthew, 'In/Outside Scotland: Race and Citizenship in the Work of Jackie Kay', in Berthold Schoene (ed.), *The Edinburgh Companion to Contemporary Scottish Literature* (Edinburgh: Edinburgh University Press, 2007), pp. 219–26.

Buchanan, Ian and John Marks (eds), *Deleuze and Literature* (Edinburgh: Edinburgh University Press, 2000).

Burnside, John, *Otro Mundo es Posible: Poetry, Dissidence and Reality TV* (Edinburgh: Scottish Book Trust, 2003).

—, 'Travelling into the Quotidian: Some Notes on Allison Funk's "Heartland" Poems', *Poetry Review* 95 (2) (2005), pp. 59–70.

—, 'Mind the Gap: On Reading American Poetry', *Poetry Review* 96 (3) (2006), pp. 56–67.

Cahoone, Laurence (ed.), *From Modernism to Postmodernism* (Oxford: Blackwell, 1996).

Carruthers, G., D. Goldie and A. Renfrew (eds), *Beyond Scotland: New Contexts for Twentieth-Century Scottish Literature* (Amsterdam: Rodopi, 2004).

Carson, Ciaran (trans.), *The Inferno of Dante Alighieri* (London: Granta, 2002).

Christianson, Aileen and Alison Lumsden (eds), *Contemporary Scottish Women's Writing* (Edinburgh: Edinburgh University Press, 2000).

Clandfield, Peter, '"What Is In My Blood?": Contemporary Black Scottishness and the Work of Jackie Kay', in Teresa Hubel and Neil Brooks (eds), *Literature and Racial Ambiguity* (Amsterdam: Rodopi, 2002), pp. 1–25.

Clark, T. J., 'Origins of the Present Crisis', *New Left Review* 2 (March–April, 2000), pp. 85–96.

Cockin, Katharine: 'Rethinking Transracial Adoption: Reading Jackie Kay's *The Adoption Papers*', *A/B: Auto/Biography Studies* 18 (2) (2003), pp. 276–91.

Conn, Stewart, *Distances: A Personal Evocation of People and Places* (Dalkeith: Scottish Cultural Press, 2001).

Corbett, John, *Written in the Language of the Scottish Nation: A History of Literary Translation into Scots* (Clevedon: Multilingual Matters, 1999).

Corbett, John, Derrick McClure and Jane Stuart-Smith (eds), *The Edinburgh Companion to Scots* (Edinburgh: Edinburgh University Press, 2003).

Corelis, Jon, 'From Scotland to Suburbia: A Landscape of Current British Poetry' *Chapman* 87 (1997), pp. 4–16.

Craig, Cairns, *Out of History: Narrative Paradigms in Scottish and British Culture* (Edinburgh: Polygon, 1996).

—, 'Scotland and Hybridity', in G. Carruthers, D. Goldie and A. Renfrew (eds), *Beyond Scotland: New Contexts for Twentieth-Century Scottish Literature* (Amsterdam: Rodopi, 2004), pp. 220–51.

Craig, Cairns (ed.), *The History of Scottish Literature: Volume 4: Twentieth Century* (Aberdeen: Aberdeen University Press, 1987).

Crawford, Robert, *Identifying Poets: Self and Territory in Twentieth-Century Poetry* (Edinburgh: Edinburgh University Press, 1993).

Crawford, Robert (ed.), *Contemporary Poetry And Contemporary Science* (Oxford: Oxford University Press, 2006).

—, *Scotland's Books: The Penguin History of Scottish Literature* (Harmondsworth: Penguin, 2007).

— and Hamish Whyte (eds), *About Edwin Morgan* (Edinburgh: Edinburgh University Press, 1990).

— and David Kinloch (eds), *Reading Douglas Dunn* (Edinburgh: Edinburgh University Press, 1992).

— and Anne Varty (eds), *Liz Lochhead's Voices* (Edinburgh: Edinburgh University Press, 1994).

— and Mick Imlah (eds), *The New Penguin Book of Scottish Verse* (London: Penguin, 2001)

Cronin, Michael, *Translation and Globalization* (London: Routledge, 2003).

Crotty, Patrick 'Between Home and Rome', review of Don Paterson's *Landing Light*, *Times Literary Supplement*, 12 December 2003, p. 5.

Dentith, Simon, 'Harnessing Plurality: Andrew Greig and Modernism', in Berthold Schoene (ed.), *The Edinburgh Companion to Contemporary Scottish Literature* (Edinburgh: Edinburgh University Press, 2007), pp. 184–93.

Dósa, Attila, '"The Kind of Poetry I Mean": Notes on Douglas Dunn's Criticism of Scottish Poetry', *Studies in Scottish Literature* 32 (2001), pp. 55–66.

Dowson, Jane and Alice Entwistle, *A History of Twentieth-Century British Women's Poetry* (Cambridge: Cambridge University Press, 2005).

Duncan, Lesley and Elspeth King (eds), *The Wallace Muse: Poems and Artworks Inspired by the Life and Legend of William Wallace* (Edinburgh: Luath Press, 2005).

Dunn, Douglas, 'Writing Things Down', in C. B. McCully (ed.), *The Poet's Voice and Craft* (Manchester: Carcanet, 1994), pp. 84–103.

Dunn, Douglas (ed.), *Twentieth-Century Scottish Poetry* (London: Faber, [1992] 2006).

Dyer, Richard, 'Jackie Kay', in Susheila Nasta (ed.), *Writing across Worlds: Contemporary Writers Talk* (London: Routledge, 2004), pp. 237–49.

Entwhistle, Alice, 'Scotland's New House: Domesticity and Domicile in Contemporary Scottish Women's Poetry', in Berthold Schoene (ed.), *The Edinburgh Companion to Contemporary Scottish Literature* (Edinburgh: Edinburgh University Press, 2007), pp. 114–23.

Fagles, Robert (trans.), *The Aeneid* (London: Penguin, 2006).

Fazzini, Marco, 'Edwin Morgan: Two Interviews', *Studies in Scottish Literature* 29, (1996), pp. 45–57.

—, 'An Interview with Douglas Dunn in 1997', *Studies in Scottish Literature* 31, (1999), pp. 121–30.

—, 'Alterities from Outer Space: Edwin Morgan's Science-Fiction Poems', in Marco Fazzini (ed.), *Resisting Alterities: Wilson Harris and Other Avatars of Otherness* (Amsterdam: Rodopi, 2004), pp. 225–41.

— (ed.), *Alba Literaria: A History of Scottish Literature* (Venezia Mestre: Amos Edizioni, 2005).

Finlay, Alec and Kevin MacNeil (eds), *Wish I Was Here: A Scottish Multicultural Anthology* (Edinburgh: Pocketbooks, 2005).

Ford, Patrick K. and J. E. Caerwyn Williams, *The Irish Literary Tradition* (Cardiff: University of Wales Press, 1992).

Fox, Stephen, 'Edwin Morgan and the Two Cultures', *Studies in Scottish Literature* 33–4 (2004), pp. 71–86.

Fraser, Lilias, 'Kathleen Jamie interviewed', *Scottish Studies Review* 2 (1) (2001), pp. 15–23.

Friel, Raymond, 'Women Beware Gravity: Kathleen Jamie's Poetry', in *Southfields: Criticism and Celebration* (London: Southfields, 1995), pp. 29–47.

—, 'Don Paterson Interviewed', in Robert Crawford et al. (eds), *Talking Verse* (St Andrews and Williamsburg: Verse, 1995), pp. 192–8.

Fulton, Robin, *Contemporary Scottish Poetry: Individuals and Contexts* (Loanhead: Macdonald, 1974).

Gairn, Louisa, 'Clearing Space: Kathleen Jamie and Ecology', in Berthold Schoene (ed.), *The Edinburgh Companion to Contemporary Scottish Literature* (Edinburgh: Edinburgh University Press, 2007), pp. 236–44.

Gardiner, Michael, 'Towards a Post-British Theory of Modernism: Speech and Vision in Edwin Morgan', *Pretexts: Literary and Cultural Studies* 11 (2) (2002), pp. 133–46.

—, *The Cultural Roots of British Devolution* (Edinburgh: Edinburgh University Press, 2004).

—, *Modern Scottish Culture* (Edinburgh: Edinburgh University Press, 2005).

—, *From Trocchi to Trainspotting: Scottish Critical Theory since 1960* (Edinburgh: Edinburgh University Press, 2006).

—, 'Literature, Theory, Politics: Devolution as Iteration', in Berthold Schoene (ed.), *The Edinburgh Companion to Contemporary Scottish Literature* (Edinburgh: Edinburgh University Press, 2007), pp. 43–50.

Gibson, Andrew, *Towards a Postmodern Theory of Narrative* (Edinburgh: Edinburgh University Press, 1996).

Gifford, Douglas and Alan Riach (eds), *Scotlands: Poets and the Nation* (Manchester: Carcanet, 2004).

— and Dorothy MacMillan (eds), *A History of Scottish Women's Writing* (Edinburgh: Edinburgh University Press, 1997).

Gish, Nancy K., 'Adoption, Identity, and Voice: Jackie Kay's Inventions of Self', in Marianne Novy (ed.), *Imagining Adoption: Essays on Literature and Culture* (Ann Arbor: University of Michigan Press, 2004), pp. 171–91.

Glen, Duncan, *The Poetry of the Scots: An Introduction and Bibliographic Guide to Poetry in Gaelic, Scots, Latin and English* (Edinburgh: Edinburgh University Press, 1999).

— and Tom Hubbard (eds), *Fringe of Gold: The Fife Anthology* (Edinburgh: Birlinn, 2008).

Gohrbandt, Detlev and Bruno von Lutz (eds), *Seeing And Saying: Self-Referentiality In British And American Literature* (New York: Lang, 1998).

Gow, Carol, Review of Alan Riach's *First and Last Songs*, *Lines Review* 137 (1996), pp. 59–61.

Hames, Scott, 'Don Paterson and Poetic Autonomy', in Berthold Schoene (ed.), *The Edinburgh Companion to Contemporary Scottish Literature* (Edinburgh: Edinburgh University Press, 2007), pp. 245–54.

Herbert, W. N. and Matthew Hollis (eds), *Strong Words: Modern Poets on Modern Poetry* (Tarset: Bloodaxe, 2000).

Hobsbaum, Philip, 'Speech Rather Than Lallans: West of Scotland Poetry', *Lines Review* 113 (January 1990), pp. 5–10.

Hubbard, Tom (ed.), *The New Makars: Contemporary Poetry in Scots* (Edinburgh: Mercat, 1991).

—, 'Skulls and Stoaters', *Poetry Ireland Review* 93 (2008), pp. 90–3.

Hubel, Theresa and Neil Brooks (eds), *Literature and Racial Ambiguity* (Amsterdam: Rodopi, 2002).

Hughes, Robert, *Nothing If Not Critical* (New York: Penguin, 1990).

Jaggi, Maya and Richard Dyer, 'Jackie Kay in Conversation', *Wasafiri: Journal of Caribbean, African, Asian and Associated Literatures and Film* 29, (1999), pp. 53–61.

Jamie, Kathleen interviewed by Richard Price, *Verse* 8 (3)/9 (1) (1992), pp. 103–6.

Jones, Chris, 'Edwin Morgan in Conversation', *PN Review* 31 (2) [160], (2004), pp. 47–51.

—, *Strange Likeness: The Use of Old English in Twentieth-Century Poetry* (Oxford: Oxford University Press, 2006).

Kavanagh, Patrick, *Collected Prose* (London: MacGibbon and Kee, 1967).

Keith, Michael and Steve Pile (eds), *Place and the Politics of Identity* (London: Routledge, 1993).

Kemp, Sandra and Judith Squires (eds), *Feminisms* (Oxford: Oxford University Press, 1997).

Kennedy, David, '"Aesthetic Pain": Authenticity and Literary Anxiety in Douglas Dunn's *Elegies*', *English* 55 (213) (2006), pp. 299–309.

Kerridge, Richard and Neil Samuels (eds), *Writing the Environment: Ecocriticism and Literature* (London: Zed Books, 1998).

Kerrigan, Catherine (ed.), *An Anthology of Scottish Women Poets* (Edinburgh: Edinburgh University Press, 1991).

Kinnahan, Linda A, *Lyric Interventions: Feminism, Experimental Poetry, and Contemporary Discourse* (Iowa: University of Iowa Press, 2004).

Klein, Holger, Sabine Coelsch-Foisner and Wolfgang Görtschacher (eds), *Poetry Now: Contemporary British and Irish Poetry in the Making* (Tübingen: Stauffenburg, 1999).

Kossick, Kaye, 'Roaring Girls, Bogie Wives and the Queen of Sheba: Dissidence, Desire and Dreamwork in the Poetry of Kathleen Jamie', *Studies in Scottish Literature* 32 (2001), pp. 195–212.

Leonard, Tom (ed.), *Radical Renfrew: Poetry from the French Revolution to the First World War* (Edinburgh: Polygon, 1990).

Longley, Edna, *Poetry in the Wars* (Newcastle-upon-Tyne: Bloodaxe, 1986).

Lucas, John, 'Souls, Ghosts, Angels, and "Things Not Human": John Burnside, Alice Oswald and Kathleen Jamie', *PN Review* 34 (1) [177] (Sept.–Oct.) (2007), pp. 27–32.

MacCabe, Colin, *James Joyce and the Revolution of the Word* (London: Macmillan, 1979).

McClellan, Sarah, 'The nation of mother and child in the work of Jackie Kay', *Obsidian III* 6 (1) (2005), pp. 114–27.

McClintock, Anne, *Imperial Leather: Race, Gender and Sexuality in the Colonial Context* (London: Routledge, 1995).

McClure, J. Derrick, *Language, Poetry and Nationhood: Scots as a Poetic Language from 1878 to the Present* (East Linton: Tuckwell Press, 2000).

—, 'Scots – A Language for Poetic Translation?' *Metamorphoses* (Spring, 2008) pp. 116–59.

McCrone, David, *Understanding Scotland: The Sociology of a Stateless Nation* (London: Routledge, 1992).

MacDiarmid, Hugh, *The Golden Treasury of Scottish Poetry* (London: Macmillan, 1940).

McManus, Tony, *The Radical Field: Kenneth White and Geopoetics* (Dingwall: Sandstone Press, 2007).

McMillan, Dorothy, 'Here and There: The Poetry of Kathleen Jamie', *Études Écossaises* 4 (1997), pp. 123–34.

— and Michael Byrne (eds), *Modern Scottish Women Poets* (Edinburgh: Canongate, 2003).

Macnaughtan, Maureen, 'The Duncan Glen Interview', *Fife Lines* 1 (1998), pp. 57–9.

MacNeacail, Aonghas, 'Being Gaelic, and Otherwise', *Chapman* 89–90 (1998), pp. 152–7.

Malroux, Claire, 'Translating Douglas Dunn into French; Or, How to Steer between the Prosaic and the Lyrical', *Forum for Modern Language Studies* 33 (1) (1997), pp. 21–6.

Mark, Alison and Deryn Rees-Jones (eds), *Contemporary Women's Poetry: Reading/Writing/Practice* (Basingstoke: Palgrave, 2000).

Michaux, Armand (ed.), *English Studies 2: Essays in Honour of Marie-Thérèse Schroder-Hartmann* (Luxembourg: Publications du Centre Universitaire de Luxembourg, 1990).

Monnickendam, Andrew, 'Changing Places with What Goes Before: The Poetry of Kathleen Jamie', *Revista Canaria de Estudios Ingleses* 41 (2000), pp. 77–86.

Morgan, Edwin, *Scottish Satirical Verse: An Anthology* (Manchester: Carcanet, 1980).

—, *Nothing Not Giving Messages* (Edinburgh: Polygon, 1990).

—, 'A Mirrear Dance Mycht na Man See', *Times Literary Supplement* 20 (1998).

—, 'Transgression in Glasgow: A Poet Coming to Terms', in Richard Phillips, Diane Watt and David Shuttleton (eds), *De-Centring Sexualities: Politics and Representation Beyond the Metropolis* (London: Routledge, 2000), pp. 278–91.

—, 'Flying with Tatlin, Clouds in Trousers: A Look at Russian Avant-Gardes', in G. Carruthers, D. Goldie and A. Renfrew (eds), *Beyond Scotland: New Contexts for Twentieth-Century Scottish Literature* (Amsterdam: Rodopi, 2004), pp. 95–108.

Mulrine, Stephen, 'Mayakovsky and Morgan', in Bill Findlay (ed.), *Frae Ither Tongues: Essays on Modern Translations into Scots* (Clevedon: Multilingual Matters, 2004), pp. 145–70.

Munro, Gillian (ed.), *Cànan agus Cultar: Rannsachadh na Gàidhlig 4* (Edinburgh: Dunedin Academic Press, 2008).

Neill, William, *Seventeen Sonnets by G. G. Belli, Translated from the Romanesco* (Kirkcaldy: Akros, 1998).

Ní Annracháin, Máire, 'Shifting Boundaries: Scottish Gaelic Literature after Devolution', in Berthold Schoene (ed.), *The Edinburgh Companion to Contemporary Scottish Literature* (Edinburgh: Edinburgh University Press, 2007), pp. 88–96.

Nicholson, Colin, *Poem, Purpose and Place: Shaping Identities in Contemporary Scottish Verse* (Edinburgh: Polygon, 1992).

—, *Edwin Morgan: Inventions of Modernity* (Manchester: Manchester University Press, 2005).

—, *FiveFathers: Interviews with Late Twentieth-Century Scottish Poets* (Tirril: Humanities-Ebooks, 2007).

—, 'Towards a Scottish Theatrocracy: Edwin Morgan and Liz Lochhead', in Berthold Schoene (ed.), *The Edinburgh Companion to Contemporary Scottish Literature* (Edinburgh: Edinburgh University Press, 2007), pp. 159–66.

Norquay, Glenda and Gerry Smyth (eds), *Across the Margins: Identity, Resistance and Minority Culture Throughout the British Archipelago* (Manchester: Manchester University Press, 2002).

Olson, Charles, 'Projective Verse', in *Collected Prose* (Berkeley: University of California Press, [1950] 1997), pp. 239–49.

O'Rourke, Daniel (ed.), *Dream State: The New Scottish Poets* (Edinburgh: Polygon, [1994] 2002).

—, 'The Dark Art of Poetry', *Brick* 75 (2005), pp. 19–33.

Paterson, Don, 'The Dilemma of the Peot'[sic], in Tony Curtis (ed.), *How Poets Work* (Bridgend: Seren, 1996), pp. 155–72.

— and Charles Simic (eds), *New British Poetry* (Saint Paul: Graywolf Press, 2004).

Rees-Jones, Deryn, *Carol Ann Duffy* (Plymouth: Northcote House, 1999).

Roberts, Andrew Michael and Jonathan Allison (eds), *Poetry and Contemporary Culture: The Question of Value* (Edinburgh: Edinburgh University Press, 2002).

Robertson, James, *Fae the Flouers o Evil: Baudelaire in Scots* (Kingskettle: Kettillonia, 2001).

—, *Voyages of Intent: Sonnets and Essays from the Scottish Parliament* (Edinburgh: Luath, 2005).

Robertson, Robin, 'Love and Loss': An Interview with Nicholas Wroe (2008), www.guardian.co.uk/books/2008/mar29/featuresreviews

Rowland, Antony, 'Love and Masculinity in the Poetry of Carol Ann Duffy', *English* 50 (198) (2001), pp. 199–218.

—, (ed.), *The Poetry of Carol Ann Duffy: 'Choosing Tough Words'* (Manchester: Manchester University Press, 2003).

—, 'Patriarchy, Male Power and the Psychopath in the Poetry of Carol Ann Duffy', in Daniel Lea and Berthold Schoene (eds), *Posting the Male: Masculinities in Post-War and Contemporary British Literature* (Amsterdam: Rodopi, 2003), pp. 125–39.

Schlag, Evelyn, 'Secrets: On Translating Douglas Dunn's Elegies into German', *Forum for Modern Language Studies* 33 (1) (1997), pp. 37–45.

Schoene, Berthold, 'Going Cosmopolitan: Reconstituting Scottishness in Post-Devolution Criticism', in Berthold Schoene (ed.), *The Edinburgh Companion* to *Contemporary Scottish Literature* (Edinburgh: Edinburgh University Press, 2007), pp. 7–16.

Sinclair, Lise, 'Literature across Frontiers: Poetry Translation on the Border of Dialect', *New Shetlander* 233 (2005), pp. 25–8.

Skinner, Jonathan, 'Nationalist Poets and "Barbarian Poetry": Scotland's Douglas Dunn and Montserrat's Howard Fergus', *Forum for Modern Language Studies* 40 (4) (Oct.) (2004), pp. 377–88.

Smalley, Rebecca, 'The Englishman's Scottishman, or Radical Scotsman?· Reading Douglas Dunn in the Light of Recent Reappraisals of Philip Larkin', *Scottish Literary Journal* 22 (1) (1995), pp. 74–83.

Smith, Iain Crichton, *Towards the Human: Selected Essays* (Edinburgh: Macdonald, 1986).

Somerville, Gillian and Rebecca Wilson (eds), *Sleeping with Monsters: Conversations with Scottish and Irish Women Poets* (Edinburgh: Polygon, 1990).

Stafford, Fiona, 'A Scottish Renaissance: Edwin Morgan, Douglas Dunn, Liz Lochhead, Robert Crawford, Don Paterson, Kathleen Jamie', in Neil Corcoran (ed.), *The Cambridge Companion to Twentieth-Century English Poetry* (Cambridge: Cambridge University Press, 2007), pp. 230–44.

Stryk, Lucien, *The Penguin Book of Zen Poetry* (London: Penguin, 1991).

Taylor, Andrene M., 'Black British Writing: "Hitting Up Against" a Tradition of Revolutionary Poetics', in Victoria Arana (ed.), *'Black' British Aesthetics Today* (Newcastle upon Tyne: Cambridge Scholars, 2007), pp. 16–30.

Thomson, Derick, *Companion to Gaelic Scotland* (Glasgow: Gairm, 1994).

Walker, Marshall, *Scottish Literature Since 1707* (London and New York: Longman, 1996).

Wallace, Gavin, 'Voyages of Intent: Literature and Cultural Politics in Post-Devolution Scotland', in Berthold Schoene (ed.), *The Edinburgh Companion to Contemporary Scottish Literature* (Edinburgh: Edinburgh University Press, 2007), pp. 17–27.

Watson, Roderick, *The Literature of Scotland* (London: Macmillan, [1984] 2007).

—, 'The Double Tongue', *Translation and Literature* 9 (2) (2000), pp. 175–88.

—, 'Alien Voices from the Street: Demotic Modernism in Modern Scots Writing', *Yearbook of English Studies* 25 (1995), pp. 141–55.

—, 'Absent Others: Edwin Morgan and Love Poetry', *Études Écossaises* 4 (1997), pp. 109–21.

—, 'Edwin Morgan: Messages and Transformations', in Gary Day and Brian Docherty (eds), *British Poetry from the 1950s to the 1990s: Politics and Art* (London: Macmillan, 1997), pp. 170–92.

White, Kenneth, *Coast to Coast: Interviews and Conversations 1985–1995* (Glasgow: Mythic Horse Press, 1996).

—, *On Scottish Ground: Selected Essays* (Edinburgh: Polygon, 1998).

—, *House of Tides: Letters from Brittany and other Lands of the West* (Edinburgh: Polygon, 2000).

—, *Geopoetics: Place Culture World* (Glasgow: Alba Editions, 2003).

—, *The Wanderer and His Charts* (Edinburgh: Polygon, 2004).

—, *Across the Territories: Travels from Orkney to Rangiroa* (Edinburgh: Polygon, 2004).

Whyte, Christopher, *Modern Scottish Poetry* (Edinburgh: Edinburgh University Press, 2004).

—, (ed.), *An Aghaidh na Sìorraidheachd: Ochdnar Bhàrd Gàidhlig/In the Face of Eternity: Eight Gaelic Poets* (Edinburgh: Polygon, 1991).

— (ed.), *Gendering the Nation: Studies in Modern Scottish Literature* (Edinburgh: Edinburgh University Press, 1995).

Williams, Raymond, *On Television: Selected Writings*, ed. Alan O'Connor (London: Routledge, 1989).

Wilson, Fiona, 'Radical Hospitality: Christopher Whyte and Cosmopolitanism', in Berthold Schoene (ed.), *The Edinburgh Companion to Contemporary Scottish Literature* (Edinburgh: Edinburgh University Press, 2007), pp. 194–201.

Notes on Contributors

Cairns Craig is Glucksman Professor of Irish and Scottish Studies and director of the AHRC Centre for Irish and Scottish Studies at the University of Aberdeen. He is a fellow of the Royal Society of Edinburgh and of the British Academy. He was general editor of the four-volume *History of Scottish Literature* (1987–9). His books include *Out of History* (1996), *The Modern Scottish Novel* (1999), *Associationism and the Literary Imagination* (2007) and *Intending Scotland* (2009).

Marco Fazzini teaches English and Post-Colonial Literatures at the University of Ca' Foscari (Venice). He has translated the poetry of Douglas Livingstone, Philip Larkin, Norman MacCaig, Hugh MacDiarmid, Charles Tomlinson, Kenneth White and Geoffrey Hill. His most recent publications include *Crossings: Essays on Contemporary Poetry and Hybridity* (2000), and *Alba Literaria: A History of Scottish Literature* (2005).

Alan Gillis teaches at the University of Edinburgh. His first collection of poetry, *Somebody, Somewhere* (2004) was short-listed for the Irish Times Poetry Now Award and received the Rupert and Eithne Strong Award for best first collection in Ireland. His second collection, *Hawks and Doves* (2007), was shortlisted for the T. S. Eliot Prize. He is the author of *Irish Poetry of the 1930s* (2005).

Tom Hubbard, based at NUI Maynooth, is an honorary fellow of the University of Glasgow, and editor of *The New Makars: Contemporary Poetry in Scots* (1991). From 2000 to 2004 he was editor of BOSLIT (*Bibliography of Scottish Literature in Translation*), and in 2006 was visiting professor at the University of Budapest. His first novel, *Marie B.* was published in 2008; and his most recent collection of poetry in Scots and English is *Peacocks and Squirrels* (2007)

Peter Mackay is a research fellow at the Seamus Heaney Centre for Poetry at Queen's University, Belfast. He works on contemporary Scottish and Irish poetry, in English, Irish and Scottish Gaelic, and is currently writing monographs on Sorley MacLean and the influence of William Wordsworth on the work of Seamus Heaney.

Kirsten Matthews is a research assistant in the Department of Scottish Literature in the University of Glasgow. She submitted her doctoral thesis on the autobiographical writing of Hugh MacDiarmid in May 2008. She has published on a variety of Scottish poets including Hugh MacDiarmid, Edwin Muir and Robert Henryson.

Matt McGuire is a lecturer at the University of Glasgow. He has published widely on both Scottish and Irish literature and he is the author of *The Essential Guide to Contemporary Scottish Literature* (2008). His work has appeared in the *Edinburgh Review, Scottish Studies Review* and *The Edinburgh Companion to Contemporary Scottish Literature* (2007).

Colin Nicholson is Professor of Eighteenth-Century and Modern Literature at Edinburgh University where he teaches a course in Modern and Contemporary Scottish Poetry. During the 1990s he edited the *British Journal of Canadian Literature*; and he is the author of *Edwin Morgan: Inventions of Modernity* (2002) and *Fivefathers: Interviews with Late Twentieth-Century Scottish Poets* (2007).

Niall O'Gallagher is an honorary research associate in Glasgow University's Department of Celtic. He is co-editor of *Scottish Literature, Postcolonial Literature* (Edinburgh University Press) and *Sùil air an t-Saoghal* (Clò Ostaig), a collection of essays on international contexts for Scottish Gaelic writing. He is currently working on a monograph entitled *Alasdair Gray and Empire*.

Alan Riach is Professor of Scottish Literature at Glasgow University. He has published four books of poetry, *This Folding Map* (1990), *An Open Return* (1991), *First & Last Songs* (1995) and *Clearances* (2001), and his books of criticism include *Hugh MacDiarmid's Epic Poetry* (1991) and most recently, *Representing Scotland in Literature, Popular Culture and Iconography: The Masks of the Modern Nation* (2005).

Fiona Wilson teaches at Sarah Lawrence College, New York. A scholar and poet, she writes often on Scottish literature and has published articles in the *International Journal of Scottish Literature, Keats-Shelley Journal*, Byron *Journal*, and *Wasifiri*, along with chapters in *Romanticism's Debatable Lands* (2007), and *The Edinburgh Companion to Scottish Literature* (2007). She is former Chair of the Scottish Literature Discussion Group of the Modern Language Association of America.

Index